PRAISE FOR *TGIF*

Those of us in the workplace need frequent reminders to keep God first. Like manna that nourished God's people in the wilderness, Os Hillman's new book will feed your heart, mind and spirit each day with timeless truth and rich perspective.

John D. Beckett
Author, *Mastering Monday: A Guide to Integrating Faith and Work*
CEO, Beckett Corporation

I'm convinced that Satan has very little interest in the "good" things a person might do as long as that person is not on track for his or her eternal purpose—the unique reason he or she is on the earth. No one I know has a clearer vision for God's purposes and for releasing working people into their purposes than Os Hillman. Thank God for the new *TGIF*.

Linda Rios Brook
Author, *Frontline Christians in a Bottom Line World*

Great movements often produce great leaders. Os Hillman is one such leader in the burgeoning workplace ministry movement in America and around the world. Investing your devotional time each day with Os through his all-new *TGIF* will pay dividends for decades to come. I recommend it wholeheartedly.

Mark Cress
President/CEO, Corporate Chaplains of America

God has blessed Os Hillman with a special gift of insight into Scripture, which he applies in very practical ways to everyday challenges found in the workplace. As a Catholic involved in an ecumenical workplace ministry, I find his reflections inspiring to all Christians, whatever their denomination.

Bill Dalgetty
President, Christians in Commerce

Os has been at the center of the Faith at Work movement for the last 15 years. His first book of devotionals, *TGIF: Today God Is First,* started a stir and was a touchpoint for thousands of Faith at Work seekers. I believe this next set of testimonials of God working in the marketplace will mark a new touchstone for those desiring to deepen their walk with Jesus in the marketplace. A must-read for those who are seeking to understand God's call in the workplace.

Dennis J. Doyle
CEO, Welsh Companies

This daily inspiration is a great source of encouragement and empowerment for everyday life. Be refreshed and revived for cutting-edge living.

Dr. Pat Francis
Senior Pastor, Kingdom Covenant Centre
Toronto, Canada

Os Hillman presents a current word of truth for God's ministers in the marketplace. He reveals how the kingdom of God can be implemented on Earth as it is in heaven—a word of truth in due season for what God is seeking to accomplish.

Dr. Bill Hamon
Bishop, Christian International Ministries Network
Author, *Apostles, Prophets and the Coming Moves of God*

I have now worked closely with Os Hillman for five years and find him to be one of the most knowledgeable and passionate leaders in the global workplace movement. You will be challenged as you use his new book of *TGIF* daily reminders.

Kent Humphreys
President, FCCI/Christ@Work

As a pastor, my heart is blessed and challenged each morning as I read the Christ-honoring words of Os Hillman. Read and be blessed.

Johnny Hunt
Senior Pastor, First Baptist Church
Woodstock, Georgia

TGIF has been a daily inspirational and transformational tool that God has used in my life for many years, particularly with the scriptural application in a workplace context. We have also used *TGIF* to encourage the members of the Coca-Cola Christian Fellowship to apply their faith in the workplace!

Steve Hyland
Director of Retail Merchandising, Coca-Cola North America

As much as we seek to honor God with our best, it's easy to get caught up in the busyness of business. *TGIF* brings inspiration to our days, fresh wisdom to our work and clarity to our calling.

Larry Julian
Author, *God Is My CEO* and *God Is My Success*

Helping people read the Bible in a way that connects creatively with the challenges and questions of daily life and work is no easy task. I commend Os Hillman for the way his devotional reflections consistently bring encouragement and inspiration to thousands of Christian workers every day.

Alistair Mackenzie
Director, Faith at Work
New Zealand

Whatever your situation may be, *TGIF* will impact your life. It did mine. Whether you are on a wave of success or on a stony path in the valley, this book will be your highlight in the early morning hours or in the evening hours together with your spouse in front of the fireplace. It will encourage you, comfort you or provide you with prophetic guidance.

Jurg Opprecht
Founder and President, The Business Professional Network
Owner, Lenkerhof Alpine Resort, Switzerland

Humanity's desperate search for truth and immortality results in either triumph or tragedy. *TGIF* is a veritable daily banquet, serving up biblical truths that satisfy the soul and perfectly timed tidbits that prepare readers in many nations to experience God's holy calling and purpose.

Gerry Organ
Former Executive Director, Christian Business Ministries Canada (CBMC)

Os Hillman is a man touched by God and weakened by Him for service and insight. He is the kind of person who changes people's lives, not just their opinions. *TGIF* will help make it so for its readers.

Dennis Peacocke
President, Strategic Christian Services
Author, *Doing Business God's Way*

Os Hillman delivers yet another masterpiece! Os has gone to the diamond mines of God's Word and pulled out treasure after treasure that will enrich your life beyond measure. God has spoken to me profoundly through Os's daily devotionals, building my faith, strengthening my resolve and softening my heart. The marketplace is a better place because of the invaluable contribution made by Os Hillman and this book!

Michael Q. Pink
Author, *Selling Among Wolves*

Recognizing that what God's people do in their workplace is a true Christian ministry might be the most radical change I have seen in the Church during my 50-plus years as a Church leader. Os Hillman has been at the forefront of this movement, and the godly wisdom that he shares in these 365 power-packed messages will keep you on top spiritually.

C. Peter Wagner
Presiding Apostle, International Coalition of Apostles

With so many committed Christians caught between what they *hear at church* on Sunday and what they *do at work* Monday through Friday, Os Hillman connects the dots in this book by providing easy-to-read antidotes for daily workplace success. This book is a must-read for anyone who desires to see God's grace move in the workplace. Os has hit another homerun!

Robert Watkins
Founder, Kings and Priests International

Os Hillman has compiled and written one of the best daily devotional books I have ever read. There is spiritual nutrition on every page. I guarantee a year full of nourishment.

Pat Williams
Senior Vice President, Orlando Magic
Author, *The Warrior Within*

TGIF

TODAY GOD IS FIRST

DAILY WORKPLACE INSPIRATION

OS HILLMAN

Regal

From Gospel Light
Ventura, California, U.S.A.

Published by Regal Books
From Gospel Light
Ventura, California, U.S.A.
Printed in the U.S.A.

Library of Congress Cataloging-in-Publication Data
Hillman, Os.
  TGIF : daily workplace inspiration / Os Hillman.
    p. cm.
  ISBN 978-0-8307-4479-4 (hard cover) — ISBN 978-0-8307-4513-5 (international trade paper)
  1. Businesspeople—Prayers and devotions. 2. Business—Religious aspects—Christianity—Meditations. 3. Devotional calendars. I. Title. II. Title: Daily workplace inspiration.
  BV4596.B8H545 2007
  242'.68—dc22
                                                                                                2007006331

1 2 3 4 5 6 7 8 9 10 / 10 09 08 07

Rights for publishing this book in other languages are contracted by Gospel Light Worldwide, the international nonprofit ministry of Gospel Light. For additional information, visit www.gospel lightworldwide.org.

To Jesus, the author and finisher of my faith.

This is what the LORD says: "Let not the wise man boast of his wisdom or the strong man boast of his strength or the rich man boast of his riches, but let him who boasts boast about this: that he understands and knows me, that I am the LORD, who exercises kindness, justice and righteousness on earth, for in these I delight," declares the LORD (Jeremiah 9:23-24).

I will give you the treasures of darkness, riches stored in secret places, so that you may know that I am the LORD, the God of Israel, who summons you by name (Isaiah 45:3).

ACKNOWLEDGMENTS

I wish to thank several people who assisted me with this project.

First, I give much thanks to Regal Books and their team for supporting the work of Christ in the workplace. We need more publishers like Regal who see this as a worthy category to publish.

Second, I want to thank my wife, Angie, who is my constant sounding board for devotional ideas and feedback. She is my soul mate, friend, wife and greatest supporter.

Third, I want to thank my staff at Marketplace Leaders. Sandy Severnak provided feedback and initial editing to my first draft and is a great encourager to our work at Marketplace Leaders. Joey Watkins is our operations manager and allows me to give time away from the office to complete writing projects like *TGIF*. And Karen Walsh has been a great asset to our Faith and Work online store and overall team effort. I am fortunate to have such a great team.

In 1994, my life changed dramatically as a result of a series of personal and business crises. It was during that season of adversity that would ultimately last for seven years that I began to write for the first time. As I searched the Scriptures in hopes of finding comfort, I began to write on the things that God was showing me. I then began to share these insights with others by sending daily email messages to friends and associates. By 2000, this email list had grown from 40 friends to tens of thousands of people around the world. That same year, I compiled those writings and published them in a devotional book.

God proved His faithfulness over and over during that season, and He eventually restored all that I lost. From my experiences during this season of my life, I learned two very important things: first, that God desires to know us intimately; and second, that He has called each of us to reflect His glory in our work life. Perhaps Jeremiah 9:23-24 says it best:

> This is what the LORD says: "Let not the wise man boast of his wisdom or the strong man boast of his strength or the rich man boast of his riches, but let him who boasts boast about this: that he understands and knows me, that I am the LORD, who exercises kindness, justice and righteousness on earth, for in these I delight," declares the LORD.

Friend, can you see that God's desire is to have a personal relationship with you? Can you see that His nature is kindness, justice and righteousness? Do you realize that He often takes us, His saints, into dark places in order to reveal secret things to us? As it states in Isaiah, "I will give you the treasures of darkness, riches stored in secret places, so that you may know that I am the LORD, the God of Israel, who summons you by name" (45:3). Adversity is often required for God to reveal things that can only be exposed in the hidden places of hardship. God plans to use those difficult times in our lives to impact the lives of others.

You and I were not placed here solely for ourselves or for God alone but also for others who need encouragement in their journey. *TGIF* is the result of God revealing treasures out of darkness in the secret places of His presence.

Men and women in the workplace often write to me from across the world and say the same thing: "You read my mind today. You said what I needed in my life right when I needed it most." These letters have shown me that others throughout the world have experienced the same challenges I faced in my work-life call. Whether a person is an executive, a mother of five, a teacher, a nurse or a Christian vocational minister, the issues are often the same. Men and women need to be validated as full-fledged ministers of the gospel of Jesus Christ, even in their secular workplaces.

God does not want us to have an attitude that is reflected in the more common use of the acronym TGIF—Thank God It's Friday. Rather, He desires for us to look forward with anticipation every Monday through Friday so that His presence can be experienced in our daily working lives. This is the place of calling for all of us who work. We should look expectantly to each day with the goal of making God *first* in our personal lives and in our work lives.

I hope that this new collection of 365 daily inspirational messages will encourage you no matter where you are in your walk with God. For those of you who are reading these for the first time, I pray that they will help you take the presence of Christ into the place where you spend 60 to 70 percent of your daily life: the workplace. For those who are reading this as their second collection of TGIF, I pray that you will be encouraged, just as you were by the first book.

When we come to know Christ intimately and understand that God has ordained each of us for a specific purpose, we learn that God desires us to *live out* our purpose (His purpose) through our calling in our spheres of influence and in our work. By living out our calling where we spend most of our time Monday through Friday, we can transform our families, workplaces, communities, cities and nations. May we begin each day declaring, "Today God is first!"

God bless you.

For Christ in the workplace,
Os Hillman

TGIF

TODAY GOD IS FIRST

THE WORK OF GOD

*May the favor of the Lord our God rest upon us; establish the work of
our hands for us—yes, establish the work of our hands.*

PSALM 90:17

In the fifteenth to sixteenth centuries, Martin Luther brought the *word* of
God back to the people. Today, God is bringing His *work* to His people. God
never intended the clergy to be the primary distribution channel of His gospel.
You and I—those of us in the workplace—are the distribution channel.

The local church is simply the franchise to equip and release God's
army into the world to affect every aspect of society. Today, God is establishing mini-franchises in the forms of prayer groups and Bible studies in the
workplace. He is igniting the silent remnant of workplace believers who have
never realized that their work really is their ministry. It is a holy calling on
par with vocational ministry.

Our local franchises (churches) should be viewed as mini-battleships
designed to raise an army of qualified warriors who can pray, create and influence their workplaces and industries with a biblical worldview. We must be
reminded of God's perfect plan found in Ephesians 4:11-13:

> It was he who gave some to be apostles, some to be prophets, some
> to be evangelists, and some to be pastors and teachers, to prepare
> God's people for works of service, so that the body of Christ may be
> built up until we all reach unity in the faith and in the knowledge
> of the Son of God and become mature, attaining to the whole
> measure of the fullness of Christ.

The next time you are tempted to pass ministry responsibility on to your
pastor, remember what Ephesians 4 says. After all, there are no part-time Christians in God's kingdom. We may get our checks in secular fields, but our ministry is full-time.

MOSES' STAFF

So Moses took his wife and sons, put them on a donkey and started back to Egypt. And he took the staff of God in his hand.

EXODUS 4:20

When God called Moses from his 40 years in the desert to lead the people out of Egypt, He first changed Moses' paradigm about his shepherd's staff. Moses' staff had originally represented his life as a shepherd, but God now told him that He was going to perform miracles through his staff (see Exodus 4:17).

During the time of Moses, a shepherd was considered to be a very lowly profession by the Egyptians. Moses had to endure a time of breaking in the desert to separate him from all that he learned in Egypt so that he could be used by God to lead the Israelites out of Egypt. In the same way, many times the way God calls us into His purpose in our work life is through a hardship of some kind.

God will often break our staff, or our vocation, in order to reshape and recommission us. The purpose of the breaking is not to destroy us but to bring us to a place of willingness in which we lay down our vocations so that God can use them for His purposes. The breaking prepares our heart for the new calling.

God required Moses to lay down his staff so that he would see it as something that had power. Moses had to lay down that which represented his life and calling so that God could transform it and raise it up for His purposes. Once Moses laid down his staff and then took it back up, a significant change took place. It was no longer his shepherd's staff; it was the staff of God.

God's staff has power. After Moses' staff became God's, it was used as the instrument of deliverance and transformation for the people of God. It delivered people out of the slavery of Egypt through one of the most dramatic miracles of all time—the parting of the Red Sea (see Exodus 14:16). Moses' staff transformed a people from slavery to freedom and was used as a symbol of his God-given authority.

How about you? Are you willing to let God use your "staff" to bring a people out of bondage?

THE 9 TO 5 WINDOW

Then Moses said to him, "If your Presence does not go with us, do not send us up from here. How will anyone know that you are pleased with me and with your people unless you go with us? What else will distinguish me and your people from all the other people on the face of the earth?"

EXODUS 33:15-16

A few years ago, the AD 2000 movement was a major emphasis in the Church. The goal of the movement was to reach the 10/40 window, a reference that relates to the tenth parallel and the fortieth parallel of the globe. It had been determined that this region was where the most people resided who had never heard the message of the gospel.

Today, there is a new move of God that is focused on the 9 to 5 window. This window represents all those who work—regardless of whether they are homemakers, construction workers, nurses, executives, Fortune 500 CEOs, or pastors and vocational ministers. The one thing most of us have in common is that we work. However, the one thing most workers have failed to do is bring Jesus into their work lives. But God is changing this.

God is helping workplace believers today to understand the importance of bringing the presence of Jesus into their work lives so that He may be shared with those who have yet to receive salvation. God is calling us to move past principle-based living to presence-based living. It is only when we bring God's presence into our work lives that we will see real transformation in ourselves and others.

God is calling us to establish church plants in this new frontier. These "churches" are not comprised of buildings but of groups of people who come together in the name of Jesus. So today, bring the Church to the workplace by focusing your mission activity on the greatest mission field of the twenty-first century: the 9 to 5 window.

A NEW CREATION

Therefore, if anyone is in Christ, he is a new creation;
the old has gone, the new has come!
2 CORINTHIANS 5:17

A "mulligan" is a golf term that allows a player to play a second shot off the first tee if the first shot is poor. It's a second chance to get a fresh start without penalty.

Sometimes in life we need a mulligan—a new start. Thankfully, we can have that new start in Christ. He represents the invitation to throw away our first life and begin anew with Him as a new creation.

The Promised Land represented a new life for the people of Israel. It is also symbolic of a new life in Christ. It states that we are no longer going to be driven by the appetites of our old nature but that Christ now lives in us so that we can live a righteous and holy life. It does not mean we're perfect; we're just forgiven.

New life in Christ has nothing to do with church attendance or even doing good things. It has to do with knowing Christ and inviting Him to be our savior. Christ said there would be many people who would claim Him as their Savior but never really know Him. In other words, Christ said there would be no evidence of the living Savior in them.

Many will say to me on that day, "Lord, Lord, did we not prophesy in your name, and in your name drive out demons and perform many miracles?" Then I will tell them plainly, "I never knew you. Away from me, you evildoers!" (Matthew 7:22-23).

Jesus invites everyone to partake of the new life He offers. We only must believe, invite Him to remove our sins and allow Him to live as Lord through our lives. "Here I am! I stand at the door and knock. If anyone hears my voice and opens the door, I will come in and eat with him, and he with me" (Revelation 3:20).

If you've never had a mulligan in life, now is the time to let Jesus give you a brand-new start. Ask Him for that new start today.

DISCOVERING YOUR PURPOSE

You know me inside and out, you know every bone in my body; You know exactly how I was made, bit by bit, how I was sculpted from nothing into something.
PSALM 139:15, *THE MESSAGE*

If you are going to discover how God wants to use your life and work, you must know why you were created. If you try to determine your purpose in life before understanding why you were created, you will inevitably get hung up on your accomplishments as the basis for fulfillment in your life. This will only lead to frustration and disappointment.

First and foremost, God created you to know Him and to have an intimate relationship with Him. In fact, God says that if a man is going to boast about anything in life, he should "boast about this: that he understands and knows me" (Jeremiah 9:24). Mankind's original relationship with God was lost when Adam and Eve sinned. However, Jesus' death on the cross allows us to restore this relationship with God and have an intimate fellowship with Him. The apostle Paul came to understand the importance of this when he said, "I gave up all that inferior stuff so I could know Christ personally, experience his resurrection power, be a partner in his suffering, and go all the way with him to death itself" (Philippians 3:10, *THE MESSAGE*).

Establishing this relationship with God is vital to understanding your purpose. If you don't have fellowship with Christ, you will seek to fulfill your purpose out of wrong motives such as fear, insecurity, pride, money, relationships, guilt or unresolved anger. God's desire is for you to be motivated out of love for Him and to desire to worship Him in all that you do. As you develop your relationship with God, He will begin to reveal His purpose for your life. "For I know the plans I have for you,' declares the Lord" (Jeremiah 29:11).

Today, ask God to help you discover your unique purpose.[1]

SACRED VERSUS SECULAR

*The LORD God took the man and put him in the Garden of Eden
to work it and take care of it.*
GENESIS 2:15

Imagine for a moment that Jesus has just completed His three years of train-ing with the disciples. He has been crucified and is now commissioning the Twelve to go into the world and disciple the nations.

Now imagine Him saying to them, "Dear brothers, it is now time for you to share what you have learned from Me. However, as you share with others, be sure that you keep what I taught you separate from your work life. The principles I have shared with you only apply in situations outside your work life, so don't try to make them fit into this context. Keep this in mind when thinking about praying for the sick or the lost. These truths will not work in the marketplace."

Sound preposterous? It may, but this is the mind-set that many people have in our world today. "What happens on Monday has no relationship to what takes place on Sunday," they say. To them, the spiritual does not mix with the everyday world of the workplace.

When Jesus came to Earth, how did He come? He came as a carpenter. He was a man given to work with His hands and to provide an honest serv-ice to His fellow man. He did not come as a priest, although He was both a king and a priest (see Revelation 1:6). When it came time to recruit those who would ultimately found the Church, He chose 12 men from the workplace—a fisherman, a tax collector, and so on.

None of Jesus' disciples were priests from the synagogue, which would be a natural place from which to recruit if you were going to start a religious movement. Instead, Jesus called them all from the marketplace of life. Was it any accident that Jesus called men and women from the marketplace to play such a vital role in His mission? I think not.

So today, embrace your work life as a holy calling.

THE QUESTION OF CALLING

I pray also that the eyes of your heart may be enlightened in order that you may know the hope to which he has called you, the riches of his glorious inheritance in the saints.
EPHESIANS 1:18-19

I walked up to a man and said, "Hello, my name is Os. What's yours?" His name was also Os—Os Guinness. It was the first time he had ever had such an experience. We chuckled about sharing a unique name.

Os Guinness was named after Oswald Chambers. He was born in England, just as Chambers was, and has become a well-known contemporary writer. He has a real interest in the subject of people's "calling," just as I do. One of his masterful works, entitled *The Call*, shares some important truths about calling:

> What do I mean by "calling"? For the moment, let me say simply that "calling" is the truth that God calls us to himself so decisively that everything we are, everything we do, and everything we have is invested with a special devotion and dynamism lived out as a response to his summons and service.
>
> There is a distinction between a later, special calling and our original, ordinary calling. Selfishness prefers the first, but stewardship respects both. A special calling refers to those tasks and missions laid on individuals through a direct, specific, supernatural communication from God. Ordinary calling, on the other hand, is the believer's sense of life-purpose and life-task in response to God's primary call, "follow me," even when there is no direct, specific, supernatural communication from God about a secondary calling.
>
> In other words, ordinary calling can be seen in our responsibility to exercise a high degree of "capitalist-style" enterprise about how we live our lives. . . . In this sense no follower of Christ is without a calling, for we all have an original calling even if we do not all have a later, special calling. And, of course, some people have both.[2]

We are all called to Someone first, and then something. As we grow in our knowledge and obedience to Christ, God fulfills our calling in life.

JESUS WAS A WORKPLACE MINISTER

"Isn't this the carpenter? Isn't this Mary's son and the brother of James, Joseph, Judas and Simon? Aren't his sisters here with us?" And they took offense at him.

MARK 6:3

In 2005, a movie entitled *The Passion* was released that chronicled the last 24 hours of Jesus' life. During a flashback scene, Jesus was seen in His carpentry shop making a table as His mother stood by, playfully observing. It was a very beautiful scene that reminds us that Jesus was a carpenter for most of His adult life. In fact, most of the people in Jesus' hometown of Nazareth probably viewed Him as more qualified to be a carpenter than the Son of God, because that is the history they knew of this young working-class man.

Consider that in the New Testament, of Jesus' 132 public appearances, 122 were in the marketplace. Of the 52 parables Jesus told, 45 had a workplace context. Of the 40 miracles recorded in the book of Acts, 39 occurred in the marketplace. Jesus spent His adult life as a carpenter until the age of 30, when He went into a preaching ministry in the workplace. And 54 percent of Jesus' reported teaching ministry arose out of issues posed by others within the scope of daily life experience. Saint Bonaventure said of Jesus, "His doing nothing 'wonderful' [during His first 30 years] was in itself a kind of wonder."

Work, in its different forms, is mentioned more than 800 times in the Bible—more than all the words used to express worship, music, praise and singing combined. God created work, and He is a worker. "My father is always at his work to this very day, and I too, am working" (John 5:17).

So the next time you are tempted to minimize your daily work as anything less than a holy calling, remember that Jesus was a workplace minister as a carpenter in His community. He has called you and me to likewise reflect His glory in our work.

WHEN YOUR SAILS NO LONGER HAVE WIND

He stilled the storm to a whisper; the waves of the sea were hushed. They were glad when it grew calm, and he guided them to their desired haven.
PSALM 107:29-30

Imagine for a moment that you have begun an exciting sailing adventure. You've been trained to navigate and sail on the ocean and to be ready should trouble arise. You are confident that you can handle the challenge. However, midway in the journey, your resources dry up.

It almost seems as though God has intentionally destroyed all the skills you have to deal with the weather and the obstacles. Your sails are now damaged. Even your engine has broken down. And to make matters even worse, your oars were lost overboard. You are stuck in the middle of the ocean, and there is no wind to propel your boat. You are, as they say, "up the creek without a paddle."

All of this leads you to the end of yourself, and you cry, "Lord, I don't know why You brought me out here only to die." You receive no response, no relief to your plight. The silence is deafening.

Finally, the Lord speaks. "Yes, you are right," He says. "I did bring you out here. I did destroy your sails. I did break your engine. And yes, I do want you *dead*. Not in a physical sense, mind you, but in a spiritual sense—in order that you may *live*. You see, My child, you are nothing without Me. You cannot do anything without My grace and power in your life."

You quietly yield. Suddenly, a gentle wave lifts the front of the boat. An easterly wind blows through the broken sail, moving the boat in the right direction. You realize that God is moving your boat! Your role now is to steer it.

Do your sails have wind to move you? Is your engine broken? Does it feel like God has propelled you into the open sea only to stop midway with no options? Perhaps He is saying it is time to *die* in order that He might *live* through you. Give the Lord total control today and you will see His wind moving through your tattered sails.

YOUR SECULAR WORK IS MINISTRY

*Whatever you do, work at it with all your heart, as working for the Lord,
not for men, since you know that you will receive an inheritance from the Lord
as a reward. It is the Lord Christ you are serving.*
COLOSSIANS 3:23-25

As I sat across the table from the well-known seminary professor and former missionary, he asked me a very direct question: "So, Os, tell me about this faith at work movement." I thought for a moment and then said, "Well, there's really nothing complicated about it. I believe every person's work can be viewed as a ministry if done with a motive to glorify God based upon Colossians 3:23."

"How can all work be ministry if you're not sharing the gospel in that job?" He replied. "You would have to be actively sharing your faith for it to be construed as ministry."

"No, that's not true," I responded. "The work itself is ministry because the word for ministry and service come from the same Greek root word *diakonia*. When you are serving others, even through your secular work, and are doing it with a motive to glorify God, it is ministry. In fact, Colossians 3:23 says you'll receive an inheritance when you do."

We continued to banter back and forth on the issue. I continued, "God created even secular work to meet human needs. Man began to divide work into spiritual and non-spiritual terms, which introduced a form of dualism. But God never secularized our work. He desires our work to be worship."

We concluded our meeting in disagreement. However, a few months later, I met my friend at a booksellers' convention. "Hey, you were right, Os!" He said. "I've done my study, and work really is ministry because it is *service*." This man went on to write a book on the subject that described this in detail. He explained how if you are a dentist and are filling a person's teeth, you are ministering to that patient. Or if you are a musician and are playing in an orchestra, you are ministering to the audience. Or if you are a pilot and are flying an airplane, you are ministering to the passengers. He concluded that all of this clearly fits biblical *diakonia*.

It was the first time I had ever won a theological argument with a theologian!

KNOWING AND DOING GOD'S WILL

Trust in the LORD *with all your heart and lean not on your own understanding; in all your ways acknowledge him, and he will make your paths straight.*
PROVERBS 3:5-6

George Mueller was a pastor in England during the nineteenth century who knew what it meant to live a life that was focused on knowing and doing the will of God. God led George in a walk of faith that has become an incredible testimony to all who hear his story.

Whenever George lacked for something, he prayed for the resources. During his ministry in Bristol, England, George built 4 orphan houses that initially cared for 2,000 children. When he died at the age of 93, more than 10,000 children had been provided for through his orphanages, and he had distributed more than 8 million dollars—all of which had been given to him in answer to prayer.

How did he know and do the will of God? "I never remember . . . a period," he stated, "that I ever sincerely and patiently sought to know the will of God by the teaching of the Holy Ghost, through the instrumentality of the Word of God, but I have been always directed rightly." George summed up the way he entered into a heart relationship with God and learned to discern God's voice as follows:

> I seek at the beginning to get my heart into such a state that it has no will of its own in regard to a given matter. Having done this, I do not leave the result to feeling or simple impression. If so, I make myself liable to great delusions. I seek the will of the Spirit of God through, or in connection with, the Word of God. The Spirit and the Word must be combined. Next, I take into account providential circumstances. These often plainly indicate God's will in connection with His Word and Spirit. I ask God in prayer to reveal His will to me aright.

Thus, through prayer to God, the study of the Word and reflection, George would come to a deliberate judgment according to the best of his ability and knowledge. If his mind remained at peace—and continued to do so after two or three more petitions—he would then proceed accordingly.[3] Consider these five steps when discerning God's voice in your life.

SECRET PLACES

*I will give you the treasures of darkness, riches stored in secret places, so that you
may know that I am the LORD, the God of Israel, who summons you by name.*

ISAIAH 45:3

When God takes you to a depth of soul experience, be alert to new truths and
new perspectives. During these times, God will often lead you to amazing new discoveries. These encounters can be storehouses of unexpected riches for the soul.

Bible teacher F. B. Meyer once observed, "Whenever you get into a
prison of circumstances, be on watch. Prisons are rare places for seeing
things. It was in prison that Bunyan saw his wondrous allegory and Paul
met the Lord and John looked through heaven's open door and Joseph
saw God's mercy. God has no chance to show His mercy to some of us
except when we are in some distressing sorrow. The night is the time to see
the stars."[4]

As I mentioned, I began writing *TGIF: Today God Is First* daily devotionals in the midst of a seven-year period of darkness. During my dark times,
God revealed things to me that have since benefited others. Writing has
become a central focus of God's work in me. If I had not gone through the
dark times, I wouldn't be an author today.

We must live each day to the fullest. We can't live in the past or in the
future. We must live in the moment God gives us right now. Our time of
deliverance will come according to God's schedule. Meanwhile, we need to be
faithful in doing what God has given us to do and be content where He has
placed us.

When we go through a trial of adversity, we need to understand that
God is performing radical surgery on our lives. The purpose of this surgery
is not to destroy us but to give us a new heart. God uses times of trial to
make fundamental changes in who we are and who we will become.

He will always reveal treasures from these secret places if we are willing
to walk through the process patiently.

LIVING FOR A CAUSE GREATER THAN YOURSELF

Defend the cause of the weak and fatherless;
maintain the rights of the poor and oppressed.
Rescue the weak and needy;
deliver them from the hand of the wicked.

PSALM 82:3-4

God raises up leaders to take on causes that are much greater than themselves. These causes are often birthed as a result of a personal crisis or conviction that then leads to a larger cause.

Martin Luther King, Jr., had a personal conviction that racial discrimination was wrong. He sought to abolish discrimination through preaching and nonviolent demonstrations. It wasn't long before his conviction became the conviction of others and his activism became a movement larger than that of any one person in history.

William Wilberforce also embraced a great cause. He was a political statesman in England in the 1800s who came to Christ when he was 28 years old. After his conversion, he began to have personal convictions about slavery in England and decided to commit his life to the goal of destroying slavery. He finally achieved this goal after 50 years of work. His labor resulted in the creation of 64 world-changing initiatives before his death in 1833.

Born in 1272, William Wallace grew up under persecution from the English king Edward I (also known as Edward Longshanks). When Wallace was older, he led a rebellion against England that resulted in freedom for the nation of Scotland. The popular movie *Braveheart* was based on William Wallace's story.

Has God placed a personal conviction in your life? God often raises up leaders and begins movements as a result of a person's conviction or crisis in his or her life.

BIG ASSIGNMENTS

The Israelites journeyed from Rameses to Succoth. There were about six
hundred thousand men on foot, besides women and children.
EXODUS 12:37-38

How does God prepare someone for big assignments? Consider the mission given to Moses. He was called to deliver an entire nation from slavery. The assignment was to bring 600,000 men, on foot, out of Egypt and into the Promised Land. In addition, there were the women and children. Talk about a big assignment! Imagine the logistics of such an endeavor.

God prepared Moses by allowing him to grow up from infancy under the ways of Egypt. He learned about Egyptian customs and idols and was a favored son of Pharaoh. Then God revealed his birthright. From that point on, Moses realized that although God had placed him in the court of the Egyptians, he was not one of them. He was being called back to his own people. At first, Moses tried to deliver his people using the ways of Egypt. But this was not God's way, so God banished him to the land of Midian for additional training.

God guided Moses to Midian because the Midianites were of the seed of Abraham and retained the worship of the true God among them. For the next 40 years, God allowed Moses to learn the trade of shepherding sheep. He discovered how to move sheep around the arid land to places where water and grass could be found.

In this way, the desert became a place of preparation for one of the greatest assignments ever given to one man. Did you hear what I just said? Yes, the desert was the place of preparation. Moses was battle-trained in the same environment in which he would spend another 40 years to bring a stubborn and willful people out of slavery.

What kind of assignment is God preparing you for? Does He have you in the desert of preparation? Learn well the lessons you encounter there. You may find you are called to be a deliverer just like Moses.

THE NEW EMPLOYEE

But we have this treasure in jars of clay to show that this
all-surpassing power is from God and not from us.

2 C ORINTHIANS 4:7

What would happen if Jesus took your place for a year in your workplace?
Let's consider some hypothetical things that He might do:

- He would do His work with excellence. He would be known
  around the office for the excellence He modeled in His work (see
  Exodus 31:3).
- He would develop new ideas for doing things better (see Ephe-
  sians 3:20).
- He would hang out with sinners in order to develop a relationship
  with them and in order to speak to them about the Father (see
  Matthew 9:12).
- He would strategically pray for each worker about their concerns
  and their needs. He would pray for those who even disliked Him (see
  Matthew 5:44).
- He would rally the office to support a needy family during Christ-
  mas (see Jeremiah 22:16).
- He would offer to pray for those who were sick in the office and see
  them get healed (see Matthew 14:14).
- He would honor the boss and respect him or her (see Titus 2:9).
- He would consider the boss as His authority in His workplace (see
  Romans 13:1).
- He would be truthful in all His dealings and never exaggerate for
  the sake of advancement (see Psalm 15:2).
- He would be concerned about His city (see Luke 19:41).
- He would always have a motive to help others become successful,
  even at His own expense (see Proverbs 16:2).

Hmm. Sounds like some good ideas we could each model.

IT'S TIME FOR A FUNERAL

I have been crucified with Christ and I no longer live,
but Christ lives in me.
GALATIANS 2:20

"There's nothing wrong with you that a good funeral won't solve," I said to the woman. "I'll even send you flowers!" She smiled in response. I was speaking figuratively to this woman who was stressing out about an issue in her life.

Her problem was the same problem most of us have—too much of "us" and not enough of Jesus and the cross. Many of our daily problems in life can be solved if we come to an end of ourselves so that Jesus can take over. I believe this is what the psalmist meant when he said, "Precious in the sight of the LORD is the death of his saints" (Psalm 116:15).

The apostle Paul also recognized the need for a funeral when he penned these words:

What shall we say, then? Shall we go on sinning so that grace may increase? By no means! We died to sin; how can we live in it any longer? Or don't you know that all of us who were baptized into Christ Jesus were baptized into his death? We were therefore buried with him through baptism into death in order that, just as Christ was raised from the dead through the glory of the Father, we too may live a new life (Romans 6:1-4).

Whenever we stress over a matter, get angry over a daily circumstance or seek to have our own way, it is a sign that there is still life in the grave. We need to fill it with dirt and smother the life of our flesh so that Christ may live freely, unhindered by our "old" self.

Send yourself some flowers today. Have a good funeral.

THE PARTNERSHIP

*When they came to the threshing floor of Nacon, Uzzah reached out and
took hold of the ark of God, because the oxen stumbled. The LORD's anger
burned against Uzzah because of his irreverent act; therefore God struck
him down and he died there beside the ark of God.*

2 SAMUEL 6:6-7

David was the ultimate marketplace leader. He began his life as a shepherd.
He later became a warrior and then a king. He never lost a battle. He amassed
wealth and was responsible for building the greatest physical testimony to
the living God on Earth when he established the plan for his son Solomon
to build the Temple of God in Jerusalem.

David decided that he wanted to honor the Lord by bringing the Ark
of the Covenant home from Balah of Judah. He prepared greatly for this
glorious day and worshiped God during the entire trip. However, during
the journey, a crisis took place. David had decided to move the Ark using a
cart drawn by oxen, but when the cart tilted, one of his favorite men
grabbed for the cart in an effort to sturdy it and was immediately struck
dead by God. Yes, by God!

David was devastated. He thought he was doing a good thing. He became
so angry with God that he delayed the transfer of the Ark for three months.
From this point forward, David's belief about God radically changed.

The problem was that David had passion without knowledge. God
had decreed that the Ark could only be carried with poles by the priests.
Had David consulted the priests about his desire to bring God's presence
into the city, he would have been informed of these requirements before
moving the Ark. The lesson here is that David moved out of presumption—and it cost him dearly.

Today, the role of priest is to equip the saints for the work of ministry
(see Ephesians 4:11). Saints do have a responsibility to seek God on their
own, but God desires a partnership between the workplace minister and the
pulpit minister. We are a team, and we need one another to accomplish
the task of bringing God's presence into the city.

COMPETITION IN THE KINGDOM

*LORD, you have assigned me my portion and my cup;
you have made my lot secure. The boundary lines have fallen for me
in pleasant places; surely I have a delightful inheritance.*

PSALM 16:5-6

There is absolutely no place for competition in ministry or marketplace activities. The Scripture tells us that we are not only to bless our competition but are also called to bless our enemies.

We can do this because our security and provision are not based on posturing ourselves against one another but on fulfilling what God has called us to do. When we take a proactive step to bless another, we actually apply a Kingdom principle that results in greater blessing to others, the kingdom of God and even to ourselves.

Our ministry tries to help other ministries like our own. Some would say that we are in danger of losing market share or even our donors, but this is the worldly model of competition. Those who cannot bless others are insecure in their own calling and in God's ability to provide for their own enterprise.

God has already allocated His portion for you before the foundation of the world. You cannot out-give God. As you do your work unto Him, God allows you to receive the fruit of your work.

If you fully obey the LORD your God and carefully follow all his commands I give you today, the LORD your God will set you high above all the nations on earth. All these blessings will come upon you and accompany you if you obey the LORD your God: You will be blessed in the city and blessed in the country . . . The LORD will send a blessing on your barns and on everything you put your hand to. The LORD your God will bless you in the land he is giving you (Deuteronomy 28:1-3,8).

Life is to be lived vertically before the Lord, not horizontally. When we worry about the activities of others, we acknowledge our lack of faith in the One who called us. We need to trust in the Lord and seek to satisfy Him, rather than the world.

LOST DONKEYS

Now the donkeys belonging to Saul's father Kish were lost.
1 Samuel 9:3

In 1 Samuel 9–10, God used adversity to call the first king of Israel. In these chapters, we find Saul working in the family business, employed by his father, Kish. Then adversity struck.

Some of Kish's donkeys went missing. In biblical times, donkeys were the primary means of transporting goods and thus were very valuable. So Kish told his son Saul to take a servant with him and go find the missing donkeys. Saul and the servant traveled the countryside for three days in search of the missing donkeys—but without results. Saul thought his father might worry about him, so he told the servant, "Let's go back."

The servant replied, "Look, in this town there's a man of God, a prophet. Let's go see him and maybe he will tell us which way to take." In today's terminology, it was time to call in a consultant.

So Saul and the servant went through the town. There, they found the prophet—a man named Samuel—walking toward them along the street. As Samuel walked toward Saul, God told him, "The man who is approaching is the one I told you about. He will be the leader of My people."

Saul stopped Samuel in the street and said, "Sir, would you please tell me how to find the house of the prophet?"

"I'm the prophet you're looking for," Samuel replied. "Today you'll have dinner with me, and tomorrow I'll tell you everything that is in your heart." Shortly after this meeting with Samuel, Saul became king.

Saul's pathway to leadership led through the experience of a business setback: a missing herd of donkeys. God arranged every step of Saul's journey.

It was *God* who sent the donkeys away, which made it necessary for Saul to go searching for them. When Saul was ready to give up the search, *God* arranged for the servant to suggest they look for a prophet in a nearby city. Then *God* spoke to the prophet and told him to expect Saul's arrival. There was not a single detail left to chance. God's plan worked flawlessly.

So it is in your life and mine. God is in control of every detail.

HIS WORK, HIS WAY

So I have caused you to be despised and humiliated before all the people, because you have not followed my ways but have shown partiality in matters of the law.
MALACHI 2:9

My work, my way—when you and I live in this world without Christ, we live just as Esau lived his life. Esau despised his birthright and failed to enter into a relationship with God that would have allowed him to fulfill his destiny. In essence, Esau fulfilled *his work, his way*. His life represented the carnal life of the flesh.

His work, my way—when you and I become born again by the Spirit of God, we begin to focus our attention on living for Christ. We realize it is His work we are doing, but it takes time before we learn what it means to do *His work, His way*.

My work, His way—as the Holy Spirit does His work in us, we learn to walk with God. We learn what it means to see our work as His work, and we desire to do it His way. The Israelites were guilty of not knowing how to do *their work, His way*. Because of this, they were unable to move into the Promised Land.

His work, His way—when we begin to walk with God, we realize that all we do is His work and that He calls us to do it His way. When we walk with God in this manner, we begin to see the kingdom of God manifested in our working lives. We begin to experience His power and learn what it means to do *His work, His way*.

In order to experience God in this manner, each of us must give our working lives to the Lord and ask him to teach us His way. Moses asked God, "If you are pleased with me, teach me your ways so I may know you and continue to find favor with you" (Exodus 33:13). Moses realized that he needed God to teach him His ways in order for him to prosper in his relationship with God.

What best describes your life today? Your work, your way? Your work, His way? His work, your way? Or His work, His way?

Pray that you learn to do *His work, His way*.

MARKET RESISTANCE

If any of you lacks wisdom, he should ask God, who gives generously to all without finding fault, and it will be given to him.

JAMES 1:5-6

George Washington Carver is a prime example of a man who was ahead of his time. Born around 1861 during the Civil War, he was a man who should have been a victim to his circumstances. Discriminated against constantly, he lost his mother to slave traders. As a young boy, he cried out to God in the midst of his circumstances, and God heard him. God gave George an indomitable persevering spirit, and he was highly motivated to learn.

Carver's passion for learning led him to discover that Southern farmers, who had planted cotton for hundreds of years, needed to plant a new crop. By continually planting cotton, the soil had become worn out and, as a result, the farmers were going into interminable debt.

To restore the soil, Carver advised the farmers to plant peanuts and sweet potatoes. After much persuasion, the planters gradually increased their peanut and sweet potato acreage until these became the primary crops grown in the South. However, there was not a substantial market for the peanuts and sweet potatoes at the time, so many of the planters were forced to let the product rot in the fields. The farmers ended up losing more money than before.

This situation placed a great deal of pressure on Carver. So he took the problem to God in prayer and said, "Mr. Creator, why did You make the peanut?" Many years later, Carver shared that God led him back to his lab and worked with him to discover some 300 marketable products from the peanut, including lard, mayonnaise, cheese, shampoo, instant coffee, flour, soap, face powder, plastics, adhesives, axle grease and pickles.

Likewise, from the sweet potato Carver made more than 100 discoveries, among them are starch, library paste, vinegar, shoe blacking, ink and molasses. Because of these new products, the demand for peanuts and sweet potatoes grew and literally transformed the Southern economy.[5]

Has God made you an inventor? Ask Him to help you bring your product to market.

MASQUERADING AS A DENTIST

For you died, and your life is now hidden with Christ in God. When Christ,
who is your life, appears, then you also will appear with him in glory.
COLOSSIANS 3:2-4

"Hello, my name is Dr. Bengel. I am a Christian masquerading as a dentist.
What is your name?" I laughed when I met this man for the very first time.
He was boldly proclaiming that he wanted to be known by who he was in
Christ instead of who he was in his occupation.

If Christ is Lord over all of life, then He must be Lord over work as well.
Our identity must be wrapped up in who we are, not just what we do. As Paul
wrote, "Whatever we do for work, we should do it 'in the name of the Lord
Jesus'" (Colossians 3:17), that is, with a concern for His approval and in a manner that honors Him.

The Spirit empowers us to live and work with Christlikeness. Christ gives
the Holy Spirit to help us live in a way that pleases Him, which has enormous
implications for how we do our jobs.

A common measure of the significance of a job is its perceived value
from the eternal perspective. Will the work last? Will it really count for eternity? The assumption is that God values work for eternity but not work for
the here and now. However, God values all work, even when the product or
service has no perceived religious value.

Keep the following in mind when you are tempted to deem secular work
as second-class Christianity: God Himself has created a world that is time-
bound and temporary (see 2 Peter 3:10-11); He promises rewards to people
in everyday jobs, based on their attitude and conduct (see Ephesians 6:7-9;
Colossians 3:23–4:1); He cares about the everyday needs of people, as well
as their spiritual needs; and He cares about people who will enter eternity. To the extent that a job serves the needs of people, He values it because
He values people.[6]

Your work does matter to God. You are called to first be a Christian, but
one who masquerades as a doctor, a lawyer, a construction worker, a secretary, or whatever job you have.

CALLED TO SOMEONE VERSUS SOMETHING

*But the Lord said to Ananias, "Go! This man is my chosen instrument
to carry my name before the Gentiles and their kings and before the people
of Israel. I will show him how much he must suffer for my name."*

ACTS 9:15-16

Sometimes we can place the idea of calling too much on the *thing* we do versus the *One* we are called to serve. For example, Paul said that he was "called to be an apostle" (Romans 1:1). This has made some feel that if they do not have a special calling, they are second-class citizens.

Paul saw his calling like any other believer's call—to salvation and obedience. We cannot negate the fact that God did call Paul in a dramatic encounter with the Lord that had broad significance to the rest of the Body of Christ. Nor can we ignore the fact that there are assignments that are going to impact the Body of Christ more than others. However, this is not the case for every believer, and we should not feel slighted should we not have the same level of call.

Every believer shares the same basic calling with Paul as a bondservant of Jesus Christ. In Romans 1:5-6, he writes:

> Through him and for his name's sake, we recieve grace and apostleship to call people from among all the gentiles to the obedience that comes from faith. And you also are among those who are called to belong to Jesus Christ.

Paul was telling the Roman Christians that their call was the same as his. They were not all apostles, but they were all called of Jesus Christ.

For most of us, God will work out His calling on our lives in many different and varied ways. Like Paul and the rest of the New Testament Christians, we are all called with the same glorious calling and thus stand as equals before God.

FROM THE DESERT TO THE PROMISED LAND

The manna stopped the day after they ate this food from the land;
there was no longer any manna for the Israelites, but that year they
ate of the produce of Canaan.

JOSHUA 5:12

God calls you to eat from the fruit of your own work. During the exodus from Egypt, Israel had to eat manna, the supernatural provision of God, because they were not able to make a living in the desert. However, the moment they stepped into the Promised Land, the manna stopped because God had brought them into a new place. The new land could yield food and provision for the families. They simply had to work it.

For most of us, God has provided an ability to derive our provision from the work He has called us to do. God made a covenant that provision would always be there if we are faithful to His commands:

> You will be blessed in the city and blessed in the country. The fruit of your womb will be blessed, and the crops of your land and the young of your livestock—the calves of your herds and the lambs of your flocks. Your basket and your kneading trough will be blessed. You will be blessed when you come in and blessed when you go out (Deuteronomy 28:3-6).

However, in order for this promise to be fulfilled, we must fulfill His requirements. We must love the Lord our God with all our hearts and minds (see Mark 12:30). And we must avoid having any idols in our lives that will take the place of God.

Every believer is called to come out of "Egypt" and enter into his or her own Promised Land. God has already set aside the land for you. It is your responsibility to prepare yourself to be able to derive the fruit from your land. "The LORD will open the heavens, the storehouse of his bounty, to send rain on your land in season and to bless all the work of your hands" (Deuteronomy 28:12).

GREEK VERSUS HEBRAIC

I will bend Judah as I bend my bow and fill it with Ephraim. I will rouse your sons, O Zion, against your sons, O Greece, and make you like a warrior's sword.
ZECHARIAH 9:13

In the Early Church, emphasis was placed on developing a heart toward God. This was the Hebraic way, because at that time the Scriptures were not accessible like they are for us today. God related to His people on a more personal and intimate level, and obedience was the key to a healthy relationship with Him. Decisions were not made based on reason and analysis alone, but on obedience. "The fear of the LORD is the beginning of wisdom" (Psalm 111:10).

This is why many of the miracles performed in the Bible went against natural reason (the feeding of the 5,000, crossing the Red Sea, retrieving a coin from a fish's mouth, walking around Jericho to win a battle). God constantly wanted to check the leader's obedience, not his or her knowledge.

In the Early Church, the rabbi was there primarily for quality control, not as the primary teacher and speaker. He did not even address the people from an elevated platform. The whole congregation was in a more circular format, each sharing what they believed God was saying. The focus was on the power of God working through every person, not just one individual (see 1 Corinthians 14:26).

Relying on knowledge and reason alone only came into the Early Church with an uncritical study of the Greek philosophers in subsequent centuries. It was during this time that the Church began to affirm oratory skills among Church leaders. Gradually, over many centuries the focus on knowledge and reason apart from intimacy of God has become more accepted in the Church.

Loss of intimacy with God has been the result of this influence of the Greek spirit. The primary focus has become teaching and discipleship instead of the development of a personal and intimate relationship with God. This alteration has resulted in a form of religion that is without power (see 2 Timothy 3:5).

Is your focus on gaining more knowledge or on growing in intimacy and power with Jesus? He desires to know you intimately.

OUT OF YOUR COMFORT ZONE

And God is able to make all grace abound to you, so that in all things at all times, having all that you need, you will abound in every good work.

2 CORINTHIANS 9:8

Have you ever been given an assignment at work that was beyond your perceived ability?

When I was in my late twenties, I made a career change that necessitated a job change. I decided to apply for a job that involved selling advertising on golf scorecards. Usually, this meant going into small towns and making sales calls to small business owners. Not an easy job for a rookie in his first sales job.

At first, the two non-Christian owners refused to hire me because my answers to their interview questions led to me discussing my faith in Christ. They felt I should be in the ministry, not in sales. However, they reluctantly decided to take a chance on me and sent me to small towns in Kentucky to sell golf scorecards in the middle of winter. Little did I know that they were trying to set me up for failure. They did not think I had any chance of success.

So I got into my Volkswagen bus and headed for the hills of Kentucky. As I took on my new job, I told the Lord that I was not qualified and that He would have to help me to be successful. After a week of selling (and sleeping in my car at night), I returned with a full inventory of sales from several cities.

When I walked into the office with orders and checks in hand, they looked at me with total surprise. They could not believe I had been successful. I went on to work for two years at this company, to become an executive and to play a key role in leading one of the partners to Christ.

Do you have a major challenge in your work life? Ask God to help you to be successful in your assignment. God delights in showing His power to His children so that they can abound in their good work.

FATHER, SON AND HOLY SCRIPTURES?

Jesus answered: "Don't you know me, Philip, even after I have been among you such a long time?"

JOHN 14:9

The disciples had been with Jesus for three years. They had seen Jesus perform many miracles—dead men came back to life, the sick were healed, water was turned to wine. However, even after these experiences, they lacked one important thing: intimacy with Jesus. They didn't really *know* Christ.

This must have been a great disappointment to Jesus. He had invested so much into developing a close and intimate relationship with the Twelve. Consider that they had spent three years with their Master and learned much about Him during those years, yet they had knowledge without intimacy. They experienced God's power individually, and He even performed miracles through their lives.

Sometimes it is easier to do the work of God without intimacy with God. A friend of mine once commented about the current condition of many of the mainline churches today: "You'd think the trinity was *the Father, Son and Holy Scriptures* versus the Father, Son and *Holy Spirit.*" There's never been a better description of the Church today.

This is a challenge to me in my own walk with God. It is easy for me to fall into the trap of working so hard *for* Jesus that I forget to work *with* Jesus. Yet Jesus desires intimacy more than works. He tells us in John 15:5, "I am the vine; you are the branches. If a man remains in me and I in him, he will bear much fruit; apart from me you can do nothing. If anyone does not remain in me, he is like a branch that is thrown away and withers; such branches are picked up, thrown into the fire and burned." Whatever works we do must be a fruit of our intimacy with Him.

Lord, help us not to just know about You. We desire to know You.

FORGIVING OURSELVES

If we confess our sins, he is faithful and just and will forgive us our sins and purify us from all unrighteousness.

1 JOHN 1:9

A murderer was condemned to life in prison. Then one day, something amazing happened. The guard came and opened the jail cell and said, "You are free to go. Someone else is taking your place."

"How can this be?" the prisoner replied. "I am still guilty!"

"Your debt has been paid. You are free to leave," said the guard once more.

But the prisoner decided not to leave. "I cannot allow another to pay my debt," he said. Because of his pride, he chose to remain in bondage.

Sometimes, the hardest person to forgive is ourselves. It is often especially hard for those of us who deem ourselves to be high achievers. We think that we are above failure. However, the Bible says that we all sin and that it is impossible for us to remedy our sins by ourselves. "If we claim to be without sin, we deceive ourselves and the truth is not in us. If we claim we have not sinned, we make him out to be a liar and his word has no place in our lives" (1 John 1:8,10). The question is not whether we will sin, but what we will do in response to our sin.

When we sin, there is only one thing for us to do: Go to the cross. Jesus paid for our sins through His death on the cross. We can picture ourselves writing our sin on a white piece of paper, pinning it to the cross and then leaving it there. When Jesus looks at us, He no longer sees our sin—He only sees the cross.

When we come to Jesus with our sin, there is nothing more that we can do besides confessing and renouncing our offenses. Sometimes this may require restitution with others, but once we confess our sin and ask forgiveness, we are no longer on the ledger of debts.

So why not choose to walk free? The cell has been opened.

WHY WORK?

For even when we were with you, we commanded you this: If anyone will not work, neither shall he eat. For we hear that there are some who walk among you in a disorderly manner, not working at all, but are busybodies. Now those who are such we command and exhort through our Lord Jesus Christ that they work in quietness and eat their own bread.

2 THESSALONIANS 3:10-12, *NKJV*

Jesus probably spent most of His life working in His family's carpentry business. We know almost nothing of His youth from adolescence until He began His public ministry at about age 30. But we know that His father was a carpenter (see Matthew 13:55) and that Jesus also practiced the trade (see Mark 6:3). Carpenters worked with wood, metal and stone to produce furniture and farm implements and construct houses and public buildings.

Jesus may have continued His occupation even after He began to teach and travel. Rabbis (or teachers) of the day commonly spent anywhere from one-third to one-half of their time working (most likely with their hands) to provide for themselves. And while Jesus' opponents, many of them rabbis, attacked Him on numerous grounds, they never accused Him of laziness or freeloading. Indeed, He was known to them as a carpenter.[7]

Jesus' reputation for working passed on to the Early Church. For instance, Paul told the Thessalonians that anyone with an ability to work should do so. Unless God has called a person to live by faith (see Matthew 10:9-10; 1 Timothy 5:17-18), work is God's mandate for every believer and is the place where we can best express the nature of God in everyday life.

Our work allows us to demonstrate integrity. Our work allows us to provide for our families and others in need. Our work allows us to connect with nonbelievers. Our work allows us to live out God's calling on our lives. Our work allows us to experience His power in the midst of daily challenges. Our work can be a place of worship when we do it with a motive to glorify Him.

Today, view your work the way God views your work. It is your primary call.

GREATER WORKS SHALL YOU DO

Jesus of Nazareth was a man accredited by God to you by miracles,
wonders and signs, which God did among you through him,
as you yourselves know.

ACTS 2:22

Jesus did all of His miracles as a man, not as God (see John 5:19). Let that sink in for a moment. This is a profound truth that has major implications for you and me. It changes everything. Pastor Bill Johnson writes:

> Jesus could not heal the sick. Neither could He deliver the torment-ed from demons or raise the dead. To believe otherwise is to ignore what Jesus said about Himself, and more importantly, to miss the purpose of His self-imposed restriction to live as a man.
>
> Jesus said of Himself: "I tell you the truth, the Son can do noth-ing by himself; he can do only what he sees his Father doing, because whatever the Father does the Son also does" (John 5:19-20). In the Greek language the word "nothing" has a unique meaning—it means *nothing*. Just like it does in English! He had *no* supernatural capabil-ities whatsoever!
>
> While He is 100 percent God, He chose to live with the same lim-itations that man would face once He was redeemed. He made that point over and over again. Jesus became the model for all who would embrace the invitation to invade the impossible in His name. *He per-formed miracles, wonders, and signs, as a man in right relationship to God . . . not as God.*[8]

Jesus said that you and I would do even greater works than He did. "I tell you the truth, anyone who has faith in me will do what I have been doing. He will do even greater things than these, because I am going to the Father" (John 14:12-13). The question for each of us is how dependent and obedient we are to the Holy Spirit so that we can experience this same power.

CREATING A MEMORY

The greatest among you will be your servant.
Matthew 23:11

Ken Blanchard, the author of *One Minute Manager*, once shared a story about what can happen when individuals in a company, no matter where they are on the totem pole, model servant-leadership. In Blanchard's story, a business consultant for a mid-western grocery chain was training more than 3,000 employees to approach their jobs with the goal of *creating a memory* for their customers. "This is what will distinguish your store from all the others," she stated.

When Johnny, a 19-year-old bag boy with Down syndrome, heard this, his first response was, "I'm just a bag boy." Nevertheless, he went home and shared with his mother what the consultant had said. Johnny and his mother began to ponder how he could create a memory for his customers. Johnny had a habit of collecting inspirational sayings that he would often read. So he decided he would begin by printing out these sayings and placing one in each of his customers' bags. When customers came through his line, he would place the sayings in their bag and say, "I've included some of my favorite sayings in your bag in the hope they will encourage you today. Thanks for shopping with us."

After just a few weeks, an amazing thing happened. One day, the store manager noticed that all the customers were lined up at only one cashier station, even though there were other stations open. The manager began to panic, thinking the other stations were broken, but after further investigation he found this was not the case. Actually, customers wanted to come through Johnny's line in order to get his saying of the day.

One woman came up to the manager and said, "I used to come to the store only once a week, but now I come every day!" Johnny's example spread to other departments in the store. The florist began giving a flower to each florist customer. The meat department put Snoopy stickers on each meat order with a special greeting. This one act by a bag boy had changed the entire climate of the store.[9]

Like Johnny, Jesus was all about creating memories. How can you create a memory for someone in your workplace today?

MANIFEST VERSUS MARKET

*Take the staff, and you and your brother Aaron gather the assembly together.
Speak to that rock before their eyes and it will pour out its water.*
NUMBERS 20:7-8

The Bible says that Moses had a unique walk with God. Numbers 12:3 states that Moses was the most humble man on Earth, and God even spoke with Moses face to face (see Exodus 3:4-22).

When Moses met God at the burning bush, God told Moses that He would perform miracles through his staff. And He did. God turned Aaron's staff into a snake in the court of Pharaoh. Moses brought plagues upon the nation and parted the Red Sea with his staff. He even struck the rock with his staff to bring forth water.

But later, God called Moses to operate on a new level. Instead of having Moses use his workplace tool (his staff) to perform miracles, God called Moses to manifest the miracles through his *words*: "Speak to the rock" (Numbers 20:8). But Moses, frustrated by the stiff-necked people he was leading, instead struck the rock out of anger. Amazingly, and in spite of his disobedience, God still allowed Moses to get water out of the rock.

God will often work through our anointing even when we do it in our flesh just for the sake of others. But beware, my friend: It will come at a great cost. Like Moses, when we do things our way, we will not enter our Promised Land and may lose our inheritance.

God will sometimes call us to manifest breakthroughs by speaking to the problem. We need to be available to the Holy Spirit when God calls us to use our authority in order to manifest His power in a situation that needs a breakthrough.

Friend, God is calling you to manifest His kingdom through a higher level of relationship with Him. Are you willing?

THE QUALITY OF A MAN'S WORK

And we pray this in order that you may live a life worthy of the Lord and may please him in every way: bearing fruit in every good work, growing in the knowledge of God.

COLOSSIANS 1:10

There was once an elderly carpenter who was ready to retire. He told his employer of his plans to leave the business and live a more leisurely life with his wife and extended family.

The contractor was sorry to see his good worker go and asked if he could build just one more house before he left as a personal favor. The carpenter said yes, but his heart was not in his work. He resorted to shoddy workmanship and inferior materials. It was an unfortunate way for him to end his career.

When the carpenter finished his work and the builder came to inspect the house, the contractor handed him the front door key. "This is your house," he said. "It's my gift to you."

What a shock! What a shame! If the carpenter had only known that he was building his own house, he would have done it all so differently. Now he had to live in the home he had built none too well.

So it is with us. We build our lives in a distracted way, reacting rather than acting, willing to put up with less than the best. At important points, we do not give the job our best effort. Then, with a shock we look at the situation we have created and find that we are living in the house we have built. Like the carpenter, if we had realized this was the case, we would have done it differently.

Think of yourself as the carpenter. Think about your house you are building in life. Each day you hammer a nail, place a board or erect a wall. Build wisely. It's the only life you will ever build. Even if you live it for only one day more, that day deserves to be lived graciously and with dignity.

As an anonymous author once wrote, "Your life today is the result of your attitudes and choices in the past. Your life tomorrow will be the result of your attitudes and the choices you make today."

BEING CHOSEN

"Come, follow me," Jesus said, "and I will make you fishers of men."
At once they left their nets and followed him.
MATTHEW 4:19-20

Do you recall how good it felt when you were chosen to be on a team? It made you feel special to be preferred over another person.

During the time of Jesus, rabbis were well known in their community. Each rabbi had a following of students. Jesus was developing as a "superstar" rabbi. He was unlike the others because He often confronted the accepted thinking of other rabbis and Pharisees. The younger men had great respect for Jesus, the rabbi.

To be selected by Jesus would have been a great honor, because most rabbis usually selected only the cream of the crop in the community as their disciples (see John 15:16). By these standards, Peter and the other disciples would not have qualified. But Jesus had a purpose in mind for Peter and the disciples.

God is the one who calls people into relationship with Himself and to their calling in life. It is for His purposes, not our own. Jesus chose each of His disciples from the workplace instead of the rabbinical schools. They did not choose Jesus; Jesus chose *them*.

Likewise, Jesus has called us into relationship with Him because His desire is for us to be faithful priests in our work life, family and city. "I will raise up for myself a faithful priest, who will do according to what is in my heart and mind" (1 Samuel 2:35). He desires that we be willing participants in His agenda.

Sometimes we think it's all about us. But it has to be all about Jesus in order for us to fulfill what is in His heart and mind for His overall Kingdom plan. He doesn't *need* us; He has *chosen* to use us.

God has an agenda for planet Earth. He has chosen you and me as the primary instruments for accomplishing His plan. Are you willing to be His faithful priest and to do what is in His heart and mind? Why not say yes to His agenda?

HOW GOD USES PAIN

I form the light and create darkness, I bring prosperity and
create disaster; I, the LORD, do all these things.
ISAIAH 45:7

God will use pain in order to create a love relationship with His creation. This statement may challenge your theology. However, consider the fact that God allowed Jesus to experience incredible pain in order to create an opportunity for Him to have a relationship with His creation. Consider how Jesus created a relationship with Paul. He blinded Paul in order to bring him into a relationship with God and use him for God's purposes. And consider how God recruited Jonah for the mission He had for him.

This is not God's first choice for His creation. Romans 2:4 reveals that God's preference is to show mercy and kindness: "Or do you show contempt for the riches of his kindness, tolerance and patience, not realizing that God's kindness leads you toward repentance?" The problem is that there are few people who respond to the goodness of God.

God loves people more than He loves their comfort. Sometimes, the process of pain is the only way He can alert us to our need for intimacy with Him. He desires relationship with us and will go to great lengths to create such a relationship in order for us to receive the rewards and inheritance He has for us.

God will allow crises to come into our lives to motivate us to obey Him in order to get out of the pain of our situation. Many times God allows us to stay in this condition in order to demonstrate His love and faithfulness during our pain. Gradually, we discover something knew about God and often have a personal encounter with Him that changes us. Our very nature is affected by this God encounter.

Take a moment today to consider how God has used moments of pain or crises in your life to accomplish His purposes.

STRANGE INSTRUCTIONS

And this is love: that we walk in obedience to his commands.

2 JOHN 6

A distinguished Indian evangelist named Sadhu Chellappa was on a mission trip to a village north of Madras when he suddenly sensed God say to him: *"Leave this house quickly and run away!"* This was not exactly a convenient thing to do. But Chellappa was accustomed to accepting even strange instructions from the Lord without debate, so he dressed quickly and ran into the darkness.

After a while, he was in open country. As he passed beneath a large tree, he felt God tell him, *"Stay here and start to preach!"* Now, even for an experienced evangelist, this was puzzling—because there was no one to be seen. Why did God want him to preach to an empty field in the middle of the night? But he stopped under the tree and began to preach the gospel.

Finally, he reached the point in which he called on his unseen listeners to give their lives to Jesus. To his surprise, he suddenly heard a voice answer from the top of the tree. A man climbed down, crying, and tearfully gave his life to Jesus. When Chellappa asked why he was in a tree out in the middle of nowhere, the man admitted, "I came out here to hang myself."[10]

How is your obedience quotient? God calls us to be obedient to that small voice inside that can direct us to sometimes do strange things. Jesus was obedient in *all* things. Likewise, we must strive for perfect obedience: "For just as through the disobedience of the one man the many were made sinners, so also through the obedience of the one man the many will be made righteous" (Romans 5:19).

God can do exceedingly great things through one man or woman who is willing to be obedient to God's voice. Ask for His grace today to be obedient to His voice.

BEING A SPIRITUAL HEAD

Now I want you to realize that the head of every man is Christ,
and the head of the woman is man, and the head of Christ is God.
1 CORINTHIANS 11:3

The Body of Christ is known in Scripture as the Bride of Christ. Jesus will return to a spotless Bride because of the sacrifice He made on the cross; but in the meantime, He is interceding for His Bride before the Father. His is a picture of self-sacrifice for the Bride. That is what being the head of a business or a family means—love and sacrifice.

God specifically calls the husband to model this kind of relationship toward his wife. He is to be an example of love and sacrifice. He is to intercede and sacrifice for his earthly bride just as Jesus did for His holy Bride. For example, Jesus holds the man responsible for the condition of the spiritual relationship in marriage. He holds him responsible for protecting and nurturing his bride.

This is illustrated in the following two examples in Scripture. When Adam and Eve sinned in the Garden of Eden, the first person God sought out was Adam, the man. He asked Adam, "Where are you?" (Genesis 3:9), with the implication that Adam had somehow not protected Eve from the serpent.

A second example is found in the story of Ahab and Jezebel. Jezebel was married to Ahab, the king of Israel. They were evil rulers. Jezebel conspired to murder a man named Naboth because he refused to sell his vineyard. God judged this act of murder by sending the prophet Elijah to Ahab. He held Ahab responsible for an act carried out by his wife.

God told Elijah, "Say to him, 'This is what the LORD says: Have *you* not murdered a man and seized his property?' Then say to him, 'This is what the LORD says: In the place where dogs licked up Naboth's blood, dogs will lick up your blood—yes, yours!'" (1 Kings 21:19).

Husbands, you are called to love, honor and protect your wife. You are called to wash her with the Word of God and to be her spiritual head and her protector. You are to lay your life down for her daily. Only then will you model what it really means to be the head.

UNIVERSITY OF ADVERSITY

We are hard pressed on every side, but not crushed; perplexed,
but not in despair; persecuted, but not abandoned; struck down,
but not destroyed. We always carry around in our body the death of Jesus,
so that the life of Jesus may also be revealed in our body.

2 CORINTHIANS 4:8-10

Most great leaders would never have been so great without earning an advanced degree at the University of Adversity. For example, John Bunyan (1628-1688), the author of *The Pilgrim's Progress*, grew up in poverty and taught himself to read. As a young man, he struggled with feelings of not being forgiven by God, and was tortured by visions of eternal punishment. His devout wife helped him to overcome his fear, but then, while she was still in her twenties, she died of a sudden illness.

In his grief, Bunyan devoted himself to preaching. The English government, however, repeatedly imprisoned him for preaching without a license. On one occasion, Bunyan was sentenced to three months in prison, but when he told the officials he intended to go on preaching, his sentence was extended to 12 years.

Yet while he was in prison, Bunyan experienced God's presence in a special way. In fact, it was in his cell that he penned his enduring classic, *The Pilgrim's Progress*. It is indeed a book that could only have been written by a soul that had been refined by the fires of adversity.

A. W. Tozer once wrote, "It is doubtful whether God can bless a man greatly until he has hurt him deeply." God has a mission for your life and mine. But before we can carry out our mission, we will often go through the boot camp of adversity. If this is where you find yourself today, ask God to give you His grace to walk through this time with you. He promised He would never leave or forsake us.

"YOU WANT TO DO WHAT?!"

For nothing is impossible with God.

LUKE 1:37

I walked into the doctor's office for my pre-op visit. The doctor came in and told me all about my arthroscopic knee surgery procedure. "So, doc, I have been told this is pretty routine," I said. "If that is the case, I have a golf outing I am responsible for that is four days after the surgery. Is there any chance I would be able to play golf that soon?"

"Not a chance," the doctor responded. "You need to let go of that idea. You will definitely not be able to play golf four days after surgery. It may be minor, but it is still surgery." I was disappointed, but I eventually resigned myself to host my friend's fiftieth surprise birthday celebration as a spectator. Nevertheless, having no shame, I prayed anyway that God would let me play.

The day of my surgery arrived. After the procedure, I was given my crutches and greeted in the recovery room by my wife, Angie. About 30 minutes later, she wheeled me out to the car. The next day I noticed that I had no soreness or discomfort. I questioned whether I had even had surgery. But the three incisions and the photographs assured me that it had taken place.

By that afternoon, I could put all my weight on my right leg without discomfort. I put away the crutches and began walking unaided. Then the doctor called from the hospital to inquire about my progress. Angie answered the phone. "Is he supposed to have soreness and pain from this procedure?" she inquired.

"Oh, yes. He should be pretty sore and experience some pain," said the doctor.

"Well," she said, "he has no pain and no soreness. He is walking like he has never had surgery!"

"That is hard to believe," said the doctor. "In fact, that is incredible!"

The next day, I could go up and down steps with full weight on my right knee. Then, only four days after surgery, I played 18 holes of golf for my friend's fiftieth birthday celebration. The day after the golf outing, I awoke with no soreness and no pain.

Do you need something special from God? As the apostle Paul said, "Do not be anxious about anything, but in everything, by prayer and petition, with thanksgiving, present your requests to God" (Philippians 4:6-7). Nothing is impossible with God!

YOUR MINISTRY TO THE POOR

*Is it not to share your food with the hungry and to provide the
poor wanderer with shelter—when you see the naked, to clothe him,
and not to turn away from your own flesh and blood?*

ISAIAH 58:7

For many years, I read this passage without responding to it personally.
I would read it and then move on to the rest of my Bible reading without
taking any action steps. It was just another verse of Scripture. Then one day,
the Holy Spirit asked me a question: "Os, how are you ministering to the
poor in My name?" It was a very convicting question.

As I began to ponder the matter, I realized that I had no specific focus
on the poor in my workplace ministry. Sure, I gave to a local church that
often gave to the poor, and I may have given a donation to the needy here
or there. However, I was not directly involved in any specific activity that
served the poor. God was challenging me to change this in my life.

I began praying about this, and soon God connected me with a Christian leader in the nation of Uganda. I had never been to a third-world
nation, nor had I ever seen poverty up close and personal. I decided that
this was God's answer to my prayer.

Paying all my own expenses, I traveled to Uganda. I visited the camps
where thousands of people came to live—having abandoned their lands
because of a 20-year rebel war. Even children had been killed and
maimed in the fighting. During my stay, I experienced limited access to
electricity and other basic amenities we take for granted in the West. The
way of life in Uganda was a stark contrast to how so many people in
North America live.

The Lord does not ask us to give what we don't have. However, I do
believe that each of us should ask God what we have to offer. That is what
Elisha asked of the widow in 2 Kings 4:2—and God performed a miracle
through what she had.

Ask God today what you have in your hand that you can give to
the poor.

WITHHOLDING YOUR NATURAL GIFTING

My message and my preaching were not with wise and persuasive words,
but with a demonstration of the Spirit's power, so that your faith might not
rest on men's wisdom, but on God's power.

1 CORINTHIANS 2:4-5

In the work world, we are trained to press through obstacles no matter the cost. However, perseverance that is not directed by the Holy Spirit is only sweat and toil. We must learn to walk the fine line between these two concepts. Watchman Nee wrote:

> I believe many people are so rich and strong that they give no ground for God to work. I frequently recall the words, "helpless and hopeless." I must tell God, "all that I have is Yours, I myself have nothing. Apart from You I am truly helpless and hopeless." We need to have such a dependent attitude toward God that it is as if we cannot inhale or exhale without Him. In this way we shall see that our power as well as our holiness all comes from Him. Oh how God delights in seeing us coming hopeless and helpless to Him. A brother once asked me, "What is the condition for the working of the Spirit?" To which I replied that . . . the Holy Spirit must first bring us to a place where we can do nothing by ourselves.[11]

Of course, God gives us our natural skills, and He will use them. Yet it can be hard at times to tell whether the things happening in our lives are a result of God working through us or our natural skills alone. We need to try to distinguish the difference without over-analyzing (which can result in paralysis by analysis).

The apostle Paul understood that it was not his ability to deliver eloquent sermons that changed people but the power of God working through him.

We bring glory to the Father when God's power comes through our work.

DO YOU KNOW WHO YOU ARE?

*Continue your love to those who know you, your righteousness
to the upright in heart.*

PSALM 36:10

Someone once said, "Success is when those who know you the best are those who love you the most."

Years ago, a man named Jahari developed a self-assessment tool that can help us understand how we relate to others. This tool, known as the Jahari Window, allows us to realize where we are in our ability to know who we are and for others to know who we are. Real transparency in communication takes place when those with whom we associate know who we are after we discover who we really are. See if you can identify in which category you might fall among these four.

Transparent life. People who lead transparent lives know who they are and others know them for who they are. Nothing is hidden. They have come to know who they are as individuals. Basically, people get what they see in them. The transparent life is the life we should desire.

Bull in the china shop. People who lead this type of life are blinded to the character flaws that others recognize in them. In order to become a transparent person, they must get feedback from those around them about the blind spots in their personality. They must ask for the feedback and be willing to respond to the input of others.

Aloof/hidden secrets. These individuals live in a secret world. They don't allow others to know about themselves. They know themselves but are fearful of letting others know them.

Hidden potential. This is a combination of the bull in the china shop and aloof/hidden secrets personalities. It is the saddest of all conditions. These people don't know themselves, and others don't know them either. Both parties have to invest the energy to communicate and get feedback from one another.

How about you? What do others really know about you? Have you allowed yourself to get close enough to others to share who you really are inside? Why not take a step to find out who you really are in the eyes of others. It could change your life.

THEY'RE ALWAYS WATCHING AND LISTENING

About midnight Paul and Silas were praying and singing hymns to God,
and the other prisoners were listening to them.
ACTS 16:25-26

It didn't take long for nonbelievers in the secular workplaces where I've worked to realize that I was different. I didn't participate in the jokes, the dirty language or the criticism of the management. I didn't judge my coworkers for their behavior, because they were merely acting the way they should act as people who did not have Christ in their lives.

I viewed my coworkers as prisoners awaiting their salvation, and I thought I might be the instrument to lead them to their Savior. In the workplace, I was often known as the "religious guy." It wasn't because I was particularly vocal or because I tried to separate myself; it just happened naturally.

Having Christ in me naturally made me stand out. Jesus called us to be the salt and light of any life situation. Because the secular workplace economy is contrary to the kingdom of God economy, it is only natural that we should stand out in any situation.

When Paul and Silas were in prison, their lifestyle of worship and prayer in the midst of the horrible conditions of a dirty prison stood out in stark contrast to their circumstances. They didn't pray and sing to impress their cellmates; they simply did what was natural to them. Still, the other prisoners were listening.

No matter where you are, others are watching you to determine if your faith is real or if you're an imposter. The world is looking to discredit your faith. You are a witness always, whether or not you choose to be.

"The jailer called for lights, rushed in and fell trembling before Paul and Silas. He then brought them out and asked, 'Sirs, what must I do to be saved?'" (Acts 16:29-30). When you begin to reflect the love and power of Christ in your life, you won't have to have an evangelism program to win others into the Kingdom. It will be a fruit of your life. The "fish" will actually jump into the boat!

Beware how you conduct your life today. The prisoners are always watching and listening.

MICROSOFT MARY

Trust in the LORD with all your heart and lean not on your own understanding;
in all your ways acknowledge him, and he will make your paths straight.
PROVERBS 3:5-6

I travel a lot. One of the greatest modern-day inventions is the GPS system for
cars. GPS stands for Global Positioning System, a navigational system tied
to a satellite that can pinpoint your location and chart directions to any
destination you select.

I remember when my wife, Angie, and I used one of these in Germany and
Switzerland. We were able to program the GPS in English. When we began our
drive, a pleasant voice came on and said, "Turn left in 200 yards." We called
our invisible road counselor "Microsoft Mary."

At first, we weren't sure whether we could trust Mary to lead us in the
direction we needed to go. We looked at the map to see if she was correct in
her instructions. Soon, however, we were trusting her for every detail. If we
needed reassurance, we simply pushed a button to replay the audio instructions. We traveled all over Switzerland with Microsoft Mary. She brought us
to the exact street address we were looking for every time. We were amazed
at how Mary got us around so easily.

Jesus sent the Holy Spirit to help you and me navigate through life.
Jesus said, "But when he, the Spirit of truth, comes, he will guide you into
all truth. He will not speak on his own; he will speak only what he hears, and
he will tell you what is yet to come" (John 16:13-14).

There is a story told about people in the Chinese underground church
having to rely on the Holy Spirit to tell them when and where they were to
meet. It was too dangerous to announce public meetings, so each member
had to ask the Holy Spirit the time and place. Remarkably, they would all
arrive at the same place at the same time.

Is the Holy Spirit active in your work life? Are you asking for His direction to succeed in your work? Microsoft Mary may help us navigate traffic,
but Jesus sent the Holy Spirit to help you navigate life. Ask Him to guide
you today.

WALK AS JESUS DID

*This is how we know we are in him: Whoever claims to
live in him must walk as Jesus did.*
1 JOHN 2:5-6

I have always found the above verse very intimidating. It says that if we are truly living in Christ, we must walk as Jesus did. How did Jesus walk?

Jesus healed the sick. He perceived the needs and situations of others supernaturally. He spoke boldly into the lives of the unsaved. He met people's needs by leading them to the kingdom of God. I can only conclude from this verse that if we are each called to live this way, Jesus will also equip us to do so.

How did Jesus walk? He walked on Earth as a human being, not as God, yet He was God. He performed miracles as a human being who tapped into the power of His heavenly Father. This is why He can exhort us to live like He did—not as deity, but as a human being who could appropriate all the Father had for Him. This is what Jesus meant when He said we are to live as He lived. We are to exercise obedience and faith, just as He did.

I believe we live in a day that requires more than proclamation evangelism to break through in the workplace. We live and work in a skeptical society. It takes more than reasoning to see those in the workplace come to Christ. The workplace is trained to see past phonies, so it will require the genuine love and power of Christ manifested to break through to a Muslim coworker, a power-driven executive or a foul-mouthed construction worker.

Jesus modeled this way of reaching the lost. He did not use reasoning to convince a person to follow Him but often received supernatural revelation about a need in a person's life. Such was the case of the Samaritan woman. This encounter not only led to a woman placing her faith in the Messiah but also to the transformation of a city.

Next time you have an encounter with an unsaved associate, find out about a need he or she has and ask God how you can meet it through His power.

FULFILLING YOUR PURPOSE

*O LORD, you have searched me and you know me. You know when I sit
and when I rise; you perceive my thoughts from afar. You discern my going out
and my lying down; you are familiar with all my ways. Before a word is
on my tongue you know it completely, O LORD.*

PSALM 139:1-4

Your purpose in life is chosen by God. It is not negotiable. It is like calling water wet—there is no changing that fact, and there's no changing God's purpose for your life. While you may not *fulfill* the purpose for which you were made, you still *have a purpose* that God intends for you to fulfill.

This is your blueprint from God. In the same way that He had a specific purpose in mind for Jesus when He sent Him to Earth, He has a specific purpose in mind for your life. This doesn't mean, however, that there is one highly specific niche for you to fill, and that if you miss it, too bad.

It is my belief that you can achieve your purpose in many different and creative ways. (This should take the pressure off!) You won't throw your entire life off course by choosing the wrong college, job or spouse. God is much bigger than any miscalculation or disobedience on your part. "The Lord will fulfill his purpose for me" (Psalm 138:8). Isn't that comforting to know?

Defining your purpose will help you to determine the activities in which you should be involved. Like Jesus, you should not involve yourself in activities that contradict God's purpose for your existence. Of course, each of us must ask *why* we are involved in an activity. Is it a God activity or just a good activity? Remember, Jesus only did something if He saw the Father doing it—and He was able to see what His Father was doing because of His intimate relationship with Him.

Today, take steps to ensure that you are aligned with your purpose.

WHEN SATAN ATTACKS YOUR DESTINY

When the Philistines heard that David had been anointed king over Israel,
they went up in full force to search for him, but David heard about it and went
down to the stronghold. Now the Philistines had come and spread out in the
valley of Rephaim; so David inquired of the LORD, "Shall I go and attack
the Philistines? Will you hand them over to me?"

2 SAMUEL 5:17-19

When you are about to enter into your destiny, there will always be opposition from Satan designed to prevent you from fulfilling your destiny.
When Jesus was born, Herod tried to kill Him. When Jesus was baptized
and then went into the wilderness to fast for 40 days, Satan came to tempt
Him in an effort to derail His destiny.

When David was anointed king over Israel, God's destiny was revealed
for all to see—even Satan. So Satan raised up the Philistines to try to sabo-
tage David's destiny. However, we see that David did two things in response.
First, he retreated to his stronghold. It was a place of protection—a quiet
place. Second, he inquired of God for the strategy to defeat his enemy. God
revealed that strategy to him, and David went on to defeat the Philistines.
In fact, David *never* lost a battle, because he learned to inquire of God for the
strategy to defeat his enemies.

Do you know God's intended destiny for your life? Beware of Satan's
strategy to attack you in the place of your destiny. His desire is to take you
off this divine path.

We must follow David's example in response to the enemy of our souls.
We must retreat to our stronghold, seek the Lord and listen for His answer.
Only then will we fulfill the purpose for which God created us.

ONE CALL, MANY JOBS

*LORD, you have assigned me my portion and my cup;
you have made my lot secure. The boundary lines have fallen for me
in pleasant places; surely I have a delightful inheritance.*
PSALM 16:5-6

Most of us will have many jobs during our lifetime. As I look back over my past, I've had quite a varied history of jobs that included being a waiter, a retail clerk, a golf pro, an advertising sales executive, an ad agency executive and an ad agency owner. Today, I am a writer and lead an international workplace ministry.

All of these jobs were important because they gave me a level of experience from which I now express God's ministry. I am able to relate to those in the workplace because of my varied work experience throughout my career. I've also been exposed to many different denominational streams in the Body of Christ that are now important to my current ministry.

With each of our jobs and life experiences, God is building something in us that He will use for His purposes now and in the future. Oswald Chambers wrote, "In the beginning we do not train for God, we train for work, for our own aims; but as we go on with God we lose all our own aims and are trained into God's purpose. Unless practical work is appointed by God, it will prove a curse."[12]

Jesus was prepared for His ultimate calling by working in His father's carpentry shop. Consequently, more than 54 percent of Jesus' teachings arose out of issues from daily life experiences. Likewise, Joseph was prepared to be the head of a nation by serving time in prison and being a slave in Potiphar's house. And Moses was prepared to lead a nation out of slavery by serving in Pharoah's house and later working for 40 years as a shepherd.

Do not despise the small jobs, for they are stepping stones to a greater purpose in God's plan for your life and for God's preparation for your ultimate destiny. Some of these jobs are necessary for the message He is forming in you.

Pray that God accomplishes His intended outcome in you through the work you are doing today.

PRAYERFULLY ARRANGED MARRIAGE

The effective, fervent prayer of a righteous man avails much.
JAMES 5:16, *NKJV*

In his book *MegaShift*, author James Rutz tells a wonderful story of God's supernatural hand in answering prayer. In 1977, Rutz had a friend named Barclay
Tait who decided to hitchhike to a Christian conference in Front Royal,
Virginia. On that trip, as Barclay was reading his Bible, a tall and thin hiker suddenly appeared. Barclay explained that he had come there to fast and meditate.

"Well, I'm an intercessor," Dave, the hiker, replied. "What would you
like me to pray for?" Barclay was a bit overwhelmed, but he managed to
reply, "Uh, frankly, I'd like prayer for a wife." The mysterious hiker jotted the
request down in his notebook and then walked on.

Several years later, Barclay, now living in North Carolina and married to
a woman named Sherry, was invited to join a gathering of Christians in the
town of Asheville. When he arrived at the meeting, the host saw him and
suddenly stopped dead in his tracks. "I know you!" he exclaimed. "You're
Barclay Tait!" Barclay drew a blank.

"Just a minute," the man said. "I have something I want to show you."
He went upstairs and then reappeared a few moments later holding a well-
worn ledger book. "See here? This is where I wrote your prayer request in
column one when I met you in Front Royal in 1977: 'Barclay Tait: God's
choice for a wife.'" Barclay looked down at the journal entry. It was the most
detailed prayer journal he had ever seen.

"I prayed for you for seven years," proclaimed Dave. "Then in the middle of the night on December 30, 1984, God woke me up out of a sound
sleep and said, 'Write in your journal, "Prayer answered."' So I did. See? Here
in column two, 'Prayer answered.'"

Barclay and Sherry stared at each other a moment, and then their eyes filled
with tears. "That was the day we were married," Barclay quietly told Dave.[13]

How is your prayer life lately? Take a moment today to ask someone
what you can pray about for him or her. Commit to praying daily for that
person and watch how God intervenes through your prayers.

HER FIRST CAR

Now Samuel did not yet know the LORD:
The word of the LORD had not yet been revealed to him.
1 SAMUEL 3:7

Charis, my 16-year-old daughter, was of driving age. She had saved her hard-earned money to match her father's contribution to buy her first car, and it was now time to begin the hunt. I told her that we needed to pray for God to lead us to that perfect car. She was excited about the possibilities.

I began combing the newspaper and the internet to find the right car. We prayed that we would find the right car, even one in the gray or silver color and model that she wanted. After several weeks, Charis became discouraged and began to tear up, saying, "We will never find a car for this price." I told her that the car was out there but that we had to be patient to allow God to provide in His time. This didn't go over well.

Finally, one day I came upon a car that seemed to fit our criteria. I called the owner. The parents of the boy who owned it answered the call and gave me more information. I liked the parents right away. They had a nice spirit about them.

We drove over to the house, and there in the front yard was a silver sports car—the model she had been looking for, complete with a fantastic stereo and speaker system. We also noticed a small fish symbol on the back bumper, which indicated that the owner might have been a Christian. "These people appear to be believers!" I exclaimed to my daughter.

We met with the owners and talked about the price. It was a little more than our budget, so we asked if they could meet our price. They did. My daughter had her new car with a personal imprint from God to show her that He was the source of the new car.

One of the most important roles that you and I have as parents is to transfer our faith to our children. There comes a time when children need to take ownership of their own faith in the Lord, rather than living off of Mom or Dad's faith. Today, consider how to pass your faith to your children.

GOD HAS NEED OF YOUR DONKEY

Go to the village ahead of you, and at once you will find a donkey tied there, with her colt by her. Untie them and bring them to me. If anyone says anything to you, tell him that the Lord needs them.

MATTHEW 21:2-3

In Bible times, donkeys were a primary means for distributing goods and services. They represented commerce in Scripture. In the above passage, Jesus told the disciples He had need of someone's donkey to ride into Jerusalem, the religious and spiritual center of their society. His entrance into the city would later become known as the triumphal entry.

I am sure the disciples must have been uneasy with their master's request to untie a perfect stranger's donkey and take it. After all, He was asking them to take what was then equivalent to a modern-day man's truck—and men love their trucks! Yet Jesus was illustrating that He wanted to use that man's donkey, or that which represented their work, to bring glory to the Father.

A while back, my wife, Angie, and I were attending a Christian business conference in Singapore. The night before I was to speak for a second time, I was prompted to add a teaching segment on this passage of Scripture in Matthew 21:2-3.

The next morning, Angie and I went to breakfast. While we were eating, a lady named Maggie joined us. Maggie was from Malaysia and was an intercessor for the conference. She had fasted for 40 days in preparation for the event.

"So, Maggie," I said, "has the Lord spoken to you about this conference?"

"Oh yes," she said, very excitedly. "On September seventeenth, the Lord said that the Singapore business people needed to give their donkeys to the Lord."

Angie and I looked at one another in amazement. God was confirming His Word to me from the night before. So that day, the focus of our conference became the need for the Singapore business people to "give their donkeys" to the Lord.

Friend, have you ever dedicated your work life to the Lord? Today, why not commit your donkey to Him. He will use it to bring glory to Himself and fulfill your life more than you could ever imagine.

TURNING THE DAUGHTER'S HEART TO THE FATHER'S

He will turn the hearts of the fathers to their children, and the hearts of the children to their fathers; or else I will come and strike the land with a curse.

MALACHI 4:6

I came into the room and greeted my wife. Within a few moments, I began to cry uncontrollably. My wife was naturally concerned, as she had never seen me do this before.

I had just returned from dinner with my 18-year-old daughter and had listened to her tell me how fearful she was of the future. At the time, I was concluding a commitment to a seven-year child support and alimony from a divorce that had taken place many years earlier. The impact of the divorce was still apparent in my daughter's life. It was something I had fought against but lost. I was angry and broken over what she was feeling, and it all came to the surface like a boil that needed to burst.

A few months later when I was speaking at a conference in Minneapolis, a dear friend came up to me and said, "Os, we want to pray for you and Angie downstairs. Can you come down?" We went downstairs to meet them and sat down. Then, my friend and his friend, Ron, began to pray for us.

Ron began to speak about my life in very specific terms. "You have a daughter? The Lord says she has a gift in writing . . . poetry . . . and she has creative gifts. The Lord says she has been in a stronghold for many years in her life, but He is about to bring her out of that stronghold. He is turning the daughter's heart back to the father's, and He is bringing her home. The Lord says He has seen the tears you have shed for her in your bedroom."

By this time, Angie and I were on the floor weeping. We went home with this profound experience, and it has stuck with us ever since. Within a year, my daughter came to Christ and even came to live at our home for a year. God did a dramatic work and now serves Christ in her life.

Do you have a son or daughter who is not walking with God right now? Lay your desire before the Lord and ask Him to draw him or her to Himself. He can do it.

CONFIRMED BY OTHERS

The LORD was with Samuel as he grew up, and he let none of his words fall to the ground. And all Israel from Dan to Beersheba recognized that Samuel was attested as a prophet of the LORD.

1 SAMUEL 3:19-20

When I was 14 years old, I was considered to be an exceptional junior golfer. As a freshman in high school, I had already broken 70 several times and had 3 holes-in-one. I competed in the U.S. Junior Amateur and eventually turned pro after attending college on a four-year golf scholarship.

Those who knew me affirmed the gift and calling that appeared to be on my life. However, after turning professional for about three years, God redirected my life into business and vocational ministry. All of these experiences have combined over many years to contribute to the calling I am living out today.

As we mature in our natural and spiritual lives, God uses our parents, teachers, uncles, coaches and pastors to affirm the gifts and callings that are on our lives. At the time, it often seems like these people are trying to get in the way of what we want to do. However, God uses authority figures to provide key direction during the early teen and 20-something years. He is using these people to help guide us to the ultimate destiny He has for our lives.

When we are young, we are often more impressionable than at any other time in our lives. The young person who can allow wisdom to rule over immaturity and impatience is a rare individual. However, if we are able to receive from the people God puts in our lives at this stage, we will be amazed at how far ahead we are of our peers.

As A. B. Simpson says, "God is continually preparing his heroes, and when the opportunity is right, he puts them into position in an instant. He works so fast, the world wonders where they came from."

Let God do the foundation work so that He can advance you to His ultimate destiny for your life.

THE TRINITY'S TEAMWORK

Yet, O LORD, you are our Father. We are the clay, you are the potter;
we are all the work of your hand.

ISAIAH 64:8

The Father, Son and Holy Spirit make up three distinct aspects of the godhead. Each of these persons forms the Trinity and contributes to the overall work of God. The Trinity reveals God's belief in teamwork. Even God brought a team together to accomplish His purposes. *The Leadership Bible* gives us further insight into the distinct roles the Trinity plays:

> The three Persons of the Godhead are never independent but always work together in concert. Scripture records the work of the divine trinity in the creation cosmos (see Genesis 1:1-2, John 1:1-3 and Colossians 1:15-17), but this perfect and harmonious interaction was especially evident in how God made it possible for people who were formerly alienated from him to be transformed into his beloved children.
>
> Paul first spoke of the work of the Father in accomplishing our salvation in verses 3-6. The Father chose us before the creation of the world and sent his Son into the world so that through him we could be adopted into his family. Second, the apostle focused on the work of the Son in verses 7-12. Christ's blood sacrifice on our behalf paid the penalty for our sins so that we could enjoy forgiveness and lay hold of God's purpose for our lives. Third, the work of the Holy Sprit, identified in verses 13-14, seals and guarantees our spiritual inheritance. Thus, the Father initiated our salvation, The Son accomplished it and the Holy Spirit made it real in our lives. At the end of each of these three sections the phrase "to the praise of his glory" appears. The Father, Son and Holy Spirit perform distinct roles, but they work together in perfect harmony and agreement.[14]

This threefold team of the Trinity is committed to bringing us into full maturity in Jesus Christ. May the Father, Son and Holy Spirit take our feet of clay and build a solid foundation for the praise of His Son.

JOHN THE BAPTIST WAS THE GREATEST

I tell you the truth: Among those born of women there has not risen anyone greater
than John the Baptist; yet he who is least in the kingdom of heaven is greater than he.
MATTHEW 11:11-12

Elijah performed miracle after miracle. Daniel interpreted dreams for kings, and he and his friends had an impact on an entire nation. Jeremiah and Isaiah were two of Israel's greatest prophetic voices. John the Baptist did no miracles. Yet despite this fact, Jesus made a profound declaration about this man: He was the greatest among all the prophets.

Why did Jesus make such a claim? Because John the Baptist did one very important thing—he fulfilled his purpose on Earth in every way.

When the disciples asked John, "Are you the one we have been waiting for?" he responded quickly, "No." Then he made a profound statement: "A man can receive only what is given him from heaven" (John 3:27). John had a complete understanding of why he was placed on Earth—to give God glory by preparing the way for Jesus.

Jesus proclaimed that John the Baptist was the greatest because he *knew* and *fulfilled* his purpose. The angel Gabriel described John's purpose to his father by saying, "And he will go on before the Lord, in the spirit and power of Elijah, to turn the hearts of the fathers to their children and the disobedient to the wisdom of the righteous—to make ready a people prepared for the Lord" (Luke 1:17). The fulfillment of John's purpose was absolutely necessary in order to prepare the way for Jesus.

Do you know why God made you? Are you fulfilling the destiny He has planned for you since the foundation of the earth? Understanding your work-life purpose is key to receiving your inheritance.

No matter what kind of work you do, if God has called you to it, you will receive an inheritance for doing it. Paul said, "Whatever you do, work at it with all your heart, as working for the Lord, not for men, since you know that you will receive an inheritance from the Lord as a reward" (Colossians 3:23-24). You and I are called to do greater things than John the Baptist—and he was considered greatest! Start now to understand and fulfill your purpose.

BUT, MASTER . . .

Simon answered, "Master, we've worked hard all night and haven't caught anything. But because you say so, I will let down the nets."

LUKE 5:5

One of the first sermons Jesus ever gave was from a boat. It was Simon Peter's boat. Jesus used a businessman's business to preach the gospel. However, Peter had to first make his business available to the Master. When he did, something wonderful happened to his business.

Peter's fishing business was in a slump. He and the other fishermen had just fished all night but had caught nothing. Nevertheless, Peter made his boat available to Jesus to use as He wished. After Jesus used Peter's boat to preach to the multitudes, He did something interesting for Peter: He blessed his business. However, Peter almost missed the blessing because he began to argue with Jesus. Peter was looking at the market conditions instead of the instruction of Jesus.

Yet something inside of Peter made him reconsider Jesus' instruction. Jesus rewarded his obedience. "When they had done so, they caught such a large number of fish that their nets began to break. So they signaled their partners in the other boat to come and help them, and they came and filled both boats so full that they began to sink" (Luke 5:6-7).

There are a number of Kingdom principles in this story that we can apply in our work lives. First, we must be willing to let God use our work life for His purposes. Second, we must not look at circumstances and argue with Jesus when His instruction seems to contradict what we have seen or experienced. Finally, we must obey the Lord.

When we obey the Lord, we might just see Jesus use us for His glory and bless us for our obedience.

GOING AGAINST PUBLIC OPINION

On the eighth day they came to circumcise the child, and they were going to name him after his father Zechariah, but his mother spoke up and said, "No! He is to be called John." They said to her, "There is no one among your relatives who has that name."

LUKE 1:59-61

Have you ever had to go against public opinion or advice from family members or peers? When Elizabeth gave birth to John the Baptist, tradition said the baby should be named in honor of a family member. Elizabeth's family members were insistent on this point. When she didn't agree with them, they appealed to her husband, Zechariah, who supported her decision.

Zechariah and Elizabeth had been told by the angel Gabriel to name their boy "John." They were being obedient to the Lord's command, which went against tradition and public opinion.

We live in a day when leaders are often driven more by public opinion than by what is right. Living a life of obedience will often go against the tide of public opinion, but we are each called to live a life based on obedience-based decisions, not public opinion.

Jesus lived a life based on a purity of purpose and mission. The Pharisees wanted Him to conform to their rules of religious tradition, but He refused to do so. The result was that He was put to death because He lived to obey an audience of One, not the audience of public opinion.

Are you challenged to live a life of conviction versus pleasing others? Be true to what God has called you to do no matter the cost.

FILLED WITH THE HOLY SPIRIT

Then Ananias went to the house and entered it. Placing his hands on Saul, he said, "Brother Saul, the Lord—Jesus, who appeared to you on the road as you were coming here—has sent me so that you may see again and be filled with the Holy Spirit."

ACTS 9:1

Billy Graham, the great evangelist, shared a personal story about the role of the Holy Spirit in his life-long ministry and how he came to see the importance of being filled with the Holy Spirit.

In my own life there have been times when I have also had the sense of being filled with the Spirit, knowing that some special strength was added for some task I was being called to perform. We sailed for England in 1954 for a crusade that was to last for three months. While on the ship, I experienced a definite sense of oppression. Satan seemed to have assembled a formidable array of his artillery against me. Not only was I oppressed, I was overtaken by a sense of depression, accomplished by a frightening feeling of inadequacy for the task that lay ahead. Almost night and day I prayed. I knew in a new way what Paul was telling us when he spoke about "praying without ceasing." Then one day in a prayer meeting with my wife and colleagues, a break came. As I wept before the Lord, I was filled with deep assurance that power belonged to God and He was faithful. I had been baptized by the Spirit into the Body of Christ when I was saved, but I believe God gave me a special anointing on the way to England. From that moment on I was confident that God the Holy Sprit was in control for the tasks that lay ahead. That proved true.[15]

As a believer, God has provided the Holy Spirit for you and me so that we can experience the power of the gospel that allows us to live the Christian life. Today, if you have not done so, invite the Holy Spirit to fill your life to overflowing so that you can be a witness in your workplace, city and nation.

THE JUDAS TEST

If an enemy were insulting me, I could endure it; if a foe were raising himself against me, I could hide from him. But it is you, a man like myself, my companion, my close friend, with whom I once enjoyed sweet fellowship as we walked with the throng at the house of God.

PSALM 55:12-14

Betrayal is one of the most difficult tests that we will ever face because it involves being wounded by someone we trust. It's hard not to become bitter when a friend or family member wounds us. It takes a lot of Christlike grace to forgive a traitor.

You have probably faced the Judas Test yourself. The Judas Test is God's graduate level course in faith that is designed to reveal the truth about us: Are we willing to trust Him enough to forgive the Judases in our lives? The book of Hebrews warns, "See to it that no one misses the grace of God and that no bitter root grows up to cause trouble and defile many" (12:15). When we refuse to forgive, we risk infecting others with a bitter root of resentment.

Everyday, you and I work in a marketplace that is rife with betrayal, deception, duplicity and treachery. Perhaps you have been betrayed by your boss or a coworker. Or perhaps somebody betrayed a confidence or stabbed you in the back. It may have even been someone you've gone to church with or prayed with—someone you trusted as a brother or sister in Christ.

The Judas kiss stings worse than a slap across the face. Almost every leader I know has experienced that sting at one time or another. Yet God is watching to see how we respond. If we pass the test, He can then take us to the next level, the next test. *If we fail, we'll probably have to repeat the test until we learn to forgive.*

King David wrote the above psalm during one of his times of betrayal. He chose forgiveness, when his advisors often encouraged retaliation. How about you? Will you wash the feet of Judas and model the forgiveness of Jesus?

LEARNING THE ART OF FORGIVENESS

Forgive us our sins, for we also forgive everyone who sins against us.
LUKE 11:4

"I'm sorry for speaking to you harshly last night," I said. Then the Holy Spirit reminded me to add the second and most important part of my admission. "Will you forgive me?"

Without this request, we have only partially repented of our sin. It is important to humble ourselves before those we sin against. This is repentance. If we only say we are sorry, we are only stating remorse for our actions. Jesus modeled this in the Lord's Prayer: "Forgive us our sins, for we also forgive everyone who sins against us" (Luke 11:4).

When I owned my advertising agency, I once filed a lawsuit against a client who refused to pay a $140,000 bill. However, the Lord instructed me that because I had also sinned in the situation, I was to drop the suit.

My next move was to attempt to contact my former client. I tried phoning him, but he wouldn't return my calls. Finally, I reached his secretary and said, "I want you to take this message down and give it to your boss, word for word—no changes: 'I have sinned against you. I know that I don't deserve your forgiveness, but I ask your forgiveness for filing the lawsuit against you. You are no longer obligated to pay the balance you owe me if you don't feel you owe it.'"

I could hear the secretary begin to cry on the other end of the line. She couldn't believe what she was hearing. About an hour later, my former client called. We hadn't spoken for six months. Because of God's gift of forgiveness, we reconciled the relationship.

The next few years were incredibly difficult because of the financial setback I suffered, but God provided for my needs. Looking back, I realize that this was my Judas test. I passed the test when I let go of my resentment and asked to be forgiven, and God was glorified in the situation.

EXCEEDING EXPECTATIONS

*She said to the king, "The report I heard in my own country about your
achievements and your wisdom is true. But I did not believe these things until
I came and saw with my own eyes. Indeed, not even half was told me; in wisdom
and wealth you have far exceeded the report I heard."*

1 KINGS 10:6-8

"I'm shocked," said the woman on the phone. "I've just seen your picture.
I was expecting a gray-haired old man. You seem to be too young to have the
wisdom that I read in your messages."

When people meet you or experience your work skills, would they say
that you far exceeded their expectations? Do you undersell and overproduce,
or oversell and underproduce? Solomon's wisdom far exceeded any man's
wisdom, and this was evident to others. When people come in contact with
you, do they come away with a sense of greater appreciation of you after
meeting you?

"Do you see a man skilled in his work? He will serve before kings; he will
not serve before obscure men" (Proverbs 22:29). Whenever we exceed the
expectations of man, we bring glory to our heavenly Father, and He often
elevates us among men.

A man named Bezalel, for example, was handpicked by God to design the
Ark of the Covenant for Moses because of his exceptional skill. Moses then
said to the Israelites, "See, the LORD has chosen Bezalel son of Uri, the son of
Hur, of the tribe of Judah, and he has filled him with the Spirit of God, with
skill, ability and knowledge in all kinds of crafts—to make artistic designs for
work in gold, silver and bronze, to cut and set stones, to work in wood and to
engage in all kinds of artistic craftsmanship. And he has given both him and
Oholiab son of Ahisamach, of the tribe of Dan, the ability to teach others"
(Exodus 35:30-35).

If there were a Kingdom project to be done today, would God recommend
you for the job? God calls you and me to live our lives and do our work
with excellence.

THE VALLEY OF HARDSHIPS

Dear friends, do not be surprised at the painful trial you are suffering, as though something strange were happening to you. But rejoice that you participate in the sufferings of Christ, so that you may be overjoyed when his glory is revealed.

1 PETER 4:12-13

I've observed a Kingdom principle regarding adversity: *The pathway to leadership almost always takes us through the valley of hardships.* We see this principle not only in the story of Joseph, who endured 13 years of adversity, but also in the lives of many other leaders in both the Old and New Testaments.

Moses was raised in the royal splendor of Pharaoh's household in Egypt, but he was forced to spend 40 years in desert exile before God spoke from a burning bush and called him to lead the Hebrew people out of slavery. Joshua spent the years of his youth as a slave in Egypt and during his middle-aged years wandered in the desert at Moses' side. He was well acquainted with adversity when God called him to lead Israel's armies in the conquest of Canaan. The prophet Daniel had to pass through a fiery furnace and a den of hungry lions before he could reach a place of power and influence in the Babylonian courts. And we see this same pattern played out in the lives of David, Isaiah, Amos, Hosea and many other Old Testament leaders.

Turning to the New Testament, we see that even Jesus had to face adversity in the desert, suffering hunger, thirst, temptation and opposition from Satan. Only then could He begin His public ministry. Likewise, the Lord's disciples had to endure the loss of their Master, the failure of their faith and character, and the dark days of despair between the cross and the empty tomb before they could become the founding leaders of the Lord's Church.

It's hard to find anyone in Christian history that became a great leader without first traveling through the valley of hardships.

ISN'T THIS JOSEPH'S SON?

All spoke well of him and were amazed at the gracious words that
came from his lips. "Isn't this Joseph's son?" they asked.
LUKE 4:22

Jesus was an earthly common man who did daily work just like His other villagers in Nazareth. So when He began to become known as a radical rabbi who thought and did things outside the box, the first observations from those who knew Him were, "Isn't this the carpenter Joseph's son?"

This is not unlike what happens when God calls us into a more public ministry. "Isn't that John, the CPA? Isn't that Bill, the restaurant manager? Isn't that Susie, the bank executive?" The first question our critics ask is, "Where did John, Bill or Susie get religion?"

The religious spirit reveals itself in many ways in the workplace. As C. Peter Wagner describes in *Freedom from the Religious Spirit,* the religious spirit can best be defined as an agent of Satan assigned to maintain the status quo by using religious devices. The religious spirit seeks to distort a genuine move of God through deception, control and manipulation. It was the primary force used against Jesus and was designed to intimidate and turn His relationship with God into a set of rules and regulations.[16]

Satan does not want Jesus in the workplace because that is where the authority lies to change a workplace, city or nation. God desires us to bring His presence with us into our workplace every day. We should not let the enemy of our soul shame us into alienating our faith from our work.

Today, ask Jesus to go into the workplace with you. The two of you just might be the team needed to bring someone out of slavery and bondage.

LEARNING TO RECEIVE

In vain you rise early and stay up late, toiling for food to eat—
for he grants sleep to those he loves.
PSALM 127:2

One of the paradigm shifts every believer must learn once they make Jesus lord of their lives is how to move from receiving by sweating and toiling to receiving by trusting and obeying. In the Scripture, Egypt represented sweat, toil and bondage. The Promised Land, in contrast, represented a land of milk and honey received by trust and obedience.

In Joshua 24:13, we learn that our obedience will allow us to receive things we would never receive out of sweat and toil: "So I gave you a land on which you did not toil and cities you did not build; and you live in them and eat from vineyards and olive groves that you did not plant." I learned this principle myself when God began to transition me from owning and operating an advertising agency to working in vocational marketplace ministry. Many times, I could not see how God would provide for me in my work, because it was not based upon the contract-for-services model to which I was accustomed.

For example, I was once invited to speak to a small group of people on a Caribbean island. I knew it would require three days of my time and also that I would receive very little compensation. Yet the Lord instructed me to go anyway. Just as I expected, I did not receive a commensurate income for the time I invested during the three days. However, I left some of my books behind, and they began to circulate to other islands. A few businessmen received the books and invited me to speak at a conference for 22 Caribbean islands later that year.

When I went back to speak at the conference, one man in particular was touched by my teaching. On January 2, I received a check from him in the amount of $5,000. When I pondered the sequence of events that led to my receiving this provision, I realized that it was because of my obedience to the small things that God was able to give me a "land on which I did not toil."

Be faithful to the small things and God will always honor your obedience.

APPEARING TO THE LITTLE CHILD

*At that time Jesus said, "I praise you, Father, Lord of heaven and earth,
because you have hidden these things from the wise and learned, and revealed
them to little children. Yes, Father, for this was your good pleasure."*
MATTHEW 11:25-26

It was a typical Sunday morning church service. Twelve-year-old Jordan, the pastor's daughter, took her regular first-row seat opposite her mother, Pattie. Jordan was deaf and could not understand the message without a sign language interpreter, but she liked to sit with her friend in the front row regardless. On this day, there was no interpreter for the service. However, sitting next to her were her friend and her friend's mother, who both knew sign language.

They often had visiting preachers at their church. This day, the visiting preacher preached a message on "getting into the river of God." During the service, Jordan asked her friend if she saw what she was seeing.

"See what?" Jordan's friend signed.

"The angels and Jesus!" Jordan replied.

"Where?" her friend signed.

"There! By the guitar!" replied Jordan, pointing to the platform.

It was then that her mother saw the girls talking. Pattie knew that her daughter was seeing something because of the look on her face and her reactions. Jordan never took her eyes off the platform. She began describing what she was seeing to her friend's mother, who then passed the message on to Jordan's mother. Jordan described the scene in every detail. As she looked at the stage, Jesus, who was standing behind the minister, looked back at her and signed, "I love you."

Jesus often appeared to the disciples after His resurrection. Over the centuries, there have been reports of personal appearances of Jesus to both believing and unbelieving individuals. Today, we need to have faith like Jordan. Ask the Lord to make His presence known in your life.

GOING WITHOUT JESUS

After the Feast was over, while his parents were returning home, the boy Jesus stayed behind in Jerusalem, but they were unaware of it.

LUKE 2:43

Bob and Janice had five kids. When they went on any trip, Benjamin, the youngest, always slept under the seat in their minivan. One day, in the rush of preparing for their visit to the grocery store and getting the other kids situated, Bob and Janice failed to pick up Benjamin, who was standing outside at the other end of the store. As they proceeded down the road, they assumed that Benjamin was quietly sleeping in his normal place under the seat in the back of the van.

Meanwhile, after about an hour, young Benjamin was wondering why his parents had not picked him up. He went back into the store and told the manager his plight. The manager called the police. Eventually, a policeman came to pick up Benjamin.

Jesus was 12 years old when Mary and Joseph traveled to Jerusalem for the Feast of the Passover. They were evidently very distracted by the excitement and business of the Feast. In fact, Mary and Joseph began their return trip to Nazareth only to realize well into the trip that Jesus was not with them. It would be three days before they could reunite with their 12-year-old son. It caused quite a scare for Mary and Joseph, and when they found Jesus again, they reprimanded Him for wandering off.

As a parent, I find this story truly amazing. How could the parents of the Son of God not know that their son was not in their presence? Yet this story illustrates how each of us can become so busy that we just continue to operate, not realizing that Jesus is no longer with us.

We can easily walk away from fellowship with Jesus. Do not let this happen to you. He longs to have daily fellowship with you because He loves you. Today, ask yourself if Jesus is accompanying you in your daily activities. He desires to walk with you each and every day.

FINDING JEWELS IN THE DESERT

*Therefore I am now going to allure her; I will lead her into
the desert and speak tenderly to her.*

HOSEA 2:14

An ancient Arabian fable tells of three merchants who crossed the desert.
In the daytime, they would pitch tents for shelter from the desert sun. When
the stars came out, they would ride their camels in the cool of the night.
At one point, the merchants crossed a dry riverbed under the stars.

"Halt!" said a voice from the darkness.

All three men jumped down from their camels and huddled in fear.
"Who's there?" one of them said.

"Don't be afraid," said the voice in the dark. "I won't harm you if you do
as I say. See those pebbles at your feet? Each of you, pick up a pebble and put
it in your pocket." The three merchants obeyed. Each took a pebble from the
riverbed. "Now leave this place," the voice said, "and don't stop until daybreak."

The merchants mounted up. One said, "What's this all about?"

"I will only say this," the voice replied. "In the morning, you will be happy—
and sad. Now go!"

Baffled, the three merchants proceeded on their way. As they traveled,
they wondered what the voice meant by saying that they would be both happy
and sad. When morning came, the merchants stopped. Each man pulled the
single pebble from his own pocket and saw that it sparkled in the morning
sunlight. The "pebbles" were precious gems. One man had a ruby, another an
emerald, and the other a sapphire.

"Jewels!" one merchant said, his face shining with joy.

"Oh, no!" wailed the second. "There were thousands of jewels all over
the riverbed! Each of us took only one! Why didn't we grab handfuls?"

"Look!" shouted the third, pointing behind them. A desert wind had
whipped up, erasing their tracks. "We can never find our way back!"

The voice in the desert had spoken truly. The merchants were happy
and sad. They had found wealth in the desert—but they could have taken
more![17] Sometimes God leads us into the desert to discover the treasures
that can only be found there.

COMFORTING OTHERS

Praise be to the God and Father of our Lord Jesus Christ, the Father of compassion and the God of all comfort, who comforts us in all our troubles, so that we can comfort those in any trouble with the comfort we ourselves have received from God.

2 CORINTHIANS 1:3-4

In September 1966, I was at home watching *I Dream of Jeannie* when the program was interrupted by a news bulletin: "Three prominent local businessmen have died in a plane crash in the mountains of Tennessee." That's how I learned of the death of my father. I was 14 years old at the time.

It was difficult and painful growing up without a father. I loved my dad and needed him in my life. I couldn't understand why God would take him away from me so suddenly. I certainly didn't see my father's death as a blessing in any sense of the word.

Yet over the years, I have seen blessings come out of that terrible tragedy. In the years since my father died, God has brought a number of men across my path who also lost their fathers at an early age. Because of my own loss, I had an instant connection with them. We shared an experience that other people couldn't fully understand.

When I later went through a seven-year period in which I experienced major financial problems, I certainly wouldn't have said at the time that it was a blessing to endure that adversity. Yet God has since used that time of trial in my life to bring blessing to other people. It was actually a catalyst to move me into a whole new calling.

God can take our adversity—a heart attack, cancer, an automobile accident, violent crime, bankruptcy, a marriage crisis, the loss of a loved one— and transform that pain into encouragement for the people around us. We come out of those experiences stronger and better able to comfort others.

Although adversity may never be a blessing, God in His grace can bring blessing out of our adversity. The key is to release the hurt and pain to the Lord so that He can bring the needed healing to our lives. Why not give your circumstance to the Lord today and let Him use it in the lives of others? This is the first step toward healing.

DISCIPLING THE NATIONS

A good man leaves an inheritance to his children's children,
but the wealth of the sinner is stored up for the righteous.
PROVERBS 13:22, *NKJV*

In 1971, Berthold Becker was converted from being a socialist activist to a disciple of the Lord Jesus. Shortly after completing his university education, Berthold decided that he wanted to understand what it meant to experience God in his professional career. So he learned to walk with God at work in the automotive industry.

Berthold later testified how God gave him many designs for cars that became best sellers for the company. He was often referred to as the "prophet" among his non-Christian auto executives. With his wife, Barbara, as his personal intercessor, Berthold left his career in the auto industry in 1986 to begin many entrepreneurial Kingdom initiatives. One was launched in Ukraine through an initiative called GfS (*Gesellschaft für Strukturentwicklung*). Through GfS, Berthold became active in many training, consulting and joint venture situations, helping Ukrainian business start-ups.

During his travels in Ukraine, he noticed the lack of availability of good bread and decided to do something about it. He started small businesses using mobile bakeries that he bought from the Swiss Army. The German and Ukranian governments soon recognized that Berthold had been serving the nation through his business expertise and began funding his enterprises.

The Bible says, "Ask of me, and I will make the nations your inheritance, the ends of the earth your possession" (Psalm 2:8). I believe that Berthold is an example of this verse in action—an example of Christians becoming the source of blessing to a city or nation. Today, God is raising up a new breed of Christian workplace leaders. He will use anyone to impact a nation because He calls each of us to disciple the nations.

How might God want to use you in the days ahead? What idea might God give you to impact a nation?

FAILING FORWARD

Forgetting what is behind and straining toward what is ahead, I press on toward the goal to win the prize for which God has called me heavenward in Christ Jesus.
PHILIPPIANS 3:13-14

Back in the 1970s, Tom Watson was the up-and-coming golfer on the PGA Tour. But time after time, when Tom led a tournament coming into the last round, he would choke, bogey a few holes and finish in the middle of the pack. Soon, the media began calling him a "choker," which only increased the pressure and his tendency to choke.

In an interview with Guy Yocom for *Golf Digest*, Watson said, "Everybody has choked. In the 1974 U.S. Open, I kept hitting the ball to the right. My nerves wouldn't allow me to adjust. That's what choking is—being so nervous you can't find a swing or a putting stroke you can trust."

How did Watson overcome this problem? "Byron Nelson, the legendary golf pro of the 1930s and 1940s , gave me the best cure for it," Watson recalled. "[Byron said], 'Walk slowly, talk slowly, deliberately do everything more slowly than you normally do. It has a way of settling you down.'"[18] That advice helped Tom Watson overcome his nervousness. He went on to win many tournaments, including five British Opens.

We all fail at one time or another. It's part of the process that leads us to maturity and success. Most successful entrepreneurs have been through a number of failures in life, but they usually don't think of their failures as defeats. They think of them as lessons.

My failures have served to help many people who are also experiencing failure in their lives. God will always have a redeeming value in our failures if we let Him reveal His life through them. If you hope to succeed, learn everything you can from your failures. And remember, failing does not make *you* a failure.

THE COST OF UNBELIEF

And without faith it is impossible to please God, because anyone who comes to him
must believe that he exists and that he rewards those who earnestly seek him.

HEBREWS 11:6

How is your faith quotient? On a scale of 1 to 10, where would you rank your-self? Every day, I marvel at the faith most of us exercise without even thinking about it.

We drive our cars at 60 to 70 miles per hour with only a white line sep-arating us from oncoming traffic and have faith that every car going in the opposite direction will not cross into our lane. We fly on airplanes that take us over oceans, trusting the pilots with our very lives. We ride on thrilling amusement rides that travel 50 to 70 miles per hour down long and winding slopes, trusting that the operators will bring us back safely. There is a great irony in the fact that we can place our faith in such things but cannot place our faith in the hands of our Creator.

God became angry with one of His priests, named Zechariah, when he questioned God's angelic messenger about his wife becoming pregnant with John the Baptist:

> Zechariah asked the angel, "How can I be sure of this? I am an old man and my wife is well along in years." The angel answered, "I am Gabriel. I stand in the presence of God, and I have been sent to speak to you and to tell you this good news. And now you will be silent and not able to speak until the day this happens, because you did not believe my words, which will come true at their proper time" (Luke 1:18-20).

Zechariah was struck mute because of his unbelief for nine months, until the birth of John the Baptist.

What consequence have you suffered from a lack of faith? Is there an area in your life in which you have not been able to trust God? Why not repent of your unbelief and place your faith totally in His hands today.

KNOWING THE RISK AND REWARD

David asked the men standing near him, "What will be done for the man who kills this Philistine and removes this disgrace from Israel?"

1 SAMUEL 17:26

Every entrepreneur must determine the risk and reward before entering into a venture. Yet this is not the only consideration. Entrepreneurs must consider all of the factors in order to determine if God is truly leading them into that venture. They must also consider whether the timing is right to proceed.

David understood the risk /reward principle. During his days as a shepherd, he had already killed a lion and a bear. When he brought food to his older brothers in the army and heard that no one was willing to fight the giant Goliath, he became angry. However, he didn't respond out of pure emotion. He asked a very important question: "What will be done for the man who kills this Philistine and removes this disgrace from Israel?" He got the answer he was hoping for: "The king will give great wealth to the man who kills him. He will also give him his daughter in marriage and will exempt his father's family from taxes in Israel" (1 Samuel 17:25).

Do you see the reward? David would get financial wealth, a wife and would no longer have to pay taxes! What more motivation does a young Jewish boy need? Does this take away from the spiritual significance of the story? Absolutely not.

The religious spirit always tries to make the business side of faith evil. However, money and profit are not evil. It is the love of money and the pride of life that get people into trouble. David understood the proper balance between these and how they could coexist to accomplish God's purposes.

To avoid getting into trouble, simply ask this question of yourself: *What is the true motive of my heart?* If it does not have the spiritual element balanced with the business element, you may be in trouble. Then ask God four questions before you proceed in any venture: (1) Is the Holy Spirit leading me? (2) Is this the time to be involved? (3) Are the risk and reward worth it? (4) Do I have what is necessary to be successful in the venture with God's help?

After you've asked these questions, go about your task with all your heart.

THREE-PHASE OBEDIENCE

Jesus replied: "'Love the Lord your God with all your heart and with all your soul and with all your mind.' This is the first and greatest commandment. And the second is like it: 'Love your neighbor as yourself.'"

MATTHEW 22:37-39

From 1994 to 2001, I went through what I call my Joseph Pit experience. It was during this time of great adversity and great growth that I wrote my first series of *TGIF: Today God Is First* devotionals and also birthed many of the things I am doing today. During this season, I discovered a spiritual truth about how most believers experience three distinct phases of their growth toward obedience in their Christian walks.

When we first begin our spiritual journey, we often make decisions based on *convenience*. Often, we decide what the outcome is that we want and then make decisions based on the perceived outcome. If it is a positive outcome, we will then make an obedient decision. I call this outcome-based obedience.

However, God desires that each of us live a life of obedience regardless of our perceived outcome. In order to transition us to this obedience-based process, He will bring a crisis into our lives. This crisis is designed to create pain that will motivate us to seek Him in order to alleviate the pain. We have all heard of "fox-hole" Christianity. There is a place of obedience for everyone! However, this is not where God desires us to remain.

Ultimately, God desires us to live a life of obedience and intimacy that is rooted in *conviction*. During the crisis phase, we discover a personal love of God in our lives that we had never experienced before. This will then lead us into an intimate love relationship with God in which we obey His commands from a heart of love and devotion.

The Christian life can be summed up in one word: love. God's desire for each of us is to know Him intimately and to love Him with all of our heart. Have you told your heavenly Father today that you love Him?

SHEPHERD YOUR PEOPLE

*Shepherd your people with your staff, the flock of your inheritance,
which lives by itself in a forest, in fertile pasturelands.*

MICAH 7:14

You and I are called to be shepherds in the workplace. Just as Moses' staff represented his calling as a shepherd, your "staff" (vocation) represents your calling to your work-life ministry. God's first words to Moses were, "Remove your shoes, for this is holy ground." God came to Moses during his workday. Moses' work became holy because God's presence was there.

God used Moses' staff to perform miracles and deliver the people of Israel from bondage (see Exodus 4:17). He is still issuing this same call today to you and me in the workplace. As we minister through our work-life call, our inheritance will come as a result of allowing God to use our abilities. As Paul tells us in Colossians 3:23-24:

> Whatever you do, work at it with all your heart, as working for the Lord, not for men, since you know that you will receive an inheritance from the Lord as a reward. It is the Lord Christ you are serving.

What makes our work holy is the motivation by which we do it. If we work to glorify God and serve others in the process, our work becomes ministry.

Those in the workplace are like a remnant of a wayward people in a forest awaiting harvest. The workplace is a fertile pasture awaiting a shepherd who can lead the lost into a life of purpose and destiny. Will you be the instrument of God to shepherd His people out of bondage?

Ask the Lord to use you to perform miracles and to become a shepherd to those He has called you to lead. Why not start today?

POWER REPENTANCE

When Simon Peter saw this, he fell at Jesus' knees and said,
"Go away from me, Lord; I am a sinful man!"
L U K E 5:8

Are you playing Christianity or do you have a daily encounter with the living Christ? In this story in Luke, Peter was going about his workday trying to earn a day's wage in his fishing business. It wasn't going well—they had caught no fish.

When Jesus showed up on the shoreline later that day, He asked to use Peter's boat in order to teach the people. After Jesus used Peter's business for His purposes, He turned to Peter and suggested that he throw his nets out again. Peter, somewhat reluctant and argumentative, said in his hallmark attitude, "Been there, done that, Master . . . You don't know what You're talking about." How many times have you and I said the same thing? We say to ourselves, *Jesus doesn't care about my work life—He only cares about the orphans and the poor.*

However, when Peter's nets filled with fish, a strange awareness came over him: "When Simon Peter saw this, he fell at Jesus' knees and said, 'Go away from me, Lord; I am a sinful man!'" Peter was overwhelmed at the personal love and power that was directed specifically at his need at the moment—his ailing business. It was more than he could handle. God even cared about the condition of his business!

Whenever we move from playing Christianity to having a genuine encounter with the living Christ, we are confronted with our own humanity and sin as compared to the unmerited love and power of Jesus Christ that is personally directed to us. This realization should bring us to our knees. It is an awesome experience to transition from religion to relationship. Life is never the same once we have a personal encounter with our Savior.

How about you? Do you need a personal encounter with Jesus today? Ask Him to reveal His power in your work today.

RECEIVING BAD NEWS

A vast army is coming against you from Edom, from the other side of the sea . . .
Alarmed, Jehoshaphat resolved to inquire of the LORD.

2 CHRONICLES 20:2-3

Has anyone ever brought you really bad news? News so bad that when you heard it your stomach immediately became upset? News that made you go into crisis mode?

This was the situation for King Jehoshaphat. He had just been informed that his country was going to be attacked by an army much larger than his. However, instead of panicking, he immediately turned to the Lord and called for a time of a fasting and prayer. The people from every town in Judah responded.

King Jehoshaphat prayed and reminded God of His promise to Israel. Then he asked God for strategy, "for we have no power against this great multitude that is coming against us; nor do we know what to do, but our eyes are upon You" (2 Chronicles 20:12).

After his prayer, Jehoshaphat waited on God's answer. This answer eventually came through the prophet Jahaziel, son of Zechariah, who said, "Listen, all you of Judah and you inhabitants of Jerusalem, and you, King Jehoshaphat! Thus says the LORD to you: 'Do not be afraid nor dismayed because of this great multitude, for the battle is not yours, but God's'" (2 Chronicles 20:15-16).

God supernaturally wiped out their enemies that day. The Israelites didn't even have to fight—God caused the enemy to fight themselves. However, the one thing the Israelites *did* do was to praise God on the battlefield: "Now when they began to sing and to praise, the LORD set ambushes against the people of Ammon, Moab, and Mount Seir, who had come against Judah; and they were defeated" (20:22).

Note that Jehoshaphat did four things in response to bad news: (1) He called for prayer, (2) he called for fasting, (3) he asked for God's strategy, and (4) he began the battle by praising God. If you've received some bad news, follow the example of Jehoshaphat. Pray. Fast. Ask. Praise.

TWO TYPES OF PEOPLE

O LORD, by your hand save me from such men, from men,
from men of this world whose reward is in this life.
PSALM 17:14

There are two types of people in the world: those whose activities are designed to generate a reward in this lifetime, and those who live to generate a reward when they meet our Lord in heaven. Unfortunately, not every Christian models the latter type.

How do we judge whether a person is living for the future reward versus the earthly reward? There are several key indicators.

First, future-reward people tend to be givers. They make their time and resources available to be channeled for Kingdom purposes. They realize that their sowing will ultimately be rewarded at the judgment seat of Christ, where what they have done on Earth will be judged and rewarded by God (see 2 Corinthians 5:10).

Future-reward people also tend to make obedience-based decisions. They don't make decisions based on their perceived outcome. They realize that a decision based on obedience alone may not result in an immediate outcome. Jesus was a future-reward person. He was obedient to the cross, even though He knew the immediate outcome would be His own death.

Future-reward situations show up in daily life in a number of ways. Perhaps a person has wronged you and God calls you to forgive and even bless that person without expectation of his or her response. Perhaps God has called you to sow money into a ministry or another person's life without expectation of return from that person. Perhaps you have been called to serve another person in another capacity without expectation of any earthly reward. The situations we might encounter are unlimited.

Are you living a life based on future reward or short-term reward? Today, evaluate how you make decisions and how you allocate resources. This will reveal whether or not you are a future-reward Christian.

HANGING OUT WITH SINNERS

When Jesus reached the spot, he looked up and said to him,
"Zacchaeus, come down immediately. I must stay at your house today."
So he came down at once and welcomed him gladly. All the people saw this
and began to mutter, "He has gone to be the guest of a 'sinner.'"
LUKE 19:5-7

Jesus modeled four things when He lived on Earth that allowed Him to impact other people's lives. I call these the Four *B*s of Transformation.

First, Jesus *built a relationship* with people. In the marketplace, you will rarely be able to have an impact on a person without first building a relationship with him or her. The old saying "people don't care what you know until they know that you care" is especially true in the workplace. Jesus modeled this in His life every day of His public ministry.

Second, Jesus *blessed people*. He tried to meet the physical needs that people had. Many times He healed people and then told them to go and sin no more. He listened to their concerns.

Third, Jesus *began praying* for others. He prayed for deliverance for people who were demon possessed. He prayed that unbelievers would know the Father. He even prayed for Lazarus to come back from the dead.

Fourth, Jesus *brought the kingdom of God* into people's lives. He invited people to believe in Him as the Savior of the world and to partake of eternal life.

I once decided to test this model with an acquaintance. I intentionally refused to talk to this person about Jesus until I had accomplished the first three steps in our relationship. After I had fulfilled the first three steps, I presented Christ to my friend. Because the soil was prepared, he received Christ immediately.

As you consider your ministry at work, consider these four stages of relationship building before you present Christ to others. You will find that the fruit of this process will be great.

DO NOT REACH FOR THE POWER

For it is we who are the circumcision, we who worship by the Spirit of God,
who glory in Christ Jesus, and who put no confidence in the flesh.

PHILIPPIANS 3:3

A few years ago, I was asked by a large organization to meet with them about doing some cooperative projects in the faith-at-work area. I visited their headquarters and had several initial discussions. We concluded that we would proceed on a joint conference.

During my visit, I stayed overnight at the headquarters of this ministry. At 5 A.M. the next day, I was awakened and led to read Exodus 33:15. In this passage, Moses said that he could not go any farther if God did not promise that His presence would go with him. I sensed that this was to be our theme for the conference.

Later that morning, I shared that I had received this leading from the Lord with some of the people in the organization. Unfortunately, the leader of the organization did not take it seriously. I was a bit irritated and my pride was hurt, but I decided to follow a principle that I had been walking in for a few years: *Act like you have the authority but do not reach for the power.* I realized that if God had truly spoken His words into my heart, I would not have to exercise my authority to make it happen. He would orchestrate the event.

More discussion was given to the theme, but nothing was resolved. A few hours later, the conference theme came up again. I turned to a friend and read Exodus 33:15 aloud, and he got excited about using that verse as the possible theme. The leader, to my amazement, chimed in as well and said, "Yes, that should be the theme of the conference." It was a big lesson for me.

Act like you have the authority, but do not reach for the power.

THINKING OUTSIDE THE BOX

This He said to test him, for He Himself knew what He would do.
JOHN 6:6, RSV

Jesus and the disciples had just crossed the Sea of Galilee. Multitudes of people followed Him because of the miracles they had seen Him perform. Jesus was just about to speak to the people when He realized it was dinnertime and the people would be hungry. There were more than 5,000 people who needed to be fed.

Jesus already knew what He was going to do in this situation. However, He wanted to test the disciples to see if they could think beyond themselves to find a God-solution to the problem. Sadly, they failed the test. When Jesus asked the disciples to get food to feed the crowd, they immediately thought the way that most of us would think. They looked in their pocketbooks and realized that they did not have adequate resources to purchase enough food for the crowd.

It is when we come to the end of our resources that God comes in with His. When I published the first volume of *TGIF: Today God Is First* in book form, I was required to order 1,000 copies from my publisher. We had very little distribution and sales of materials at that time. So, after a few months, we still had boxes and boxes of inventory in our basement.

"These books are not doing us or anyone else any good in our basement," I said to my wife, Angie. "I think we need to go downstairs, lay hands on the books and command them to leave our basement. As it says in Mark 11:23, we can speak to the mountain and have it removed."

So Angie and I walked downstairs and prayed, "In the name of Jesus, get out of the basement and go be a blessing to someone!" Feeling very foolish, I walked upstairs. Two hours later, we received a call from a Texas-based workplace ministry that placed an order for 300 books! It was Saturday, when such businesses should be closed! Until then, we had never sold more than a few copies in one day!

When a problem arises in your work life, do you think only the logical thought? Perhaps God has created your problem as an opportunity to manifest His glory in the situation. Next time, go outside the box and see the glory of God revealed in your predicament!

TEAM BUILDING

You will be my witnesses in Jerusalem, and in all Judea and Samaria,
and to the ends of the earth.

ACTS 1:8

Building a good team is key to the success of any enterprise. Jesus chose 12 unique individuals to build His world-changing enterprise. He intentionally chose several men who had similar backgrounds—Peter, James and John were fisherman. However, two others that Jesus chose—Matthew and Simon the Zealot—came from opposing political views. From this, it is clear that Jesus first chose those who had a skill set and then changed the character of the individual. He mentored each one.

A good team needs to have team members with different viewpoints as well as those who are specialists in a particular area. For instance, it is noteworthy that Jesus chose someone like Matthew—a tax collector—who was experienced in handling money. Taking a team of 12 men around the country required money and the ability to manage it. I'm sure Jesus spent a great deal of time with Matthew mentoring him on the proper use of money. He had to reshape his thinking about money.

Once the team was formed, Jesus spent time molding the members of that team into a cohesive unit. He corrected them when correction was needed. He taught them what it meant to love one another. He washed their feet and modeled servant-leadership.

Before you put a team together, sit down and make a list of the skills you want represented on your team. Then recruit and invest spiritually in your team. Who knows, your team just might change the world as well!

RECEIVING ONLY WHAT GOD GIVES YOU

A man can receive only what is given him from heaven.
JOHN 3:27

John the Baptist was in the business of bringing sinners to the place of repentance by baptizing them and teaching them about the coming Messiah. Over time, he had developed quite a customer base of disciples. Yet when the promised Messiah showed up—the fulfillment of John's business plan—true to form, John's coworkers (or disciples) went to John to complain that the One he had testified about was stealing all of his customers.

John's response, "A man can receive only what is given him from heaven," clearly shows that he understood his purpose and role in life. He understood that we receive by understanding our purpose and what God desires us to receive in light of our purpose.

We don't need to worry about what others receive. We only need to worry if we are receiving what God wants us to receive. Many of us try to receive things God never intended us to receive or try to be someone that God never intended us to be.

A story is told about F. B. Meyer, the great Bible teacher and pastor who lived a century ago. He was pastoring a church when he began to notice that attendance was dropping. This continued until he finally asked some members of his congregation why they thought this was happening. "It is because of the new church down the road," one member said. "The young preacher has everyone talking, and many are going to hear him speak." The young preacher's name was Charles Spurgeon.

Rather than seeking to discourage this development, Meyer exhorted his entire congregation to join him and go participate in seeing this "move of God," as he described it. "If this be happening, then God must be at work," he said. Like John the Baptist, he understood the principle of receiving from God and was not threatened by the new competition in town.

Do you model a Kingdom mindset? Do you rejoice when others succeed? Are you receiving only what God desires you to receive?

MOURNING FOR YOUR CITY

When I heard these things, I sat down and wept. For some days I mourned and fasted and prayed before the God of heaven.

NEHEMIAH 1:4

Nehemiah lived in the world of politics. He was a high-ranking worker in the government of Babylon. His official title was cupbearer for King Artazerzes. Today, he would be considered the U. S. Secret Service agent who made sure the king was safe from being poisoned.

After Judah had been driven into exile, some of Nehemiah's friends returned with news about his fellow brothers and sisters in Jerusalem.

In the month of Kislev in the twentieth year, while I was in the citadel of Susa, Hanani, one of my brothers, came from Judah with some other men, and I questioned them about the Jewish remnant that survived the exile, and also about Jerusalem. They said to me, "Those who survived the exile and are back in the province are in great trouble and disgrace. The wall of Jerusalem is broken down, and its gates have been burned with fire" (Nehemiah 1:1-3).

Nehemiah's response on hearing the news is the same kind of response necessary for any Christian leader who wants to impact his or her city: He wept for the condition of his beloved city. He immediately went into prayer and asked for God's direction on how he could be a positive impact on his city. He developed a strategy to rebuild the wall of Jerusalem, and accomplished the task in only 52 days.

Do you weep for your city? Today, God is calling forth men and women from the marketplace to be a catalyst for change in their cities. Begin to pray for your city and ask God how you can be used to rebuild your city's spiritual walls.

THINKING BIG

For nothing is impossible with God.
LUKE 1:37

In July 2000, a South African businessman named Graham Power was awakened at 4 A.M. by a vision from God that came in three distinct parts. In the first part of the vision, God instructed Graham to rent the 45,000-seat Newlands rugby stadium in Cape Town for a day of repentance and prayer for the city. In the second part of the vision, Graham saw the prayer movement spreading to the rest of South Africa for a national day of prayer. In the final part of the vision, Graham saw the prayer effort spread to cover the rest of the continent.

It was only 30 days earlier that a man named Gunnar Olson had stood in front of a podium at the conclusion of a marketplace conference in Johannesburg, South Africa, and proclaimed Isaiah 60, which said to "arise and shine" over the continent of Africa and that God was going to use Africa to bless the nations.

Graham was obedient to his vision, and on March 21, 2001, a capacity crowd gathered in the Newlands rugby stadium for prayer and repentance. Soon after, a notorious gangster in the city was saved. News of the first gathering spread quickly, and in 2002 eight cities in South Africa hosted a day of prayer. Leading up to the event, young people from all over the country took part in a walk of hope from Bloemfontein to the eight stadiums where the prayer meetings were to be held. The events were broadcast on television.

By June 2006, what began as Transformation Africa became the Global Day of Prayer. Two hundred nations from seven continents around the world participated in the event. And this prayer movement is still growing.

It all started from the obedience of one businessman. What might God want to do through your life? It begins with obedience to the small things and exercising your faith to believe God can do it. Our part is obedience. His part is outcome.

THE BLACK HOLE

My grace is sufficient for you, for my power is made perfect in weakness.
2 CORINTHIANS 12:9

On February 20, 1962, at 9:47 A.M., the spacecraft Friendship 7 rose on a pillar of fire, piloted by lone astronaut John Glenn. Leaving the coast of Florida far behind, the space capsule orbited the earth three times, traveling 81,000 miles in less than 4 hours. As the craft began its descent from space, controllers in Houston received a warning signal. A sensor indicated that the capsule's heat shield was in danger of detaching. If the heat shield came loose during reentry, the capsule would burn like a meteor—and John Glenn would die.

Because radio waves cannot penetrate plasma, the spacecraft experienced a total communications blackout—what astronauts and mission controllers call a "black hole." As the minutes crawled by, the suspense mounted in the Houston control room. NASA engineers felt totally helpless. Finally, after five minutes of silence, the controllers heard Glenn's voice crackling over the radio: "*Friendship 7* to Houston . . ."

Shouts of joy shook the control room. John Glenn was coming home. Although neither Glenn nor the mission controllers knew it at the time, the heat shield was absolutely firm and reliable. The fears for John Glenn's safety during his black hole experience were unfounded.

If you've ever been through a major crisis, you probably know what a communications black hole feels like. While you are in the pit of adversity, you feel that your world is collapsing, that your life is out of control and that God is silent. The silence of a black hole is deafening. You feel isolated and alone. You question God's love, His care for you, and even His existence.

But even when it seems that God is distant and silent, your heat shield is still there, firm and reliable. In your black hole experience, God is teaching you to go deeper into your relationship with Him. You may think that your life is out of control and burning like a meteor, but in reality God—your heat shield—still protects you from the fiery forces that surround you.

Stand firm in the knowledge that God says He will never leave us or forsake us (see Hebrews 13:5).

HEARING THE VOICE OF GOD—EVEN ON THE JOB

I am the good shepherd; I know my sheep and my sheep know me . . .
My sheep listen to my voice; I know them, and they follow me.
JOHN 10:14,27

Tom Fox is a successful financial investment manager who heads up a work-place ministry in the Twin Cities area in Minnesota. He used to be troubled when he heard Christians say, "The Lord told me . . ." He certainly had never heard God speak to him like that. *What is different about those people and me?* he wondered. In the book of John, Tom had read that Jesus had said that His sheep hear His voice, but Tom didn't understand how they could do that. His pursuit to answer that question began his quest to discover how to hear God's voice himself.

Today, Tom realizes that God does speak and that we, as His children, can hear His voice. He has discovered how to hear God's words of guidance in his daily life, which includes the day-to-day operations of his business. He is also teaching others how to hear God's voice.

A friend of mine told me a story about an experience he had in Israel that demonstrates how sheep know their shepherd's voice. He and his wife were visiting some of the famous biblical sites when they saw a group of shepherds and their flocks. They watched as three different shepherds put their sheep in the same pen for the night. They wondered how in the world the shepherds would separate their sheep the next day, as none of them had any identifying marks on them.

My friend got up early the next morning to watch the shepherds gather their sheep. The first shepherd went over to the pen and called out to his sheep. One by one, his sheep (and only his sheep) filed out to follow him. The same thing happened with the other two shepherds. My friend said it was amazing to watch how only the shepherd's sheep followed him while the others remained in the pen—and all because they recognized his voice.

What a picture of Jesus' words spoken centuries earlier. Ask God to help you hear His voice—even on the job.

KINGDOM ECONOMICS

So I gave you a land on which you did not toil and cities you did not build; and you live in them and eat from vineyards and olive groves that you did not plant.

JOSHUA 24:13

In the world of business, we are taught to do whatever it takes to produce a desired outcome. Competitive forces can drive companies beyond the limits of ethics and integrity to achieve a goal. Men and women can become workaholics because of the need for competitive advantage in order to meet sales and marketing goals. This sweat-and-toil mentality contradicts God's kingdom economy.

When the people of Israel were coming out of Egypt, a place of sweat and toil and slavery, God began to teach them a new economy of receiving. Instead of sweat and toil, He wanted them to learn obedience. Their income would now be based on their obedience, not on their skill, sweat or toil.

This new Kingdom economy meant that there would be times when what a person received from his or her efforts might be less than the commensurate time invested. Yet there would also be times when a person would receive more as compared to the time he or she invested.

I used to determine whether I would meet with a person based on my perceived return on that investment. I justified that behavior as being a good steward. However, God says we are to determine if He wants us to meet with a person or to be involved with an endeavor based on His leading alone, not on the perceived outcome. It is His responsibility to bring fruit from the activity.

If you begin to practice Kingdom economy, you will discover a new freedom in your work life. Stay vertical with God and let Him determine your next activity.

BECOMING THE HEAD

The LORD will make you the head, not the tail. If you pay attention to the commands of the LORD your God that I give you this day and carefully follow them, you will always be at the top, never at the bottom.
DEUTERONOMY 28:13

At the time of this writing, Coca-Cola has a 40 percent market share in the soft-drink industry.[19] It is the number one brand in the world. When Coke enters a new business environment, it immediately has authority in that realm. The company has earned great respect because of its position in business.

George Barna, a researcher on Christian activity in the United States, states that 35 to 45 percent of people in the U. S. claim to be born again.[20] Based on the U.S. Bureau of Labor Statistics, there were 149 million adult workers in 2005. If you take 40 percent of this figure, it would mean that there are 59 million born-again Christian workers.[21] If this is the case, why aren't we having more impact on this world?

I would have to say that the Body of Christ in America is not the head but still the tail. Part of the reason for this is that we have not understood our biblical mandate to have dominion on the earth as was modeled in Genesis with Adam and Eve. When Jesus returned to Earth, He came to save that which was lost and restore this principle of dominion (see Luke 19:10). When Jesus prayed the Lord's prayer, "Our Father in heaven, hallowed be your name, your kingdom come, your will be done on earth as it is in heaven" (Matthew 6:9-10), He was praying that His dominion would be restored on Earth just as it is in heaven.

We have given over leadership in our societies to the ungodly. In order to restore God-honoring dominion, we must win the battle in seven key domains in society. These include (1) business, (2) government, (3) education, (4) arts and entertainment, (5) religion, (6) media, and (7) the family.

This battle begins by affirming men and women in the workplace as having a holy calling. Whatever work we are doing, we need to realize that God has called us to express His life in that arena in order to exert His dominion over the earth.

LIVE AS THOUGH YOU ARE DEAD

In the same way, count yourselves dead to sin but alive to God in Christ Jesus.
ROMANS 6:11

"How will I know when I am going to come out of my adversity pit?" said the woman sitting across from me. "When it doesn't matter anymore," I replied. The conversation brought back memories of when I sat across from a mentor *of mine* who said to me, "The only problem you have, Os, is that you are not dead yet. You need a good funeral." He was talking about my carnal flesh life.

In the Bible, when Joseph was made ruler over the entire kingdom of Egypt after spending many years in slavery and imprisonment, my guess is that it didn't really matter that much to him. He had thought he was going to get out of prison years earlier when he successfully interpreted the cupbearer's dream, but ended up remaining there two more years. *Why should this situation prove any different?* he must have thought to himself.

I believe that Joseph had to come to a place with God where he resigned himself to remain wherever God had chosen to keep him. He had become dead to his circumstances. We are to do the same. This does not mean we can't have a longing for better days, but just that we have a godly contentment that allows us to remain in any condition with a peace that passes all understanding (see Philippians 4:7).

The Bible says we are to live as though we are dead. Of course, we will still have emotions and dreams. Jesus said, "My soul is overwhelmed with sorrow to the point of death" (Mark 14:34), which sounds like anxiety to me, yet we know Jesus never sinned. So we can conclude that we can have concerns and emotions without crossing over into transgression. God has given us His Spirit to allow us to operate inside the storms of life without sinning.

Place your faith today into the hands of the One who can calm any storm in life.

THE RELIGIOUS SPIRIT AT WORK

For our struggle is not against flesh and blood, but against the rulers,
against the authorities, against the powers of this dark world and against
the spiritual forces of evil in the heavenly realms.

EPHESIANS 6:12

As we begin to express the life of Christ in our work lives, we need to be aware of another one of Satan's deceptions—namely, the religious spirit.

The religious spirit favors tradition over a genuine, intimate relationship with God. It influences believers to live the Christian life based on works instead of grace. It requires people to depend on their own human efforts to acquire spiritual knowledge and favor from God.

In the years before the Protestant Reformation, Martin Luther's greatest challenge was to root out the religious spirit. His religious teachers told him that there were stringent requirements for receiving the favor of God. "Remember, Martin," they said, "just to pray by yourself is not enough. The church has to pray for you too. Even when the priest has asked that you be forgiven, God will not listen unless you do good works. The more gifts you give to the church and to the poor, the more trips you make to Rome and Jerusalem, the more pleasures you give up, the better will be your chances for heaven. The best and safest way to do all this, and the one that is most God pleasing, is to give up everything and become a monk."[22]

The essence of Martin Luther's struggle to win God's favor still resides in many a Christian worker today. The religious spirit nullifies the importance of faith and grace that has been given to us through the work of the cross. We cannot gain acceptance from God by doing any works. We must simply accept His unconditional love for us today.

Know that God accepts you the way you are. You cannot do any works that will make you more acceptable to Him once you've given your heart to Him.

THE SPIRITUAL LIFE IS CAUGHT, NOT TAUGHT

Elisha then left his oxen and ran after Elijah.
1 KINGS 19:20

There is a man in my life that I consider my mentor. He came into my life during a crisis period and helped me understand my situation. I have learned a great deal from him. I have rarely spent more than a few hours in his presence at any one time. However, I did not learn from him through a formal arrangement. I mostly *caught* what I have learned. He never took me through a Bible study. He never sent me articles or things to read. I learned by being around him.

One day a crisis situation arose in my life. In the midst of my own predicament, I remembered what my mentor did in a crisis in his life and, amazingly, I appropriated faith, just as my mentor had, to my crisis. This is what I mean by *catching* the faith of another. Spiritual truth is learned through the atmosphere that surrounds us, not through intellectual reasoning.

In the Bible, when Elijah handpicked Elisha as his successor, Elisha immediately killed his 12 oxen and ran after Elijah just to be with him. No doubt he knew what a great privilege it was to be selected by the great prophet. However, it was not enough for Elisha to be handpicked. He also wanted to spend time with Elijah so that he could receive a double portion of Elijah's anointing. If you read the whole story of Elijah and Elisha in 1 Kings, you'll find that it appears that God answered this prayer.

If you want to grow in your Christian life, ask God to lead you to a man or woman who is far ahead of you spiritually, and start hanging out with them. As you walk alongside them you will begin to catch what they have. You will begin appropriating the anointing that is on their lives, and with God's grace, it will mix perfectly with your unique gifting and talents.

We need more people today who are willing to run after their "Elijahs."

SPEAK TO YOUR MOUNTAIN

"Have faith in God," Jesus answered. "I tell you the truth, if anyone says to this mountain, 'Go, throw yourself into the sea,' and does not doubt in his heart but believes that what he says will happen, it will be done for him."
MARK 11:22-23

A few years ago, I received the following letter that demonstrates the principle of using your authority to speak to your "mountain" in your workplace:

I own a video company that shoots a variety of projects. One day, my editor discovered a videographer's worst nightmare—a garbled mess of video picture and little or no audio on tapes that I had shot the weekend before. Four tapes of raw footage from two separate events were ruined.

I prayed that God would restore my tapes. I got an odd sense of peace and knew God had answered my prayer. I relayed to the group that I believed God had told me that the tapes would be fine in a day. My associate challenged me to put in the tape anyway and not wait. I put a tape in the editing deck, and right before our eyes, the tape now had a perfectly clear picture and audio where there had been no sound moments before.

The next morning, I entered my editing room with great anticipation. I put in one of the remaining damaged tapes that contained footage from a wedding, but the video was still scrambled and there was no audio. My wife heard me and came in to look over my shoulder. I prayed out loud over the ruined footage and reassured my wife that God loves us and would take care of things. I kept praying as I watched the screen.

Then suddenly, before our eyes, the tape began to clear up. Just as the pastor announced how God intimately loves us, I turned to look at my wife and saw the tears streaming down her face. Apparently, God had rigged this moment to touch her deeply on issues that only the two of them knew about. Not only did God save my business, but He also ministered to my family through this crisis-fixing miracle.

What type of mountain might God want you to speak to today?

THE GOSPEL OF THE KINGDOM

Repent, for the kingdom of heaven is near.
MATTHEW 3:2

God is doing a unique work on the earth today. There are seasons in which the Holy Spirit speaks things to the Church. During one decade there might be a focus on evangelism. During another, the focus might be on a greater awareness of the Holy Spirit. During yet another, it might be a focus on social problems in cities.

Today, God is speaking very clearly to the Church about societal transformation. Fifteen years ago, the idea of a community being totally transformed through the gospel of Jesus Christ was a foreign concept. However, according to George Otis, Jr., director of the *Sentinel Group*, there are over 500 communities that are in some form of quantifiable transformation process today.

The defining characteristic of a community that is being transformed is that socio-economic traits are positively affected: The crime rate goes down, the economy is improved, the number of Christians in the city increases, prayer increases and the city leaders become Christians. It is the manifestation of Deuteronomy 28:13: "The LORD will make you the head, not the tail. If you pay attention to the commands of the LORD your God that I give you this day and carefully follow them, you will always be at the top, never at the bottom."

In order to go beyond the gospel of salvation to the gospel of the Kingdom, we must exercise a different level of faith for our communities. Jesus talked about the kingdom of God more than 70 times in the New Testament—much more often than He mentioned salvation. While salvation is part of bringing the kingdom of God on Earth, there are many other aspects as well. We must increase our faith to the point where we are actively practicing all aspects of Kingdom life.

When the gospel of the Kingdom comes into a life and a community, everything in its wake is transformed. How might God want you to be the catalyst to bring the entire gospel of the Kingdom into the lives and communities you are called to influence?

THE REAL DEAL

*God did extraordinary miracles through Paul, so that even handkerchiefs
and aprons that had touched him were taken to the sick, and their illnesses
were cured and the evil spirits left them.*

ACTS 19:11-12

We have an expression in America that says, "He's the real deal." What we are saying is that the person in question is really who he or she appears to be. That person is not trying to be or to convince you that he or she is someone he or she is not. It is a compliment when someone says, "You are the real deal." It means that you are not a hypocrite and that you are not trying to be someone you're not.

The apostle Paul was the real deal. God began using Paul in amazing ways, as recorded in the book of Acts. God used Paul in such amazing ways, in fact, that there arose groups of people who saw Paul's power and wanted to do the same acts that Paul did. The problem was, they were not the real deal. They were trying to be someone they were not. These people were trying to appropriate the same Power Source as Paul without ever having a relationship with the Power Source. That lack of relationship nearly killed them:

> Some Jews who went around driving out evil spirits tried to invoke the name of the Lord Jesus over those who were demon-possessed. They would say, "In the name of Jesus, whom Paul preaches, I command you to come out." Seven sons of Sceva, a Jewish chief priest, were doing this. [One day] the evil spirit answered them, "Jesus I know, and I know about Paul, but who are you?" Then the man who had the evil spirit jumped on them and overpowered them all. He gave them such a beating that they ran out of the house naked and bleeding (Acts 19:13-16).

It is impossible to be the real deal without tapping into the real Power Source, the Holy Spirit. Do you want to experience miracles in your walk with God? If so, ask God to allow His power to be manifested in and through you.

FOUR TYPES OF CHRISTIANS

But if you are led by the Spirit, you are not under the law.
GALATIANS 5:18

In his book *Anointed for Business*, Ed Silvoso provides a thoughtful look at the four types of Christians in the workplace. The following four categories provide an excellent tool for self-assessment.

(1) *The Christian who is simply trying to survive.* Christians who are simply trying to survive have no purpose or zeal for integrating their faith at work. They have not seen the power or presence of God in their work lives. Such Christians segment their faith life from their work life. They lack purpose and meaning and they have little direction.

(2) *The Christian who is living by Christian principles.* The second type of Christian in the workplace includes those who are living by Christian principles. They participate in 12-step programs and read books with guaranteed formulas to help them lose weight or improve their marriages. This programmed teaching can be beneficial to change negative patterns in their lives; however, it is important to recognize that the root of this type of teaching comes largely from a Greek-based system for acquiring information, compared to the Early Church's Hebraic model of experiential learning.

(3) *The Christian who is living by the power of the Holy Spirit.* Christians who are living by the power of the Holy Spirit understand the importance of developing a heart toward God through prayer, study of the Word of God and obedience. They realize that these are the three core ingredients to experiencing the power of God in their lives.

(4) *The Christian who is transforming his or her workplace for Christ.* A wonderful by-product of living by the power of the Holy Spirit is the power to transform a workplace for God. Christians who passionately seek the manifestation of God's kingdom here on Earth will be able to realize this transformation in their workplaces. When the kingdom of God is demonstrated on Earth, it can transform the workplace and society.[23]

Which of the four categories do you fall into? Start asking God to lead you to be a category-4 Christian, and ask Him to help you transform your workplace today.

ASA, A MODEL KING UNTIL . . .

Because you relied on the king of Aram and not on the LORD your God,
the army of the king of Aram has escaped from your hand.
2 CHRONICLES 16:7

Asa was a godly king of Judah. There were two kingdoms during his reign—Judah and Israel. Israel's king was Baasha, a wicked king. To the east of Judah was Damascus, whose king was Ben-Hadad. In Judah, Asa was an amazingly faithful and righteous king for 35 years. He got rid of idol worship and even deposed his mother for the veneration of idols. Because of his godliness, God blessed Asa's rule by allowing peace in the land for 35 years.

Before Asa came into power, the nation was lost. There was no godly ruler. There were many wars, and the people began to cry out to God for deliverance. In response, God sent them Asa.

While Asa was king, Judah was attacked by Zerah the Cushite who marched against the Judeans with a vast army and 300 chariots. But Asa called upon the Lord, and God answered his prayer and delivered them from a larger and stronger army than Judah's.

However, 35 years later, Asa began to move away from trusting God and decided that he could *buy* the favor of his enemy, the king Ben-Hadad. Asa sent gold and silver to him as a bribe, asking Ben-Hadad to cancel his treaty with King Baasha and go to war on behalf of Asa and Judah. Asa's strategy worked, and he defeated Israel.

However, there was a cost: "In the thirty-ninth year of his reign Asa was afflicted with a disease in his feet. Though his disease was severe, even in his illness he did not seek help from the LORD, but only from the physicians. Then in the forty-first year of his reign Asa died and rested with his fathers" (2 Chronicles 16:12-14).

What we learn from Asa is that whenever we place our trust and obedience in the Lord, God becomes our source for security and prosperity. However, when we move away from trusting God, our security is removed and we fail to receive those things God intended us to have.

THE INTEGRITY TEST

*God, who gets invited to dinner at your place? How do we get on your guest list?
"Walk straight, act right, tell the truth. Don't hurt your friend, don't blame your
neighbor; despise the despicable. Keep your word even when it costs you, make an
honest living, never take a bribe. You'll never get blacklisted if you live like this."*
PSALM 15:1-5, *THE MESSAGE*

In 2002, U.S. companies Arthur Andersen, Enron and Salomon Brothers
were all brought down by the rogue actions of a few who failed the integrity test. The companies' corporate integrity codes failed to equip front-line
employees to make the right decisions without supervision.

Lack of integrity is nothing new. The Bible is full of examples. One of
these involves Gehazi, the assistant to the most famous prophet of his
day, Elisha. It's hard to imagine that anyone working with such an anointed man, who saw firsthand the power of God, would fail the integrity test.
But he did.

When Elisha healed Naaman (a general in the army) from leprosy, he
didn't expect to be compensated and he didn't ask for money. When Naaman
insisted that Elisha take some form of payment, the prophet answered,
"As surely as the LORD lives, whom I serve, I will not accept a thing" (2 Kings
5:16). Gehazi, however, did not agree with his employer. He saw this as a great
opportunity for gain and took matters into his own hands. In 2 Kings 5:20,
it says, "Gehazi, the servant of Elisha the man of God, said to himself, 'My
master was too easy on Naaman, this Aramean, by not accepting from him
what he brought. As surely as the LORD lives, I will run after him and get
something from him.'"

As a result of his sin, God judged Gehazi. Elisha fired him, God struck
him with leprosy and his life was never the same. Each of us has the potential of being a Gehazi if we do not have a foundation that makes us willing
to receive only what God gives us through the fruit of our obedience.

Ask God to keep your motives pure in all you do.

CAN YOUR BOSS SAY THIS ABOUT YOU?

Can we find anyone like this man, one in whom is the spirit of God?
GENESIS 41:38

I often get résumés from people wanting to come to work for us. They think that because we are a Christian organization the pressures and the environment will be better than the place where they work. That may be true, but there is a danger in this view.

The Bible says that God has defined the place and time in which we are to live. As David says in Psalm 16, "LORD, you have assigned me my portion and my cup; you have made my lot secure. The boundary lines have fallen for me in pleasant places; surely I have a delightful inheritance" (vv. 5-6).

God has uniquely gifted you to bring His presence and power in the area of your calling. Your life should be such a testimony of the power, creativity and servanthood of Jesus that it impacts your employer to the degree that he says the same thing Pharaoh said about Joseph: "Can we find anyone like this man, one in whom is the Spirit of God?" (Genesis 41:38).

When God uses your life to bring His presence into your workplace, He gives you authority there. You will begin to see others drawn to you. You may begin to be ostracized as well. This too is part of your call. But do not fear. Embrace the call.

We should not seek to remove ourselves from the pressure cooker of life, but we should instead use that pressure cooker to reveal the power and grace of God through our lives. It is in the workplace that we will receive our inheritance as we fulfill our purposes in and through our work-life call.

Today, ask God to give you supernatural wisdom and discernment to express the Spirit of God to your employer.

BALANCE THE NATURAL AND THE SPIRITUAL

*No king is saved by the size of his army; no warrior escapes by
his great strength. A horse is a vain hope for deliverance;
despite all its great strength it cannot save.*

PSALM 33:16-17

The Bible tells us not to put our confidence in things the world considers to be our protection, defense or strength. However, the man or woman who does not perform well on the job is left behind in today's competitive world. Not only is this typical of the world at large but even many Christians promote the importance of identifying our strengths, and they encourage us to move in them to accomplish God's will. Yet, throughout the Bible, we are *discouraged* from depending upon our own strengths. Instead, we are urged to rely totally upon the Lord.

God wants us to depend upon Him, and He demonstrates this throughout Scripture. For example, in Judges 7, God wouldn't let Gideon fight against another army until he reduced his own from 22,000 soldiers to a mere 300 so that Gideon could not boast about his army's strength. In Joshua 6, God told Joshua to walk around Jericho seven times and blow trumpets instead of relying upon his mighty army to overpower his enemy. In 2 Samuel 24, God judged David when he counted his troops to determine the size of his army's strength, because David took the census out of pride and overconfidence in the strength of his army.

On the other hand, Jesus instructed the disciples in due diligence through the parable of the builder, who is cautioned to consider the cost before beginning to build. Jesus says, "Suppose one of you wants to build a tower. Will he not first sit down and estimate the cost to see if he has enough money to complete it? For if he lays the foundation and is not able to finish it, everyone who sees it will ridicule him, saying, 'This fellow began to build and was not able to finish'" (Luke 14:28-30).

Today, bring every project and endeavor before the Lord as you ask for His power and grace to accomplish it using *both* your natural gifts and the Spirit of God.

THE FERTILE PASTURE

Shepherd your people with your staff, the flock of your inheritance,
which lives by itself in a forest, in fertile pasturelands.
MICAH 7:14

"I've called you to pastor the bank," said the Lord to my friend Chuck.

"Pastor the bank? How does one pastor a bank, Lord?"

"I want you to teach others the things I taught you," came the reply.

There are people who live isolated in fertile pasturelands. They long for a shepherd who will help them discover their own inheritance. They are the lost majority in the marketplace who are living lives as children, lost and aimless in a deep, dark forest.

Though most do not know it, they long for a pastor who will reveal to them their destinies. Your staff, which represents your vocation, is the means by which God is going to use you to pastor those in your sphere of influence in the workplace.

A fertile pastureland means there is a great harvest that can come if only there is someone to do what is necessary to bring a harvest from it. This is where you will derive your inheritance—the people you serve will be the spiritual inheritance God has allotted to you.

This forest is more fertile than all other potential fields because the power and authority represented by this forest has the potential to impact far greater fields. This forest has CEOs, presidents of nations, entertainment moguls, media tycoons, and educators, to name just a few. They are the shapers of society who have yet to meet their Maker.

Are you willing to use your staff to be a shepherd to those in the fertile pasturelands?

BEING PROMOTED BEYOND YOUR ANOINTING

*But he said to me, "My grace is sufficient for you,
for my power is made perfect in weakness."*
2 CORINTHIANS 12:9

Have you ever done a job so well that you were promoted outside your skill set? The exceptional salesman gets promoted to manager and fails as a manager. The secretary gets promoted to office manager but fails for lack of management skills. I have seen this happen a lot over the years. Understanding your anointing will enable you to know when you are moving in the opposite direction from what God intends for your life.

Just because you don't feel equipped to accomplish the job doesn't mean that you are headed in the wrong direction. Sometimes, God will place you in situations in which you have no natural gifting. In these cases, God puts you there to experience His power in order to accomplish your tasks. My wife, Angie, is a good example of this. Before she came to work with me full-time, she was a marketing and advertising manager for a non-profit organization. This organization hired a career consulting company to take all their employees through a series of tests to determine if each employee fit into his or her proper job function.

When the results of Angie's test were shared with the rest of her team, her profile revealed that one of her greatest weaknesses was lack of organization and focus. Her boss took exception to the assessment and publicly acknowledged that Angie was the most detailed and organized individual on the entire team. "How could that be true?" he asked.

The consultant said, "Oh, I am glad you asked that. Angie is a perfect example of someone who has overcome her weakness, because even though she recognizes this is her natural bent, she has overcome this by learning to be focused and detailed." In essence, she has yielded this area to the Holy Spirit, and God has worked through her weakness.

God sometimes moves us beyond our natural gifting and allows us to operate in a place where our natural gifts do not fit the job. Other times He is teaching us to acquire a new skill set for the given situation.

NEW PARADIGMS

Yes, he has hidden himself among the baggage.
1 SAMUEL 10:22

If you want to experience something you've never done, you must do something you've never done. In his book *Experiencing God: Knowing and Doing His Will*, Henry Blackaby writes, "You cannot go with God and stay where you are."[24]

God often has to radically change us if we are going to fulfill His purposes in our lives. For example, Saul was about to be anointed by Samuel as the first king of Israel. Samuel said to Saul, "The Spirit of the LORD will come upon you in power, and you will prophesy with them; and you will be changed into a different person" (1 Samuel 10:6). Up to this point, Saul had never prophesied or led a group of people. He had also never had to be accountable to a prophet and to God for his every action.

Right away Saul took a big step of faith and prophesied with the prophets just as Samuel said he would. How exciting that must have been. Yet when Samuel called the entire nation of Israel together to announce Saul as Israel's first king in history, Saul was nowhere to be found. When they called Saul's name, he didn't come forward. So the people "inquired further of the LORD, 'Has the man come here yet?' And the LORD said, 'Yes, he has hidden himself among the baggage'" (1 Samuel 10:22). Saul was so afraid that the Lord couldn't use him that he hid among luggage—but God *did* use him.

Saul's story reminds me of when God began moving me from a career in advertising to a new ministry to men and women in the workplace that involved writing and public speaking. Neither of these were my particular forté. Yet despite wanting to hide from the task, I was forced to do something I had never done. And because of my obedience to the task, the Lord has used me to reach many people for Him.

God continues to pick the foolish things of this world to confound the wise. Your greatest setback may be thinking that there's no way that God can use "little me." However, the reality is that He can and will, if we respond obediently to the new places He takes us.

THE WORKAHOLIC

*For you did not receive a spirit that makes you a slave again to fear,
but you received the Spirit of sonship.*

ROMANS 8:15

Living a balanced life is evidence of a Spirit-led life. Working long hours can lead to significant problems in our lives.

One reason we overwork is that we often think we must do so in order to keep up with our workload. Like any compulsive behavior, however, there is usually something beneath this reasoning. As a former workaholic myself, I can tell you that the root of overworking is often (1) a fear of loss and (2) a need for self-acceptance created by performance.

The fear-of-loss issue is often a fear of what will happen if we *don't* work long hours, and this fear is often subconscious. For example, our fear that there may not be enough money if we don't work long hours can drive us to overwork. In addition, we often have an inaccurate view of what is enough, which drives us to greater levels of achievement because we believe that a financial reward will ensure protection against potential financial disaster. As a side effect of overworking, we'll often find that those around us feel shamed if they do not work at the same level—and the cycle repeats itself, because others become intimidated by the unspoken directive that long hours are required. This leads to a whole new set of problems.

The second root of overworking is our need to gain self-acceptance and esteem from our jobs. It is rewarding to see something come from our efforts. However, when we begin to be driven to work, it becomes an unhealthy condition. We begin to gain self-esteem needs from our performance instead of from our position in Christ.

So, in order to avoid allowing work to become an idol and a compulsive behavior, we must maintain a balance in which we spend quality time with the Lord, our families and fellow believers.

Sometimes the greatest exercise of faith is to work only 40 hours a week. This ensures that the outcome of our work is dependent upon God, not our self-effort.

CLOSED ON SUNDAY

Observe the Sabbath, because it is holy to you.
EXODUS 31:14

Can a business have a Christian testimony without ever saying a word? Absolutely.

Atlanta-based Chick-fil-A, Inc., is America's second-largest quick-service chicken restaurant chain. The company's stated corporate purpose is "to glorify God by being a faithful steward of all that is entrusted to us, and to have a positive influence on all who come in contact with Chick-fil-A." This company is a great example of a business that is modeling Christian values and producing a quality product in the competitive fast-food industry. Chick-fil-A is one of the fastest-growing chains nationally, currently with over two billion dollars in annual sales.

One of the defining distinctions of Chick-fil-A is that the restaurants are not open on Sundays. From the time Truett Cathy, the company's founder, started in the restaurant business in 1946, he believed that God wanted him to honor the Sabbath by keeping the stores closed on Sundays. Although shopping mall operators challenged him on this idea many times, Truett always held that he would "have more sales in six days than those who are open for seven." This has proven to be true, and today the malls no longer hassle the company to remain open on Sunday.

When you go to a Chick-fil-A restaurant, you can tell something is different about the people and the atmosphere there. The messages in the company's kids' meals always reinforce education, values and integrity. Although the employees do not wear their faith on their sleeve, the fruit of the company is known by many—especially the many young restaurant employees who receive educational scholarships each year. The company also focuses on foster homes, character-building programs for kids, and other community services.

I have spoken at Chick-fil-A's corporate headquarters several times and have met with Truett and his son, Dan. The appearance of their headquarters conveys their values—a sense of quality without extravagance.

What type of message is your life or company preaching?

THE INTEGRITY TEST

Surely you desire truth in the inner parts; you teach me wisdom in the inmost place.
PSALM 51:6

Integrity is often defined by what we do in secret. Are our actions the same in public as they are behind closed doors? Kenneth Lay was the chairman and CEO of Enron, a multibillion-dollar energy corporation that went bankrupt at the hands of its executives because of mismanagement and misrepresentation of its financial practices. Many people lost their retirement life savings as a result.

In 1996, Kenneth Lay made a comment in a book entitled *Business as Mission:*

In my own case I grew up the son of a Baptist minister. From this background, I was fully exposed to not only legal behavior but moral and ethical behavior and what that means from the standpoint of leading organizations and people. I was, and am, a strong believer that one of the most satisfying things in life is to create a highly moral and ethical environment in which every individual is allowed and encouraged to realize their God-given potential. There are few things more satisfying than to see individuals reach levels of performance that they would have thought was virtually impossible for themselves.[25]

Something went very wrong from the time Kenneth Lay wrote those words and the time he was convicted June 6, 2006. But Lay never went to prison, because he died of a heart attack a few months after being convicted.

No one is immune from starting well and ending badly. The Scriptures are full of men and women who did great things for God but who did not finish well toward the latter part of their lives. Success is often the breeding ground for ethical failure. Oswald Chambers said, "Not every man can carry a full cup. Sudden elevation frequently leads to pride and a fall. The most exacting test of all to survive is prosperity."

Ask God today to protect you from pride that can lead to ethical failure.

A JOB VERSUS A CALLING

Whoever wants to become great among you must be your servant . . .
as the Son of Man did not come to be served, but to serve.
MATTHEW 20:26-28

My wife and I travel to my hometown every few months to visit my mom in an elderly care nursing facility for Alzheimer's and dementia patients. We often comment that it is easy to distinguish between those at the facility who see their work as a job versus those who see it as a calling.

There is one woman there that we all love. Her name is Carolyn. We know that if Carolyn is on duty, our mom will be well cared for. Carolyn exemplifies one who is doing her job because she actually loves her work. Carolyn's job involves caring for difficult patients who often have little appreciation for what she does. Her position often requires cleaning up urine and giving baths to invalid patients. When asked about her view of her job, Carolyn's response was quite remarkable: "I enjoy it."

Carolyn is so good at what she does that she was recognized by her organization as Caregiver of the Year. She didn't do her job because she wanted that recognition. Instead, recognition was one fruit of living out her calling to be a caregiver.

Carolyn sharply contrasts others who work at the same facility. It is often difficult to get them to do the basic necessities of care for your loved one. Requests are met with resistance. The attitude in which they do their job is compulsory instead of a motivation to serve.

Similar attitudes occur in almost any vocational area. Whether you go into a department store, speak with a customer service agent or go to get your tires changed, it is easy to recognize those who are living out their calling versus those who are collecting a paycheck.

Which person are you in this story? Pray that you see your work as a calling and an avenue to express the life of Jesus through your work life.

CITY TRANSFORMATION BEGINS IN TWO PLACES

While Paul was waiting for them in Athens, he was greatly distressed
to see that the city was full of idols. So he reasoned in the synagogue with
the Jews and the God-fearing Greeks, as well as in the marketplace
day by day with those who happened to be there.

ACTS 17:16-17

In order to transform a city or nation, change must take place in two areas: the marketplace and the local church. Paul was burdened for Athens when he saw all of the idols in that great city, so he began a strategy to win the city back by reasoning with people every day in the synagogue (with Jews and God-fearing Gentiles) and also in the marketplace.

Old Testament records reveal that even at the time of the Temple's construction, the foundations of a God-centered city were laid in both the marketplace and the synagogue: "He erected the pillars in the front of the temple, one to the south and one to the north. The one to the south he named Jakin and the one to the north Boaz" (2 Chronicles 3:17).

Jakin was a priest of the Lord and represented the spiritual foundation of the Church. Boaz represented the strength of the marketplace and its impact on the society through workplace ministers or kings.

God continues to move today in cities across the world through collaborative coalitions made up of priests, kings and intercessors. This is a city transformation trinity that the Holy Spirit is forming to rid our cities of idols and to restore the spiritual foundations.

When we begin to equip and release those in the workplace to fulfill their godly roles in business, government, media, arts/entertainment and education, we will begin to see the idols in our cities removed. Pray that God raises up godly workplace leaders who will lead with a biblical worldview.

BEWARE OF UNUSUAL CIRCUMSTANCES

*Now to each one the manifestation of the Spirit is given for the common good.
To one there is given through the Spirit the message of wisdom, to another
the message of knowledge by means of the same Spirit.*

1 CORINTHIANS 12:7-9

Whenever something unusual happens in daily life, it is often a sign that
God is up to something. We must have a heightened sense of awareness of
what God may want to do in these situations.

My mentor once shared how he was upgraded on an airline unexpect-
edly. On that flight, a woman who was very troubled sat down next to
him. He began to quietly pray for the woman, and God gave him supernatural insights that her problem related to the fact that she had not forgiven her mother in a family-related issue. He decided to politely share
his insight. The woman was shocked that he knew such personal knowledge of such details without ever meeting her. My mentor began to minister to her on the airplane and ultimately led her to Christ.

God is raising the spiritual bar for Christians who want to impact the
world for Christ today. He wants to break into people's lives supernaturally by giving them insights into the needs of people in order to bring them
to Christ.

Jesus often spoke supernaturally into the lives of others based on the
circumstance of the moment. He often spoke of their current condition in
life and invited them to make a change.

As you go about your day, there are often open doors for bringing Christ
into the circumstance. In fact, He is the one orchestrating the circumstance!

Next time an unusual situation develops, be aware that God may be creating such a circumstance to bring His glory into the situation.

LYDIA, A WORKPLACE MINISTER

One of those listening was a woman named Lydia, a dealer in purple cloth from the city of Thyatira, who was a worshiper of God.

ACTS 16:14

There was a businesswoman whom Paul encountered in Thyatira named Lydia. She was an Early Church entrepreneur dealing in purple cloth, the most expensive type in the first-century Middle East. Most accounts believe this was Paul's first known convert. I find it interesting that his first known convert was a woman and an entrepreneur.

"We sat down and began to speak to the women who had gathered there. The Lord opened her heart to respond to Paul's message. When she and the members of her household were baptized, she invited us to her home" (Acts 16:13-15). This encounter with Lydia and her women associates ultimately opened the way for ministry in that region. God often worked in and through women in the Early Church. Lydia was an influential business-woman, and the gospel was affecting all strata of society, just as it does today.

Lydia was a maker of beautiful cloth that was mainly used by members of the royal families and Roman senators who were required to have a purple band around the edge of their togas. Purple cloth was both valuable and expensive in the culture of the first century. It was often worn as a sign of nobility or royalty. Lydia's ministry would be to the upper-class business community.

Evidence of Lydia's conversion was immediate. She told the men that if they considered her a believer in the Lord, she would like for them to come and stay at her house. Evidently, she had plenty of room to accommodate the four of them: Paul, Silas, Timothy and Luke. After urging the men, they accepted her invitation and stayed at her house.

Lydia's heart was like the good soil in the parable of the sower. When she heard the word of God, she received it with joy and obeyed the words of the apostle. Who are the "Lydias" God has placed in your circle of influence? Pray that you will be the instrument, like Paul, to bring the gospel to influential women entrepreneurs.

SITTING AT HIS FEET

So Ruth gleaned in the field until evening. Then she threshed the barley she had gathered, and it amounted to about an ephah.

RUTH 2:17-18

The story of Ruth provides an excellent illustration of the connection between spending time in the presence of God and receiving physical provision. Naomi was married to Elimelech. They had two married sons. Ruth was married to one of the sons. Elimelech died, and 10 years later both of his sons also died. The other daughter-in-law moved back to her family, but Ruth, in spite of Naomi's encouragement to do likewise, insisted on staying with Naomi.

The only way for the family line to continue was for Ruth to marry another of Naomi's sons or, through a custom known as the kinsman redeemer, Ruth could be married to a relative in the family line.

Times were tough during Ruth and Naomi's day, and most people made a living by farming. Luckily, Naomi had a relative named Boaz who was a prominent landowner and farmer. She sent Ruth to glean in the fields of Boaz all day in hopes of picking up excess grain left behind by the harvesters.

Ruth stayed in the fields all day and yielded just one *ephah* of grain. One *ephah*, to give you a picture, is much sweat and toil for very little return. However, something happened later that made amends for this. Naomi realized that the only way Ruth was going to have any kind of future was if a kinsman redeemer came to her rescue. So she instructed Ruth to go to the threshing floor where Boaz would be and to quietly sit at his feet all night. This would be a sign of submitting her life to Boaz, and he would then have to exercise his right to be her kinsman redeemer.

Later, Boaz sent Ruth home and took the necessary steps to become her redeemer. But before he sent her home, he gave her six *ephahs* of barley—*six times what she got working all day in the fields.*

Friend, like Ruth's story illustrates, if we are going to succeed in fulfilling God's destiny for our lives, we must have a life of intimate worship and devotion to Jesus—our redeemer. Why not start spending more time at the feet of Jesus?

WHAT IS YOUR PROMISED LAND?

So I gave you a land on which you did not toil
and cities you did not build; and you live in them and eat
from vineyards and olive groves that you did not plant.
JOSHUA 24:13

God called the people of Israel to leave Egypt and come out of slavery in order to enter their own Promised Land. It meant they had to change a way of life they had known their whole lives. Instead of being told what to do everyday by a taskmaster, they were now being led by the cloud of God that led them into the desert with the ultimate goal of entering their own Promised Land.

Every believer has a Promised Land in his or her life. It is the place where you receive all that God intended for you to receive. However, many of us are still living in Egypt where we sweat and toil in response to the taskmaster of production dictated by our workplaces and our lifestyles of busyness.

We will know that we are beginning to experience our Promised Land when we experience God's rest while at the same time fulfilling our work-life call. We begin to give testimony to what Joshua says in the above verse. We begin to receive things we never built or planted. We begin to experience a level of rest in our working lives that is not characterized by sweat and toil. Things become easier because we receive them as a fruit of our call rather than as a result of toiling toward a goal.

I experienced this new way of living as I began to be obedient to doing things based on God's direction versus my perceived outcome. Provision began to follow obedience. Projects got done with little sweat. God brought people to me to get things done. I no longer had a tendency to manipulate outcomes that I desired. God was giving me my Promised Land as I yielded to Him.

Are you living in your Promised Land? If not, release the goals of your life to the Lord and simply be obedient to His voice. Ask Him for the steps you are to take to receive your Promised Land.

HEARING GOD ON THE JOB

But God chose the foolish things of the world to shame the wise;
God chose the weak things of the world to shame the strong.

1 CORINTHIANS 1:27

God is raising up a new kind of workplace believer who is experiencing the power of God in their daily work life. My friend Emeka Nywankpa, for example, was a barrister (lawyer) in Nigeria. Emeka spoke at a conference a few years ago on the subject of how the spiritual impacts the physical.

Emeka shared a story about arguing an important Supreme Court case in his country. There were five points to argue in the case. The morning the trial began, he prayed with his wife and junior lawyers in his chambers. During his prayer time, he sensed that the Holy Spirit was telling him, "Do not argue points one through four. Only argue point five." Imagine making such a change just before you argue a case before the Supreme Court!

In the courtroom, Emeka announced that he wished to drop points one through four and only wished to argue point five. The judge was shocked but gave him permission to proceed. He argued point five and sat down. The other attorney got up and for 12 minutes stumbled around trying to defend his position, unable to get a coherent word out.

Finally, he approached the bench and said, "Your Lordship, it is unfortunate that my learned friend has dropped the first four points. I wish to yield the case." The other attorney had only prepared for the first four points. Emeka won the case. God had given him a strategy to win his case supernaturally. It made no sense to him, but he obeyed and God gave him victory in a very unusual way.

Isaiah 48:17 tells us, "Thus says the LORD, your Redeemer, The Holy One of Israel: 'I am the LORD your God, Who teaches you to profit, Who leads you by the way you should go'" (*NKJV*).

When is the last time you allowed God to give you a strategy to be successful in your work-life call and bring glory to His name? This is His desire for you.

WHAT'S YOUR BRAND?

The one who calls you is faithful and he will do it.
1 THESSALONIANS 5:24

As I mentioned in a previous chapter, Coca-Cola is the number one brand in the world. Companies like Coke spend millions of dollars making their brands known in business. They want you to recognize their brand. When you think of their brand, they want you to have positive thoughts in hopes that their positioning will influence your next purchasing decision.

Even cultures and ethnic groups have a brand. Likewise, every individual has a personal brand whether or not they want it. Your brand is defined by your conduct. If you are always late, you'll soon develop a brand, or reputation, for being late. Others will even show up late because they know you will be late. If you are a person who exaggerates the truth, others will soon fail to take you seriously.

However, the opposite can also be true. Your brand can be incredibly positive. When you are a man or woman of your word who is consistent in dealing fairly and honestly with others, your brand labels you as someone who is faithful in all aspects of life.

One of God's most important brands, or characteristics, is His faithfulness. Faithfulness means fulfilling promises to others in the time that was committed. God is faithful to fulfill all His promises to His children.

Moses was also an example of faithfulness to his call: "Moses was faithful as a servant in all God's house, testifying to what would be said in the future. But Christ is faithful as a son over God's house" (Hebrews 3:5-6).

What is your brand among your peers? Is it a positive brand or does it need improvement? Allowing the Lord to make us more like Jesus is the only way our brand becomes trustworthy. Ask the Lord today to make you a faithful brand in which others can trust.

FAITH IS SPELLED "RISK"

*Then Peter got down out of the boat, walked on the water
and came toward Jesus. But when he saw the wind, he was afraid and,
beginning to sink, cried out, "Lord, save me!"*

MATTHEW 14:29-30

Jesus told Peter to get out of the boat. There is always a risk when we attempt something that has never been done before. Naysayers seem to come out of the woodwork. Why? Because it's not their vision; it's ours. Sometimes we fail at first. It's a fact that most entrepreneurs fail before they are really successful.

"Success," said Winston Churchill, "is going from failure to failure without loss of enthusiasm." Everybody fails. It's part of the process that leads us to maturity and success. Most successful entrepreneurs don't think of their failures as defeats. They think of them as lessons.

If you hope to succeed, learn everything you can from your failures. In *The Three Success Secrets of Shamgar*, Orlando Magic executive Pat Williams observed, "Our experiences may not all be triumphs and successes, but so what? Failure is usually a far better teacher than success—if we are willing to learn the lessons." Houston Astros pitcher Larry Dierker adds to the topic: "Experience is the best teacher, but a hard grader. She gives the test first, the lesson later."[26]

God never gets mired in our past failures. He is constantly viewing our lives with future success in mind, saying, "See, I am doing a new thing! Now it springs up; do you not perceive it? I am making a way in the desert and streams in the wasteland" (Isaiah 43:19).

Someone once said, "When your memories are bigger than your dreams, you're headed for the grave." God wants to give us new dreams that are bigger than anything that has ever happened to us in the past.

Don't let past failures keep you from future successes.

A NEW KIND OF ARMY

Proclaim this among the nations: Prepare for war! Rouse the warriors!
Let all the fighting men draw near and attack. Beat your plowshares
into swords and your pruning hooks into spears.
JOEL 3:9-10

God is raising up a new kind of army in these last days. It is the remnant in the Body of Christ that has the greatest potential for societal transformation of any segment of society—men and women in the workplace. It is a remnant that has been largely silent.

Plowshares and pruning hooks are agricultural instruments that farmers use in their work. The prophet Joel says these very instruments will be used in the last days as weapons of war. However, it won't be a war against man and an enemy but against the kingdom of darkness.

As we enter the last days, we will begin to see our vocations as instruments to defeat the forces of evil and usher in the kingdom of God. We will see Christ glorified in the marketplace like never before. We will see hundreds and thousands become part of a new harvest of souls in the 9 to 5 window, where many have yet to experience the saving knowledge of Jesus Christ.

What has to happen for your plowshare or pruning hook to be transformed into a weapon of love, designed to cut through the strongholds of unbelief and corruption in your workplace? You are a spiritual warrior in a worker's uniform.

God has called you to transform your view of yourself and your work. He desires to use you and your work life to impact your workplace, city and nation. Are you ready to beat your plowshare into a sword and your pruning hook into a spear?

RECOGNIZING THE RELIGIOUS SPIRIT IN THE WORKPLACE

For our struggle is not against flesh and blood, but against the rulers, against the authorities, against the powers of this dark world and against the spiritual forces of evil in the heavenly realms.

EPHESIANS 6:12

Living according to rules and regulations and by our own human efforts is a trap that we can all fall into, set by the religious spirit in the workplace. Do you know the signs of the religious spirit when it is operating in the workplace?

The religious spirit discourages a genuine move of God and will thwart the activity of God under the banner of religious righteousness and dogma. It also motivates believers to live out their faith in legalistic and rigid ways. We need to be aware of how this happens in a workplace. The following are some characteristics of how the religious spirit manifests itself in believers in workplace situations.

Workers may have difficulty praying and applying God's promises to everyday work encounters. Workers may believe that biblical truths apply only to their personal lives, families and churches, not to their jobs. Workers may focus on evangelizing coworkers but fail to do their work with excellence. Workers may give greater priority to religious activity and events than to relationships with others at work. Workers may maintain an "us versus them" attitude when relating to non-Christians in the workplace.

Workers may also refuse to join a workplace prayer group or Bible study because they feel that it is trying to replace the role of their local church. Workers may feel the need to compartmentalize faith activities to their local church alone. Workers may discount the idea that Christianity could transform a workplace, city or nation as overzealous, naïve or even doctrinally wrong.

Beware of this when trying to encourage faith in your workplace. Remember, Stephen was the first martyr in the Early Church, and he was killed at the hands of religious leaders. You will find that your greatest resistance often comes from those in the religious community.

NOAH'S BUILDING PLAN

Noah did everything just as God commanded him.
GENESIS 6:22

When God chooses to do something on Earth, He uses a man or woman to accomplish the task. Partnership between man and God is very one-sided. God gets the worst part of the deal.

In Noah's generation, God got to a very bad place with the human race. He decided to start over. He was going to wipe out the entire population and begin afresh, and He chose one man to place His entire strategy around. Can you imagine that? God placed His entire plan around one man: Noah. Why? Because God could trust him. The Bible says Noah did everything just as God commanded him. He didn't argue with God. He didn't take short cuts. He listened and he obeyed.

Who was this man Noah? The Bible says that "Noah was a righteous man, blameless among the people of his time, and he walked with God" (Genesis 6:9-10). When it came time to execute God's plan, the Lord spoke to Noah and told him to build a big boat. However, Noah had no idea what a boat was or how to build one. So, God told him how to build it. He gave him the dimensions—the height, width, space requirements—everything he needed to complete the task.

God will instruct us in performing our work, too. God is in partnership with us in our working life. He has given us the tools, the creativity and the drive to accomplish what He placed us on Earth to do. Our partnership with God requires us to listen to our senior partner, though, because He knows the exact way our project is to be done. And when we follow His direction, our project will be excellent in every way: "Thus says the LORD, your Redeemer, The Holy One of Israel: 'I am the LORD your God, Who teaches you to profit, Who leads you by the way you should go'" (Isaiah 48:17, *NKJV*).

Do you need God to show you how to succeed in your call? Ask for His wisdom and understanding. God says He will give it generously (see James 1:5).

PRAYER AT WORK

Epaphras, who is one of you and a servant of Christ Jesus . . .
He is always wrestling in prayer for you, that you may stand firm in
all the will of God, mature and fully assured.

COLOSSIANS 4:12

Many of us have been entrenched in the "secular versus sacred" model for so long that it can be difficult for us to view our work as a ministry and workplace believers as missionaries in the 9 to 5 window. However, God tells us clearly that we are to glorify Him in all that we do (see Colossians 3:17). Having people pray for us to fulfill our purpose and calling in our workplaces is consistent with the will of God for every individual.

While the idea of a workplace intercessor may be a new concept for us, we need to remember the examples we find in the New Testament of believers praying for one another, such as Epaphras's praying for the Colossians in the Scripture above.

Colin Ferreira is a friend, a board member for our ministry and an owner of an optical business in Trinidad. I first met Colin in 2001 when he invited me to speak at a Caribbean workplace conference that he was organizing. I have watched Colin develop into a Kingdom business leader.

Through a series of struggles common to most businesses, Colin began to recognize the need for more prayer coverage. One of the organizations for which he had been supplying financial and leadership support maintained a prayer ministry. Colin asked the minister who headed the organization to intercede for him and his company on an ongoing basis, and she gladly agreed.

The two met periodically to discuss prayer needs and critical issues developing within the organization, which the minister then addressed discreetly in her intercessory group meetings. Often, this woman would recognize specific problems during these prayer meetings and know how to pray for them effectively.

Is prayer a regular part of your time with God? Are you in relationship with others who are praying for you?

CAN A CITY BE TRANSFORMED?

All those who lived in Lydda and Sharon saw him and turned to the Lord.

ACTS 9:35, EMPHASIS ADDED

Can an entire city be transformed for Jesus Christ? The book of Acts reveals that at least one city was. There are four key ingredients required among Christian leaders to see a city transformed. These include prayer, humility, unity and knowledge of God's ways.

(1) *Prayer.* In every city in which transformation has taken place, believers have come together to pray for their city. Prayer changes the spiritual climate of a city. Some of the main areas of influence that must be the focus of our prayers include churches; businesses; the legal, political, educational and medical fields; and the media/entertainment industry. Workplace leaders in each of these fields must be strategically aligned with intercessors to impact their city.

(2) *Humility.* God uses men and women who recognize that they need each other and who do not seek glory for their work. God "guides the humble in what is right and teaches them his way" (Psalm 25:9). The workplace leaders that God is using today care little about being in the limelight.

(3) *Unity.* Jesus said, "May they be brought to complete unity to let the world know that you sent me and have loved them even as you have loved me" (John 17:23). God calls each of us individually and corporately to represent Christ to the world, but our independence, pride and egos often prevent us from becoming unified in the purposes of Christ.

(4) *Knowledge of God's ways.* Sometimes leaders can move in presumption instead of in a faith that is rooted in knowledge of God's ways. Such was the case of David, who wanted to bring the Ark of the Covenant into the city of Jerusalem. He was zealous for God and celebrated as he brought the Ark into the city. However, the Ark was being carried into the city on a cart instead of by priests on poles, as God required. When a man named Uzzah reached out to catch the Ark when the oxen stumbled, he was immediately struck dead by God. David was devastated. He lacked knowledge of God's ways.

Do you want to see your city transformed? Make sure the four ingredients of prayer, humility, unity and knowledge of God's ways exist in your leadership team.

THE ULTIMATE PERFORMANCE REVIEW

If what he has built survives, he will receive his reward.

1 CORINTHIANS 3:14

Have you ever had a job performance review? If you are in the workplace, you will likely have had one. Employers want to see if you have done what was desired of you and whether you have done it in the prescribed way that has produced results. If you do well, you will be affirmed and may even get a pay raise. If you fail to live up to expectations, you could even get fired.

The Bible has its own performance review. It is called the Judgment Seat: "For we must all appear before the judgment seat of Christ, that each one may receive what is due him for the things done while in the body, whether good or bad" (2 Corinthians 5:10).

The generation that came out of Egypt with Moses is going to have a bad day at the Judgment Seat. We already know God's view on the matter: "That is why I was angry with that generation, and I said, 'Their hearts are always going astray, and they have not known my ways'" (Hebrews 3:10).

The Bible says that there is a way that seems right to a man, but the end of that way is death (see Proverbs 14:12). There is a way that God wants you and me to operate on the earth. He has given us His Word—our instruction manual—in order to know His ways of doing things.

How well do you know the instruction manual? Have you read only a few parts here and there? Are you well-versed on the intricacies of His ways so that you will be able to have a glorious "performance review" when the time comes?

Take time every day to get your instructions for His ways of living your life. Your reward will be great.

A MOTHER'S WORK

Children, obey your parents in the Lord, for this is right. "Honor your father and mother"—which is the first commandment with a promise—"that it may go well with you and that you may enjoy long life on the earth."

EPHESIANS 6:1-3

One of the great tragedies of society today is the minimizing of the work performed daily by stay-at-home moms. Women who decide to stay home to raise their kids are a rare breed, indeed. They must overcome the stigma of comparison to others who pursue careers outside the home. They often fail to feel the accomplishment that comes with an out-of-the-home career. They are the unseen missionaries of our day. There will be a special reward for these selfless servants.

Without the commitment of our stay-at-home moms we would not have some of our greatest leaders. "All that I am, or hope to be, I owe to my angel mother," said Abraham Lincoln.

Though poor, Ida Stover was determined to go to college. She scraped together enough money to attend Lane College in Lecompton, Kansas, where she met fellow student David Eisenhower. She was known as a firm but gentle disciplinarian and was deeply religious. It is said she once won a prize for memorizing 1,365 Bible verses. As a pacifist, she was not in favor of her son attending West Point but decided to let him go. She was the mother of Dwight David Eisenhower, one of the greatest U.S. presidents.

Mary Litogot grew up on a farm, and met her future husband, William Ford, when he came to work on their farm. She was 12 and he was 26. They married nine years later. Mary was self-sufficient and a diligent worker. Henry later attributed his clean factories to her belief in cleanliness. She encouraged his interest in machines early on. He later said, "I have tried to live my life as my mother would have wished. I believe I have done, as far as I could, just what she hoped for me." She was the mother of Henry Ford.[27]

Has God called you to be a stay-at-home mom? Know that if you choose to do so, your obedience and sacrifice will be recognized by the Lord.

URIAH

For where two or three come together in my name, there am I with them.
MATTHEW 18:20

My friend Rick Hereen shared a story about an encounter he had where prayer revealed an amazing insight into a business owner's problem.

> A friend who is a pastor told me that a couple within his congregation were having financial trouble in their business. He asked me if I would pray for them. I agreed. The day came for me to meet the couple. I listened to their story for a while and then suggested that we begin to pray.
>
> I waited for a few moments until a word popped into my mind. The word was "Uriah." I knew that Uriah was the husband of Bathsheba and that King David had had Uriah put in the front lines of a battle where there was a high likelihood that he would be killed. Essentially, David murdered Uriah so that he could take Bathsheba away from him.
>
> When I told the couple about the word that just popped into my mind, the wife immediately dissolved into tears. "Oh, Lord," she cried, "I knew that you were going to make me confess all of these sins." She went on to describe how she had been married previously. At work she fell in love with another man (her current husband) and colluded with that man to extricate her from her marriage to her first husband. Once the first husband was out of the way (divorced, not murdered), the two were free to become husband and wife. They confessed all sorts of other sins that they had committed. In short, they didn't have a business problem—they had a sin problem!
>
> Most marketplace Christians are unfamiliar with prayer. The idea that prayer is two-way communication with God is new for many. Receiving answers to prayer is not just for especially gifted Christians. Hearing from God is for every believer.[28]

Do you have a problem in your workplace? Ask God to show you the source of the problem.

FOR SUCH A TIME AS THIS

*For if you remain silent at this time, relief and deliverance for the Jews will arise
from another place, but you and your father's family will perish. And who knows
but that you have come to royal position for such a time as this?*

ESTHER 4:14-15

Esther was a Jewish orphan living in the land of Persia (an empire that
stretched from India to Ethiopia) after her people were taken into captivity
from Jerusalem. Raised by her cousin Mordecai, she lived during the time of
Persia's King Xerxes.

During King Xerxes's reign, an edict was sent out to bring all the virgins
from the surrounding regions to the king's palace to replace Queen Vashti
who found disfavor with the king and was deposed. Esther was one of the
young women taken and was ultimately selected to be the next queen.

Mordecai had a high-ranking position in the government that allowed
him to learn of a plot by Haman, an official of the king, to kill all of the Jews.
The only way this edict would not be carried out was if Esther asked for an
audience with the king to request that the plot be abandoned on her behalf.
However, to request an audience before the king was a serious matter. If he
refused to give her audience, the penalty was immediate death.

It was at this time that Esther made her famous statement, "If I perish,
I perish" (Esther 4:16). Esther realized this could be the reason God created her—
to save her people from destruction. However, out of concern for Esther,
Mordecai explained the situation to her: "For if you remain silent at this time,
relief and deliverance for the Jews will arise from another place, but you and your
father's family will perish" (Esther 4:14). Mordecai was giving her a choice: Either
she would be used by God or someone else would be used to save their people.

Everyday you and I are given a choice in our workplace. Are we willing to be
the person God uses to impact the future destiny of a people? Many of us are
silent Christians simply letting the status quo reign while we sit watching. Who
knows—you may have been created for such a time as this to be a catalyst to
stand in the gap for some situation in your workplace, community or nation.

Be faithful to your calling.

STOP LIVING BY CHRISTIAN PRINCIPLES

Having a form of godliness but denying its power.
2 TIMOTHY 3:5

God never called you to live by Christian principles. He calls you to live in relationship with the living God, Jesus Christ. One of the weaknesses of the Church today is that we teach people principles without the relationship.

The Western Church is big on five-step programs, how-to methods, and acrostics to illustrate memorable ideas. There is a place for establishing principles to change negative behavior; but we are not called to have a relationship with principles.

Living by principles is the equivalent to living by the law in the Old Testament. It is rooted in the Greek system of learning and is dependent upon our strength instead of the Holy Spirit's leading and empowerment.

Principle-based living is powerless living. This makes our Christian experience a religion instead of a relationship. In the book of Galatians, it is written, "But if you are led by the Spirit, you are not under law" (5:18). We also read about principle-based followers in the book of Acts: "The apostles performed many miraculous signs and wonders among the people. And all the believers used to meet together in Solomon's Colonnade. No one else dared join them, even though they were highly regarded by the people" (Acts 5:12-13). These were a group of followers who liked being taught but never entered the game.

In contrast, the prophet Jeremiah tells us about the nature of God and His desire for every believer: "This is what the LORD says: 'Let not the wise man boast of his wisdom or the strong man boast of his strength or the rich man boast of his riches, but let him who boasts boast about this: that he understands and knows me, that I am the LORD, who exercises kindness, justice and righteousness on earth, for in these I delight,' declares the LORD" (Jeremiah 9:23-24).

Friend, have you been guilty of living a life based on principles instead of knowing the One who authored the principles? Invite Jesus to be Lord over your life and begin to spend time with Him every day. Ask the Holy Spirit to lead and guide you through every moment of your day.

GRADUATE-LEVEL CHRISTIANITY

Love your enemies and pray for those who persecute you.
MATTHEW 5:44

There was a man who had become a friend and mentor to me, but a conflict arose between us that we were unable to resolve. I never imagined that this man would go from being one of my best friends to an enemy. I asked God to show me how I should treat this man, and the words of Jesus came to mind: "Love your enemies and pray for those who persecute you."

"Lord," I said, "surely You don't mean I'm to *love* this man! Not after the way he's hurt me and refused to reconcile!"

As I argued with God, I remembered that Jesus, before He was betrayed, got down on His knees and washed the feet of Judas Iscariot, His enemy. The moment that scene came to my mind, I knew what God was calling me to do. I had to wash the feet of my Judas.

This man who had been my friend and mentor had also been a client of my advertising agency. He was a Christian author and speaker, and I decided to bless him by continuing to promote his ministry and his books (a foot-washing of sorts).

Did he ever come back to me and reconcile? Yes, seven years later. But even if he had never reconciled with me, I knew that I did what God called me to do. I washed the feet of my Judas. I passed the test.

God doesn't promise that if we forgive there will be a happy ending. He doesn't promise that the man who refuses to pay a bill will suddenly write a check. He doesn't promise that the one who rejects reconciliation will instantly soften his heart. Jesus forgave His executioners, but that didn't keep them from nailing Him to the cross.

The graduate-level test is not about getting the results we want. It's about proving that we trust God enough to forgive our Judases. It's a graduate-level course in Christian obedience. God wants to know if we are willing to be imitators of Jesus. How can we say we are followers of Christ if we won't wash the feet of our Judases?

WHY THE WORKPLACE?

Do not conform any longer to the pattern of this world, but be transformed by the renewing of your mind.

ROMANS 12:2

If we are going to see the transformation of workplaces, cities and nations, then we must equip, affirm and release believers into their callings in the marketplace. The marketplace is where there is real authority—authority that can change society.

I often receive requests from the media for interviews about the faith at work movement. One day a writer from the *New York Times* magazine called. After several interviews, the reporter asked me, "Can you point me to someone who can demonstrate what this looks like in a daily workplace?" I told the writer to give my friend Chuck Ripka a call. Chuck was a banker in Elk River, Minnesota, who is a great example of a Christian impacting his workplace and city for Christ.

I told Chuck that the reporter would be calling him and Chuck and I immediately began praying for the writer. A few days later, Chuck called me and said the Lord was going to use this article not only for the workplace movement but also for this writer's life.

The writer visited Chuck and the bank for two days and attended community meetings, interviewed all the employees of the bank and watched Chuck pray for many people at work.

At the end of the reporter's visit, Chuck asked the writer if he and a friend could pray for God's blessing on him. The reporter agreed, and they prayed for God's blessing on his writing skills and for the *New York Times*. They also prayed that God would help him write the article. The writer was touched. Afterward, Chuck asked the reporter about his own relationship with God, which led to him praying to receive Christ. Two weeks later, photographers came to take pictures for the article, and they too prayed to receive Christ.

When the article was published, it was one of the best, most extensive and balanced articles on the faith at work movement that has been written from a secular viewpoint.

How might God use you to impact your workplace?

WITCHCRAFT IN THE WORKPLACE

The acts of the sinful nature are obvious: sexual immorality,
impurity and debauchery; idolatry and witchcraft.
GALATIANS 5:19-20

The envelope arrived in my mailbox with the exciting announcement on the outside: "You've just won one million dollars!"

Of course, like you, I have received so many of these over the years that I automatically file it in my nearby deep file—the trash can. The sensational headline is used to get you to open the envelope, only to discover that they are trying to sell you magazines with an opportunity to be entered into a sweepstakes drawing that could allow you to win a million dollars.

Everyday we are exposed to witchcraft in the workplace. Yes, I said witchcraft. Most of us think of this ancient term "witchcraft" as something that witches do. We think it has no relevance to modern society. However, this is not the case.

Whenever you do something "for free" with the intent of deceptively coercing someone to take action, you have engaged in witchcraft. This takes place in advertising, marketing and even Christian ministries.

In order to avoid engaging in witchcraft in the workplace, ask yourself if you are deceptively attempting to persuade others to buy your product. Make sure you are conveying truth about your product and what it professes to do. Don't use gimmicky sales approaches to engage others.

Perception is not always reality. When it comes to promoting a product or service, you want people's perception to match the realty of your advertising. Then you will avoid the sin of witchcraft.

GODLY FOREFATHERS

The angel of the LORD gave this charge to Joshua: "This is what the LORD Almighty says: 'If you will walk in my ways and keep my requirements, then you will govern my house and have charge of my courts, and I will give you a place among these standing here.'"

ZECHARIAH 3:6-7

On September 17, 1796, George Washington said, "It is impossible to rightly govern the world without God and the Bible." In his "Prayer at Valley Forge," he entreated God: "Almighty and eternal Lord God, the great Creator of heaven and earth, and the God and Father of our Lord Jesus Christ; look down from heaven in pity and compassion upon me Thy servant, who humbly prostrates myself before Thee."

On another occasion he said, "To the distinguished character of a patriot, it should be our highest glory to add the more distinguished character of a Christian."

America was founded as a Christian nation—the founding fathers had a deep faith in Jesus Christ. Today, there is a movement designed to remove God from our history and our foundations. Without God, America will no longer be good. And when America ceases to be good, we will cease to be great.

England also had a great Christian statesman in its early years. A man named William Wilberforce grew to prominence at the early age of 28, when he came to faith in Christ and almost chose to give up politics to go into the ministry. But John Newton, composer of "Amazing Grace," convinced him to stay in politics. In the end, Wilberforce was credited with 69 world-changing initiatives, not the least of which was the abolishment of slavery after 50 years of work.

Pray that this generation might acknowledge and embrace their godly heritage and pray that God will raise up other leaders who lead from a godly foundation.

WHEN DOING RIGHT ENDS WRONG

Consider it pure joy, my brothers, whenever you face trials of many kinds, because you know that the testing of your faith develops perseverance. Perseverance must finish its work so that you may be mature and complete, not lacking anything.

JAMES 1:2-4

Sports can teach us many valuable life lessons, if we'll let it. I played sports growing up and was a golf professional for three years in the 1970s. Sometimes in sports we buy into the idea that if we do all the right things and execute the perfect golf swing, or the perfect baseball pitch or the perfect whatever, we are guaranteed success. Sometimes that is true: The outcome matches the execution and the goal. However, in sports, as well as in life, success is not guaranteed.

Sports psychologist Bob Rotella says, "If you bring a smothering perfectionism to the golf course, you will probably leave with a higher handicap and a lousy disposition, because your game will never meet your expectations."[29]

You can make the perfect golf swing and end up in a divot or sand bunker, or you can make a great baseball pitch and the batter will hit a homerun. The analogies are limitless.

So what do we do when the outcome is bad? We must accept that in sports, as in life, outcomes don't always end the way we hope.

In Jesus, the outcome wasn't what we could have hoped—it was greater than anything we could have hoped for. Jesus came to be Savior of the world. He was a perfect human being without sin. He did all the right things. However, the result was death on the cross. A short-term positive outcome was not God's plan for the situation—He had a bigger picture in mind.

You and I need to keep the big picture in mind when short-term outcomes don't turn out well. The Bible calls this perseverance. "Blessed is the man who perseveres under trial, because when he has stood the test, he will receive the crown of life that God has promised to those who love him" (James 1:12).

Ask God for the grace to accept bad outcomes even when you have done all the right things.

KNOW YOUR ARMOR

David fastened on his sword over the tunic and tried walking around,
because he was not used to them. "I cannot go in these," he said to Saul,
"because I am not used to them." So he took them off.

1 SAMUEL 17:39

David, the young shepherd boy, heard the challenge from the Philistines to send someone to fight Goliath. No one volunteered to fight except David, so King Saul reluctantly agreed and offered David his armor. David put on the weighty equipment but quickly concluded that he could not fight in heavy armor. He gave it back to Saul.

God equips each of us in a way that is unique to our strengths and abilities. David knew who he was and who he wasn't. David was trained as a shepherd to use another weapon—a slingshot. He showed great maturity in realizing that he could not be effective with Saul's armor.

What are the gifts and talents God has given to you? Have you ever tried to accomplish a task with tools you were not trained to use? God allows each of us to develop skills that are unique to our life. He will not call you to use someone else's tools.

However, this is only half of the equation. These talents must be mixed with faith. Talent alone is not enough. Faith alone is not enough. It is only when the two are combined that God's power is released and manifested in the physical realm.

Sometimes we admire the talents of others and seek to emulate them. The temptation arises to be someone we are not. This is a mistake. Let God work His plans through the unique you.

Then, mix your unique gifts with faith; you will be surprised at the power of God that will be manifested as a result.

ARE YOU BECOMING SECULARIZED?

*Therefore God gave them over in the sinful desires of their hearts to
sexual impurity for the degrading of their bodies with one another.
They exchanged the truth of God for a lie, and worshiped and served created
things rather than the Creator—who is forever praised. Amen.*

ROMANS 1:24-25

There is a commonly known story about a frog in a kettle. A frog is placed in a kettle of warm water. The frog does not notice that the water temperature is being turned up gradually until it is too late. He dies from the heat of the water, not realizing the danger in time.

Societies are suffering from the "frog in the kettle" analogy. They make decisions that seem innocent enough, only to realize later the impact these decisions have on their society. Whether the issue is gay rights, abortion, euthanasia or simply a lack of spiritual influence over society, the changes seem logical to the unregenerate mind but over time reveal that the moral compass of the nation has been removed.

In 1945, a book was written about the spiritual condition of England. In it, the author stated, "We are convinced that England will never be converted until the laity use the opportunities daily afforded by their various professions, crafts and occupations."[30] At the time that book was written, 30 percent of the population of England attended church. Today, less than 7 percent attend church.[31] It has become a secularized nation.

In America during the 1940s, more than 40 percent of Americans attended church.[32] Today, less than 30 percent attend church, and the number is rapidly declining. The reason is that more and more believers are seeing the local church as irrelevant to the world they live in. Surveys reveal that up to 90 percent of church members believe that though the Bible is taught, they are not being taught how to apply the Bible to the complex world of work where they spend 60 to 70 percent of their time.[33]

Pray that God will bring revival upon our nations and that His glory will be revealed in and through His Church throughout the earth. Let's get out of the kettle before it is too late.

TWO GROCERS

You must have accurate and honest weights and measures, so that you may live long in the land the LORD your God is giving you.

DEUTERONOMY 25:15

A few hundred years ago there were two Christian grocers in London. One of them said to the other, "You know, as Christians, we're supposed to have honest scales. It says so in the Bible. So how should we do that?"

"Well, I'll tell you what, I'll come and check your scales on Wednesdays to make sure they're accurate and you come on Sundays and check mine," said the other grocer. The two grocers developed a list of 12 principles that they felt should guide the way they did business.

People preferred to buy from them because they knew they would get a good product at a fair price, with honest scales. After a while, other Christian grocers decided to join in, and they formed an association of Christian grocers. In those days it was called the Most Worshipful Company of Livery Merchants.

This group led to other industries adopting a similar ideal, and they became known as Livery Companies in the City of London. There are now 300 companies in London registered as Livery Companies. The latest one was the Most Worshipful Company of Information Technologists. Everybody that joins one of these companies, even today, receives a list of the principles to which they must agree. The list contains 36 biblical principles, and they call the book *Some Rules for the Conduct of Life to Which Are Added a Few Cautions*.

The rulers of the nation in Britain began to see the effect of these companies and said, "What we need to do is make it a law for the whole nation. So instead of just these grocers having their honest scales, every scale in Britain needs to weigh accurately." The government's Weights and Measures Department, still in existence today, can trace its history back to the day when two grocers decided to keep themselves accountable to biblical principles.[34]

Are you operating based on honest weights and measures?

FULFILLING THE PURPOSE OF A GENERATION

For David . . . served the purpose of God in his own generation.
ACTS 13:36, *NASB*

Imagine for a moment that you have just died and that you are about to come before the Judgment Seat of Christ. Jesus is speaking to His angel about you. He then says these words: "You have served the purpose of my heavenly Father for your generation."

Will God be able to say you served your purpose in your generation? Imagine being able to say that. God was able to say this about the life of David, even though David made some incredibly bad choices that led to long-term consequences. However, because David repented each time he erred, his purpose was accomplished on Earth as God had designed it.

One of the prayers I often pray for people is, "Lord, may You fulfill every purpose for which You made this person. May there be no inheritance left on the table that he or she is entitled to."

That last part of the prayer is really the definition of success. Success is fulfilling the complete purpose for which God made you. It has nothing to do with wealth, accomplishments, stature in life or standard of living. It has to do with living a life of obedience to the Father. And when we live a life of obedience to the Father, we will fulfill the purposes that God had in mind when He made you and me.

In 1924, Eric Liddell, a Scottish Olympic runner whose life was chronicled in a movie entitled *Chariots of Fire*, was challenged by his missionary sister to forego running in the Olympics in lieu of going to China with her as a missionary. He responded by saying, "When I run, I feel His [God's] pleasure." Eric understood his complete purpose for his generation. As a result, he brought glory to the Father by running in the Olympics and later joining his sister in the missionary service in China.

Today, ask God to fulfill His purposes for your life in your generation.

FREEDOM AND BOUNDARIES

And the LORD God commanded the man, "You are free to eat from any tree in the garden; but you must not eat from the tree of the knowledge of good and evil, for when you eat of it you will surely die."

GENESIS 2:16-17

Everyone needs both freedom and boundaries in their work to succeed. God set up the ultimate work environment in the Garden of Eden. He gave Adam and Eve responsibility to manage the animals, the agriculture and every activity. He gave them specific instructions as to how things were to be done, but He also gave liberty of expression for fulfilling their tasks.

In addition, God told them what was off-limits. They could not eat from the tree of the knowledge of good and evil because God knew it would be bad for them. He was not trying to withhold from Adam and Eve—He was trying to protect them.

If you are a manager, it is your responsibility to clearly define the job responsibilities of those under your care. They should know what the freedoms and boundaries are in carrying out their duties. They should be given adequate freedoms along with authority to enforce the decisions that will impact whether or not they can be successful.

Once freedoms and boundaries are established, this allows a healthy accountability to take place between management and worker. Both can have healthy expectations of each other.

Do you have a clearly defined job description with measurable goals outlined? Are your freedom and boundaries clearly defined so that you know what you can and cannot do within the scope of your job? If not, you are setting yourself up for failure.

Today, evaluate your job function and make sure you have clearly defined freedoms, boundaries and expectations.

WASHING TOILETS

Those he wanted to promote, he promoted; and those he wanted to humble, he humbled.
DANIEL 5:19

My friend Paul desired a career in the building industry. Early in his career, he was working with a large ministry to help direct several of their construction projects. As the projects were completed, Paul was asked to stay on for future projects. To keep him busy, he was given a number of jobs—one of which was cleaning toilets. He recalls getting down on his knees each day and complaining to the Lord, "I'm a college graduate!"

Discouraged, Paul told the Lord, "I will not leave here until You promote me. Please give me contentment with my circumstance."

Despite his prayer, Paul felt totally forgotten by God. A few months later, Paul received a phone call from a man in the Midwest who owned five successful businesses and who wanted to interview Paul for a job. This came as a total surprise to Paul. As he drove to the interview, he told the Lord, "I only want Your will in my life, nothing else. I am content to remain obscure for the rest of my life if I have You. You must override my lack of experience for me to get this job."

The owner of the company asked Paul a surprising question: "If I asked you to clean a toilet, what would you do?" Paul sat there, stunned. He wanted to burst out laughing. Paul assured him that he would simply pick up a sponge and start cleaning.

Amazingly, Paul was hired even though other candidates were more qualified. After several months of success, Paul asked his boss why he hired him. His boss replied, "Paul, I still have a large stack of applications from people who wanted this job. Do you remember the first question I asked you in the interview? I asked each one the same question. You were the only one who said he would clean the toilet. Paul, I am a wealthy man, but I grew up dirt poor. I clean my own toilets at home. I can't have people running my businesses who are too proud to clean a toilet."

Sometimes God places us in humble circumstances to see if we will be faithful in those before He is willing to promote us to greater things.

HONOR IN BEING HELPFUL

He gave him the plans of all that the Spirit had put in his mind for the courts of the temple of the LORD and all the surrounding rooms, for the treasuries of the temple of God and for the treasuries for the dedicated things.

1 CHRONICLES 28:12

It is said of George Washington Carver that he got up early in the morning each day to walk alone and pray. He asked God how he was to spend his day and what the Lord wanted to teach him. Carver grew up at the close of the Civil War as a slave in a one-room shanty on the property of Moses Carver—the man who owned his mother.

Carver grew up at the height of racial discrimination, yet he had overcome all these obstacles to become one of the most influential men in the history of the United States. He made many discoveries with the use of peanuts and sweet potatoes. The new products he made created a demand for peanuts and sweet potatoes, and they were major contributors to rejuvenating the Southern economy.

As he made new discoveries, he never became successful monetarily. But during his lifetime, he did have success in overcoming great rejection for being black. He was offered six-figure income opportunities from Henry Ford, and he became friends with presidents of his day—yet he knew what God had called him to do.

His epitaph reads: "He could have added fortune to fame, but caring for neither, he found happiness and honor in being helpful to the world."[35]

Like Carver, each of us must connect with our primary purpose in life. We must heed Carver's example and pray that the Lord would teach us new things each day and that we would find happiness not in money, but in helping others.

MANAGING MONEY

He who loves money will not be satisfied with money,
nor he who loves abundance with its income.
ECCLESIASTES 5:10, *NASB*

A successful businessman named John once confided in another business-man known for his wisdom: "I've made a lot of money. I will soon be able to retire comfortably and do just about anything I want."

"John," the wise businessman replied, "I've noticed that every time someone thinks they've built a tree that is so tall it almost reaches heaven, God often decides to shake the tree."

The minute we start trusting in riches, God will, in fact, "shake the tree" to demonstrate that He is the source of wealth and to turn us back to trusting Him completely. He did it in my life, and He'll do it in your life too. He loves us too much to allow us to continue down the destructive path of loving money.

Money is mentioned more than 2,000 times in the New Testament. Jesus used it many times to illustrate to His followers how they needed to be good stewards of the resources He entrusted to them. He also spoke of money because He wanted to warn them to stay away from making money an idol in their lives.

Jesus was completely surrendered to His Father's will: "I tell you the truth, the Son can do nothing by himself; He can do only what he sees his Father doing, because whatever the Father does the Son also does. For the Father loves the Son and shows him all he does" (John 5:19-20).

As we look at our relationship to our heavenly Father and our use of money, it's clear that we, like Jesus, must seek to live a life that is totally yield-ed to God's purposes—especially financially.

Money, independence and security are often the reasons many start their own businesses or change jobs. Check your motives today and see if your financial life can stand Jesus' scrutiny.

Are you operating as a steward of the financial resources He has entrust-ed to you?

RECALIBRATE ROUTE!

The crooked roads shall become straight, the rough ways smooth.
LUKE 3:5

I love the Global Positioning Systems (GPS) in new cars. A voice comes on and tells me how far I have to go and when to turn. However, sometimes I get off course and the voice says, "Recalculating route." When I go off course, the GPS recalculates the route based on my wrong turn.

Sometimes we can make wrong turns in our spiritual lives. We think we are going the right direction only to discover it was never God's will to enter that relationship, make that business deal, hire that person—the examples are limitless.

There is an amazing thing about God: He can make our crooked places straight. He has an ability to make whatever blunder we make turn out right. It may mean there might be some consequences to our decisions, but He will always allow our actions to work together for good according to His purposes, as long as we repent and seek Him fully to make things right. These lessons can contribute to even greater wisdom in our lives as we learn from our mistakes.

God's omnipotence is always one step ahead of our incompetence. Do you think He knew you would make that misstep? Absolutely. Do you think your life was planned even with that misstep figured in? Absolutely.

Isn't it comforting to know that you cannot plan God out of the equation no matter how badly you mess up? He will always turn crooked places into straight places for those who are humble and contrite.

Do you need a crooked place straightened out today? Ask Him to straighten the course so that you can flow in His perfect will for your life.

TRAINED FOR WAR

Praise be to the LORD my Rock, who trains my hands for war, my fingers for battle.
PSALM 144:1

You'll never experience God in powerful ways by acquiring Bible knowledge alone. It is only when that knowledge is used in the heat of battle that you will know the reality of what you've learned intellectually. Otherwise, it remains only an exercise in spiritual gymnastics that yields little fruit.

David, for example, became a great warrior and the leader of a nation at an early age. Before these honors, though, his training ground was his job as a shepherd in the open fields. When bears and lions sought to take his sheep, he personally fought them. In this way, he was prepared for future battles. David later found that Goliath was the competition that God used to reveal how well David's training had prepared him.

Today, our local churches often look more like luxury cruise liners designed to tickle the ears, entertain its members and make them feel good. They don't often resemble a battleship designed to train an army for war. The average member still watches from the sidelines. But in sports you discover how well you handle pressure by competing. You can practice all you want but never know how you will do until you enter the game and test what you've learned when there is pressure added to the equation. Similarly, in a battle you discover how well you are trained by what you actually do on the battlefield.

Have you ever prayed with someone in public? Have you ever personally led someone to Christ? Have you ever served others for the sake of the gospel? Have you ever taught a Bible study? If you said no to these questions, then you are not engaged in the game. Today, why not ask God to give you the grace to step onto the battlefield.

SEEING GOD'S POWER IN THE CLOTHING INDUSTRY

My message and my preaching were not with wise and persuasive words,
but with a demonstration of the Spirit's power, so that your faith
might not rest on men's wisdom, but on God's power.
1 CORINTHIANS 2:4-5

Crystal is a businesswoman involved in the manufacture of designer clothing. Her designs are known for their elaborate detail and the accessories she sews into the garments. Her patterns are so popular that she had a contract with a major retail chain that agreed to carry her clothing. One day a call came from the retailer. They requested that four designs be sent to them for consideration for the next season's clothing line. Crystal agreed, knowing that meeting this particular deadline was going to be very difficult due to other circumstances that were going on in her life.

Finally, the deadline came and she had not completed the detailing and accessories on two of the four pieces of clothing she wanted the retailer to consider. She called the retailer and said that she had two pieces ready to ship but that the other two still needed to be completed. The retailer argued with her and said, "Send the others to us anyway."

The idea of sending her designs to the retailer without the finished detail, creativity and quality made Crystal very uncomfortable. Then she recalled my teaching on this principle. She decided to do something in total opposition to her perfectionist inclinations: She sent the two incomplete pieces of clothing to the retailer along with the other two finished pieces. To her shock and amazement, the retailer ended up choosing the two pieces of clothing that had not been finished and declined the other two.

Crystal later realized that God had demonstrated His power through the principle of withholding her natural gifting to show her that it was by His hand that she was successful in her business. Crystal's realization did not take away her need to be creative or skillful but instead allowed her to place greater dependence upon obedience rather than on her natural skill.

Are you willing to trust God in obedience, even against your natural abilities and inclinations?

A CONVERSATION IN HEAVEN

*I will raise up for myself a faithful priest, who will do according to
what is in my heart and mind. I will firmly establish his house,
and he will minister before my anointed one always.*

1 SAMUEL 2:35

I once imagined a meeting in heaven between the angel Gabriel and Jesus.
It went something like this:

> Gabriel, I chose 12 men from the workplace to build My Church.
> They were an unlikely group. But I wanted a people to express My
> life where they spent most of their time and experienced most of
> their challenges. However, today we have a problem. My Church is
> not being represented in the workplace. So, I've decided to call sev-
> eral people to serve Me in this arena. We must awaken the Church
> in the workplace.
>
> There is a man in Atlanta, Georgia, who reminds Me of My ser-
> vant Jacob. Boy, what a manipulator and controller he was before
> I did My work in him. Now you recall that Jacob became one of the
> patriarchs! This businessman in Atlanta has the same potential.
> He is our man to awaken My servants. However, in order to awaken
> him to My plan and My destiny for him, I must remove some of
> the things he relies upon. This will draw him to Me.
>
> It will be painful at first, but necessary. It will take seven years.
> But I plan to restore all I take from him. The result will be quite amaz-
> ing. He will engage many others. He'll usher in a whole new focus in
> My Church that has been lost since those early days. I plan to do this
> with many others as well. My plan is designed to raise up an army in
> these last days before I return. It is time for you to go now. You know
> what you must do. Be gentle but firm with My servant.

What kind of conversation might Jesus and an angel have about your
life? What catalyst is needed to bring you into alignment with the purposes
and plans of God?

SEVEN NEEDS

The weapons we fight with are not the weapons of the world.
On the contrary, they have divine power to demolish strongholds.

2 CORINTHIANS 10:4

Jerry had grown up with a father who was a successful workaholic. Although he lacked for nothing materially, he never sensed much warmth or compassion from his parents. Then, when Jerry was still in his early teens, his father died very suddenly. His large family was left with little support, and insecurity and fear became the dominating factors in the young man's life. Vowing to himself that he would never have financial need again, Jerry worked hard at his business.

Over time, the stronghold of idolatry brought reliance on the wealth he had accumulated rather than a prayerful dependency on God. Arguments over money dominated his marriage. Distrust and greed permeated his home and business relationships. No one could tell him what to do. Finally, as his marriage disintegrated and his business gave signs of going under, Jerry renounced the strongholds of insecurity and fear that had made money his idol and had shaped his disbelieving view of God's ability to meet his need.

As the Holy Spirit brought conviction of the sins he had committed against so many people, Jerry purposed to approach each individual to seek forgiveness and make restitution wherever appropriate. His priorities shifted to God and family, then to close friends and business. God began to restore balance and intimacy between Jerry and God as well as between Jerry and others.

God created human beings with seven primary needs, as represented in Genesis 1–2. Each of us has a need for (1) dignity, (2) authority, (3) blessing and provision, (4) security, (5) purpose and meaning, (6) freedom and boundary, and (7) intimate love and companionship.

Whenever we seek to meet one or more of these basic needs outside God's design, we have set the stage for the development of a generational stronghold. In the case of Jerry—who is actually me—he needed to discover the needs he was attempting to meet through a demonic stronghold of insecurity and fear.

Today, why not begin to investigate root issues that may be impacting you or your family.

CONFRONT AND SUPPORT

Barnabas wanted to take John, also called Mark, with them,
but Paul did not think it wise to take them . . . because he had deserted
them in Pamphylia and had not continued with them in the work.
They had such a sharp disagreement that they parted company.

ACTS 15:37-39

Conflict in the workplace, in ministry or even in marriage is inevitable because in each situation, we are working closely with others. God has wired each of us with different personalities so that we can view circumstances differently.

There are times when our differences cannot be resolved, which results in conflict. It doesn't mean that one person or the other is evil or sinful; it just means that the difference of opinion or the personality clash has no solution.

We see an example of this in the relationship between Paul and Barnabas, two partners in Christian ministry who had a sharp disagreement regarding a young man named John Mark. In Acts 15, Barnabas wanted to take John Mark on a missionary journey. However, Paul refused. John Mark had disappointed him once before and Paul didn't want to give him another chance. In the end, Paul and Barnabas agreed to disagree and to part company. Paul went one way; Barnabas and John Mark went another. Sometimes, that's the only solution to a disagreement.

But there's a postscript to this story: In 2 Timothy 4:11, Paul writes from his prison cell in Rome and tells Timothy, "Get Mark and bring him with you, because he is helpful to me in my ministry." Sometime after the disagreement between Paul and Barnabas, John Mark redeemed himself and became a valued partner in Paul's ministry. In fact, as Paul faced execution in Rome, he wanted his friend John Mark at his side.

Whenever there is disagreement, make sure you maintain support of the person at the same time you disagree with their position. Avoid personal attacks and implying motive behind someone else's position. This will allow you to disagree and still maintain a relationship.

FOSTERING THE RIGHT ENVIRONMENT

Be sure you know the condition of your flocks, give careful attention to your herds.
PROVERBS 27:23

Janice was a high-level executive who required excellence and exceptional performance from those under her leadership. She was the general manager of a credit card unit when 5 of her 2,000 employees were found to have deliberately hidden $24 million in losses for which she was accountable.

Janice's "no failure" policy had brought great pressure upon her employees and she had failed to recognize how this leadership style discouraged employees from bringing problems to her. She was an intense perfectionist whom others saw as intimidating and confrontational. She was extremely opinionated. Her subordinates were fearful of reporting any bad news, so they lied about it.

Do you feel like what you accomplish is never quite good enough? Do projects have to be just right? Do you feel you must give more than 100 percent on everything you do or else you will be mediocre or even a failure?

Perfectionism refers to a set of self-defeating thoughts and behaviors aimed at reaching excessively high and unrealistic goals. Perfectionism is often mistakenly seen in American society as desirable or even necessary for success. However, studies show that perfectionist attitudes actually interfere with success. The desire to be perfect can both rob individuals of a sense of personal satisfaction and cause them to fail to achieve as much as people who have more realistic strivings.

As a result of Janice's predicament, she lost her job but was later offered another chance to salvage one of the company's smaller businesses. In her new leadership position, she realized that she needed to be much more understanding of the people around her. She learned from her experience and succeeded in her next assignment with the company.

What would others say about your management style? Do you foster dialogue and encourage others to bring issues to your attention? Are you willing to work with your team to solve problems together?

THE PLACE OF NOTHINGNESS

Be still and know that I am God.

PSALM 46:10

Do you find yourself in a place of nothingness? There is a time and place in our walk with God in which He sets us in a place of isolation and waiting. It is a place in which all past experiences are of no value. It is as if God has placed a wall around us: no new opportunities—simply inactivity. It is a time of such stillness that it can disturb the most faithful if we do not understand that He is the one who has brought us to this place only for a season.

During these times, God is calling us aside to fashion something new in us. It is a place of nothingness designed to call us to deeper roots of prayer and faith. It is not a comfortable place, especially for a task-driven workplace believer. Our nature cries out, "You must do something," while God is saying, "Be still and know that I am God."

How can we tell if we are in the place of nothingness? We know the signs when we find that God has removed many things from our life and we can't seem to change anything. Perhaps we are unemployed. Perhaps we are laid up with an illness.

Many people live a very planned and orchestrated life where they know almost everything that will happen. But for people in whom God is performing a deeper work, He brings them into a time of quietness that seems almost eerie. They cannot see what God is doing. They just know that He is doing a work that cannot be explained to themselves or to others.

Has God brought you to a place of nothingness? Be still and know that He really is God. When this happens, *your nothingness will be turned into something you will value for the rest of your life.*

MOTHER TERESA

For I was hungry and you gave me nothing to eat, I was thirsty and you gave me nothing to drink, I was a stranger and you did not invite me in, I needed clothes and you did not clothe me, I was sick and in prison and you did not look after me.

MATTHEW 25:42-43

Mother Teresa gave her life to serving the needs of the poor in Calcutta, India. She revealed what she believed every believer in Jesus is called to do:

> It is not enough for us to say: "I love God," but I also have to love my neighbor. St. John says that you are a liar if you say you love God and you don't love your neighbor. How can you love God whom you do not see, if you do not love your neighbor whom you see, whom you touch, with whom you live? And so it is very important for us to realize that love, to be true, has to hurt. I must be willing to give whatever it takes not to harm other people and, in fact, to do good to them. This requires that I be willing to give until it hurts. Otherwise, there is not true love in me and I bring injustice, not peace, to those around me.
>
> It hurt Jesus to love us. We have been created in His image for greater things, to love and to be loved. We must "put on Christ" as Scripture tells us. And so, we have been created to love as He loves us. Jesus makes Himself the hungry one, the naked one, the homeless one, the unwanted one, and He says, "You did it to Me." On the last day He will say to those on His right, "whatever you did to the least of these, you did to Me, and He will also say to those on His left, whatever you neglected to do for the least of these, you neglected to do it for Me."
>
> When He was dying on the Cross, Jesus said, "I thirst." Jesus is thirsting for our love, and this is the thirst of everyone, poor and rich alike. We all thirst for the love of others that they go out of their way to avoid harming us and to do good to us. This is the meaning of true love, to give until it hurts.[36]

How might Mother Teresa's words encourage you to do things differently?

"YOU NEED POWER"

*But you will receive power when the Holy Spirit comes on you; and you will be my
witnesses in Jerusalem, and in all Judea and Samaria, and to the ends of the earth.*

ACTS 1:8

D. L. Moody was a shoe salesman until God moved him into a full-time
preaching ministry, often in the streets of Chicago. There came a point in
his journey with God when he realized he needed more in his life than
what he was experiencing:

> At the close of the Sabbath evening services [two women] would say
> to me, "We have been praying for you." I said, "Why don't you pray
> for the people?" They answered, "You need power."
>
> "I need power?" I said to myself. Why? I thought I had power.
> I had a large Sabbath school and the largest congregation in Chicago.
> I was in a sense satisfied. But then came these two godly women who
> prayed for me, and their earnest talk about "the anointing for special
> service" set me thinking. I asked them to come and talk with me, and
> we got down on our knees. They poured out their hearts, that I might
> receive the anointing of the Holy Ghost. And there came a great
> hunger into my soul. I knew not what it was. I began to cry as I never
> did before. The hunger increased. I really felt that I did not want to
> live any longer if I could not have this power for service. I kept on cry-
> ing all the time that God would fill me with His Spirit. Well, one day,
> in the city of New York—Oh, what a day! I cannot describe it. I seldom
> refer to it; it is almost too sacred an experience to me. . . .
>
> I went to preaching again. The sermons were no different; I did
> not present any new truths, and yet hundreds were converted.
> I would not be placed back where I was before that blessed experi-
> ence if you would give me all Glasgow.[37]

Do you need more in your life than what you are currently experiencing?
Ask God to fill you with His power today.

PRACTICING THE PRESENCE OF GOD

Enoch walked with God.
GENESIS 5:24

The true test of a person's spiritual life and character is not what he does in the extraordinary moments of life but what he does during the daily grind of everyday life, when there is nothing tremendous or exciting happening.

In the 1600s, there was a monk named Brother Lawrence who was a dishwasher in his monastery. There, he made a profound discovery that is true for every believer in the workplace today. He wrote, "For me the time of activity does not differ from the time of prayer, and in the noise and clatter of my kitchen, while several persons are calling for as many different things, I possess God in as great tranquility as when upon my knees at the blessed Sacrament."[38]

You see, he found no urgency for retreats, because in the common task he met the same God to love and worship as he did in the stillness of the desert. It is this kind of life that Jesus desires for each of His children.

Enoch was also a man that practiced the presence of God. The Bible does not give a detailed account of his life—all we know about him is that "He walked with God." In fact, it says in Genesis 5:22 that Enoch walked with God for 300 years. Wow! That is faithfulness!

What does it mean today to practice the presence of God daily? It means we are constantly talking to our heavenly Father about the issues in our day. It means praying about things as they come up. It means stopping at a red light and praying for the person God brings to mind. It means singing a song in your car while you are sitting in traffic.

Today, when God gives you times alone or when there are needs that arise, stop and consult your heavenly Father about the situation. Then you will be practicing the presence of God.

WHY DOES GOD ALLOW EVIL?

If you, O LORD, kept a record of sins, O Lord, who could stand.
PSALM 130:3

One of the most common questions people wrestle with in life is this: "God, if You are loving, just and all-powerful, why do You allow good people to suffer?" Many choose not to believe in God because they cannot adequately explain this question. Evangelist Billy Graham addressed this question in his book *Answers to Life's Problems*:

> We do not know all the reasons why God permits evil. We need to remember, however, that he is not the cause of evil in this world and we should therefore not blame Him for it. Remember that God did not create evil, as some believe. God created the world perfect. Man chose to defy God and go his own way, and it is man's fault that evil entered the world. Even so, God has provided the ultimate triumph of good over evil in Jesus Christ, who on the cross, defeated Satan and those who follow him. Christ is coming back and when He does, all evil will be ended forever and righteousness and justice will prevail.
>
> Have you ever thought about what would happen if God suddenly eliminated all the evil in this world? Not one person would be left, because we are all guilty of sin.[39]

Whenever we suffer, we should remember that the Son of God went before us, drinking the cup of suffering and death to the dregs. Because Christ is fully man and fully God, we know that God understands our fears, sorrows and suffering. He identifies with us. Most important of all, the Father has given us the gift of His Son so that we don't have to die and suffer forever in eternity. Because Jesus suffered and died for us, our suffering can be made like His—purposeful and meaningful.

Billy Graham may have settled some of your questions, but there are some questions that will remain unresolved until we are able to meet face to face with our Creator in heaven.

BLOCK LOGIC

For this is what the LORD Almighty, the God of Israel, says:
"Houses, fields and vineyards will again be bought in this land."
JEREMIAH 32:15

In the Scriptures, we discover a difference in the way the Hebrew mind viewed things compared to the way many Westerners relate to God. Hebrews used something called *block logic*—that is, concepts were expressed in self-contained units or blocks of thought. These blocks did not necessarily fit together in any obvious, rational or harmonious pattern.

Greek logic, which has influenced the Western world, was different. The Greeks often used tightly contained *step logic*—that is, reasoning a premise to a conclusion. Each step of this type of thinking is linked tightly to the next in coherent, rational, logical fashion.

This is why some Bible stories don't make sense to the Western mind. It is particularly difficult for Westerners—those whose thought patterns have been influenced more by the Greeks and Romans than by the Hebrews—to piece together the block logic of Scripture.

Consider Jeremiah and God's instruction to purchase land in a seemingly inopportune time. If I asked you to purchase some land when you knew that the country you were living in was about to be invaded and you were sure to be placed under arrest, how wise would you believe such an investment to be? Do you believe God would lead you to make such an investment? That is exactly what God told Jeremiah to do. However, God had a good reason for having Jeremiah make such a purchase. It was to be a testimony and a promise that God was going to restore the Jews to their land.

As Jeremiah's story points out, the Hebrews often made decisions based on obedience. Greeks (and Westerners), on the other hand, often made decisions based on logic and reason. If the Early Church had made decisions based on a pro and con method, there would be no miracles in the Bible.

We are not to question God's instructions. We are simply to obey.

WHERE DO YOU PLACE YOUR CONFIDENCE?

Satan rose up against Israel and incited David to take a census of Israel.
1 CHRONICLES 21:1

God always requires total trust in Him alone for our victories in life. Through-out Scripture we are cautioned not to place our trust in the strength of horses, other men or our own abilities. In 1 Chronicles, David's decision to take a census was a failure to keep his trust totally upon the Lord.

David's purpose in counting his population was to assess his military strength, much like the second census taken under Moses (see Numbers 1:2–3). David found 800,000 men eligible for military service in Israel, and 500,000 men in Judah (see 2 Samuel 24:9), more than double the previous head count.

David's commander evidently recognized the grave error that his king was about to make. "But Joab replied, 'May the LORD multiply his troops a hundred times over. My lord the king, are they not all my lord's subjects? Why does my lord want to do this? Why should he bring guilt on Israel?'" (1 Chronicles 21:3).

Joab was right—the census displeased the Lord. David was falling into the temptation of trusting in the size of his army rather than in the Lord. In consequence, God punished David and reduced his forces by bringing a plague that killed 70,000 men.

How do you avoid placing your trust in God today? Do you trust your bank accounts, your skills and the security of your workplace? When you begin to place your faith in these things instead of in the Provider of these things, you get into trouble with God.

What a lesson this is for each of us. Today, place your total trust in the Lord for all of your needs.

OAKS OF RIGHTEOUSNESS

They will be called oaks of righteousness, a planting of the LORD
for the display of his splendor.
ISAIAH 61:3

It was the worst time in my life. Feeling betrayed by God, I stormed out of the door and walked up the heavily wooded hill behind my house. Reaching the hilltop, I raged at God. "God!" I shouted, "Is this how you treat someone who is faithful to You?! I've waited and waited. I've worked and prayed. And for what? For this?" My lungs hurt and my throat was raw—but I had one more thing to say to God. "I hate You, God! I hate You!"

I sat down on an old oak tree that had broken at the base and was lying on the ground. For the next three hours I sobbed uncontrollably, unable to speak, unable to pray. I wondered how God could abandon me. I wondered if He even existed. Maybe I had wasted my life believing in a myth.

Finally, I got up to leave. When I looked over at the fallen oak that I had sat on, I noticed something interesting. The fallen tree was pointed toward the base of another oak tree—a tree that stood strong and tall with wide-spreading branches. At that moment I heard a quiet voice inside me say, *Today, like this broken oak tree, you are a broken man. But this brokenness was needed in order for you to become like the large, strong oak tree that stands before you.*

Years later, I would look back and know that God Himself had spoken to me out of my period of darkness and silence.

Even when I raged at God and told Him I hated Him, God was faithful and forgiving. Today, He has replaced the ashes of my despair with the oil of gladness. He has planted me firmly like a strong and sturdy oak tree, and I live my life in gratitude for His mercy.

Do you find yourself in a dark place? Share your true feelings with God. You'll be surprised how well He is willing to listen.

THE ETERNAL SALES CALL

That if you confess with your mouth, "Jesus is Lord," and believe in your heart that God raised him from the dead, you will be saved."

ROMANS 10:9

I received a phone call from a technology CEO who had begun to receive my *TGIF* devotionals a few weeks earlier. He told me that each day he read the daily message and found that it really helped him. He had called because he felt that his technology product might have some application to my ministry. I asked about how he had started getting the devotional. As he told me his story, I could tell he probably did not know the Lord personally. So I inquired further with a few more leading questions.

Gradually, he changed the subject to his product. We discussed the product for 20 minutes or so. He was about to conclude our conversation when I asked, "Could we go back to our original conversation? Tell me more about your spiritual journey and where you feel you are." He told me that he was raised in a particular Christian tradition. I shared how Christ came not to give us a religion but to have a personal relationship with us.

Eventually I asked, "What do you think keeps you from making such a commitment?"

"Well, quite frankly, I am a controller. I feel that I can't let go of control. I fear what might happen." I appreciated his honesty.

We discussed this at length, and I helped him understand that every person has a control issue to overcome. However, Christ requires us to give up control in order to give us real life. It is the great paradox of faith in Christ.

Then, I said, "So, now that we have dealt with that issue, is there any reason you would not be prepared to make that commitment to Christ?"

"Well, now that you put it that way, no, I guess there isn't," he responded. Bill prayed with me over the phone to invite Jesus to be Lord over his life, not just to be his Savior. What he intended to be a typical sales call became a call for eternity.

Perhaps there will be an opportunity at your work today to share the love of Christ with someone who is waiting to receive salvation through you.

REMEDY FOR DEPRESSION

To console those who mourn in Zion, to give them beauty for ashes, the oil of joy for mourning, the garment of praise for the spirit of heaviness.

ISAIAH 61:2-3, *NKJV*

A 1988 article in *Psychology Today* reported on an experiment involving 1,700 women under stress. The women participated in various projects that involved helping other people. Within 30 days, 85 percent of the women reported that they had been relieved of stress symptoms that included "stress-related disorders such as headaches, voice loss and even pain accompanying lupus and multiple sclerosis."[40]

I suspect that many people could save thousands of dollars on therapy and antidepressants if they would just take time to serve others. The best way to get beyond our pain is to get outside of it. I discovered this in my own journey through a particular dark time. I decided to serve others even though I was in great emotional pain. This had a remarkable positive effect on my emotional state.

When we refocus our attention on the needs of others while we ourselves are in turmoil, it allows the burden of our circumstance to be removed from us. The more we focus on our own problem the more likely we are to become depressed.

The Scripture passage above shows that Isaiah understood a principle that is still valid today. If you find yourself depressed because of a circumstance in your life, take Isaiah's advice—begin to praise the Lord in spite of the circumstances you see. Then you will see the spirit of heaviness begin to be lifted.

CONFRONTING EVIL

The LORD sent Nathan to David.

2 SAMUEL 12:1

There are times when evil must be confronted. When God judges a situation, He often uses His servants as vessels for communicating to the guilty party. Such was the case with David who tried to conceal his sin of sleeping with Bathsheba by orchestrating a cover-up plot intended to kill Bathsheba's husband on the battlefield.

In order to expose David's sin, God sent the prophet Nathan to rebuke David and to call him to change his ways. David's scandal was a wicked deed that became the most significant black mark upon David's life, but God used Nathan to repair some of the damage David had caused.

There are times in the workplace where God may want to use you as His instrument to bring righteousness to a situation. Sherron Watkins, for instance, was a finance president at Enron, the now famous Houston-based energy company that went bankrupt because of financial fraud. By the summer of 2001, Sherron had become suspicious of her company's accounting practices.

Sherron struggled to know what she should do when she discovered the scandal that was going on. She thought she might lose her job if she confronted other top-level managers. Yet, if she did not do something, it could impact the entire company and its employees. Sherron was a Christian and knew that God was calling her to do something.

At first, she decided to use constructive ways to bring the problem to her superiors. Eventually, she met with CEO Kenneth Lay and outlined the elaborate accounting hoax that she believed was going on in the company. She was ignored. Months later the company collapsed when the problems came to light, and Lay was convicted on 10 counts of conspiracy.

Sherron Watkins allowed God to use her to expose a scandal that would destroy a company. She was recognized as *Time Magazine*'s "Person of the Year" in 2002 for her role in revealing the scandal.

Are you willing to be the instrument of God, if necessary, to expose unrighteousness?

GETTING PICKED

You did not choose me, but I chose you and appointed you
to go and bear fruit—fruit that will last.
JOHN 15:16

I will never forget the day in junior high school when I went to the gymnasium to view the list of those who had made the basketball team. Several of us went excitedly to see who was on the list and who was not. I made it! The feelings of exhilaration were beyond description for a 14-year-old. While I celebrated my victory, those who didn't make it were sad and downcast.

Most of us growing up either landed on the "picked" or the "unpicked" side of life. I often hear my wife say, "I never got picked for anything. I wasn't very good in sports or music." (She wanted to play in the marching band but couldn't play and walk at the same time.)

It is easy to forget, but we have all been picked by the God of the universe to be on His team. When God chose you, He knew what He was doing. God doesn't always pick those who have the greatest skill, the greatest aptitude or even the greatest personality. However, He always has something in mind for those He picks.

There is one thing He requires of those He picks. They are to be fruit-bearers. They are not to be fruit-makers, but fruit-bearers. Our goal should be to know the One who chose us and who makes the fruit. When we really know the One who chose us, fruit will be a natural by-product.

Today, as you begin your workday, consider where you will drop some fruit. It might be praying for a coworker. It might be simply greeting someone cheerfully during lunch. It might be leading someone to the Savior today. Share your fruit freely.

AVOIDING THE GIBEONITE RUSE

The men of Israel sampled their provisions but did not inquire of the LORD.
JOSHUA 9:14

When Joshua and the Israelites entered the Promised Land, they fought many battles. In fact, they fought 39 battles in the Promised Land, as compared to only 2 during their exodus from Egypt.

While traveling to the Promised Land, God instructed the Israelites to wipe out all their enemies completely. The more battles they won, the more their reputation preceded them as they entered new territories. Such was the case when Joshua and the people came into the land where the Gibeonites lived. The Gibeonites knew they were as good as dead if they didn't do something. So they dressed up in old, worn clothes and posed as foreigners passing through. Then they asked Joshua and the people to make a peace treaty with them. An interesting thing happened.

The Scriptures tell us that Joshua and the people made a treaty with the Gibeonites because they *did not inquire of God* about these people. They assumed that what the "foreigners" said was true. This turned out to be a very bad assumption. The Israelites were forced to abide by the treaty after they discovered the true identity of the foreigners. They had been deceived. The deception resulted because Joshua failed to keep a vertical focus with God. This created a problem for Joshua and the people.

The Israelites had to pay the consequences of Joshua's failure to talk to God. They had to work to avoid cross-tribal marriages and were forced to make the Gibeonites slaves—this was something God never intended them to have to do. This resulting relationship between the Israelites and the Gibeonites was a source of compromise for the Israelites that made them susceptible to future compromises.

Many of us fall for the Gibeonite Ruse in our lives. It may be a great looking investment, a job that's going to pay more or a relationship that we deeply desire. Sooner or later we all get entangled in our own Gibeonite Ruse because we fail to inquire of God.

THE POWER OF ONE

Then the men of Judah said to the Simeonites their brothers,
"Come up with us into the territory allotted to us, to fight against
the Canaanites. We in turn will go with you into yours."

JUDGES 1:3

After the death of Joshua, there arose a wicked king named Adoni-bezek who was creating havoc in the land. He prided himself in defeating his enemies and cutting off their big toes and thumbs. He had done this to 70 kings. Without Joshua to lead them, the people wondered how they were to defeat this wicked king. Every king who had attempted to defeat Adoni-bezek had lost.

The Lord told the Israelites that they were to join forces with the other tribes in order to defeat this wicked king:

When Judah attacked, the LORD gave the Canaanites and Perizzites into their hands and they struck down ten thousand men at Bezek. It was there that they found Adoni-Bezek and fought against him, putting to rout the Canaanites and Perizzites. Adoni-Bezek fled, but they chased him and caught him, and cut off his thumbs and big toes (Judges 1:4-6).

Today, God is calling the Body of Christ together in cities to operate in unity in order to defeat the wickedness in our cities. However, the key to victory is a willingness for churches, workplace leaders and intercessors to work together as a unified army.

Jesus said, "May they be brought to complete unity to let the world know that you sent me and have loved them even as you have loved me" (John 17:23). God calls each of us individually and corporately to represent Christ to the world, but our independence, pride and individualism often prevent us from becoming unified in the purposes of Christ. The marketplace and the Church must come together to bless the city with practical initiatives that benefit the city.

When unity takes place among leadership in the Body of Christ, Jesus responds by allowing the city to respond to Jesus. You will see more fruitful evangelism, favor among city leaders and an impact on the city you never thought possible.

RESPONSES TO ADVERSITY

Though the fig tree does not bud and there are no grapes on the vines, though the olive crop fails and the fields produce no food, though there are no sheep in the pen and no cattle in the stalls, yet I will rejoice in the LORD, I will be joyful in God my Savior.
HABAKKUK 3:17-18

When we experience adversity, we generally respond in one of three ways: We become angry; we try to gut it out; or we accept it with joy.

(1) *Anger.* When adversity comes our way, we say, "Why me, Lord?" We become bitter and resentful and blame God and others for our problems. We also tend to view ourselves as victims and demand that God answer our accusing questions: "Why don't You love me, Lord?" During moments of anger, we feel entitled to life, health, wealth and happiness.

(2) *Gutting it out.* Another way we respond to adversity is by adopting a stoic attitude and repressing our emotions. We lie to ourselves and say, "I'm gutting it out. I'm demonstrating endurance." In reality, we are merely isolating ourselves with a shell of false bravado. When we gut it out, we don't meditate on God's love, we don't pray and we don't believe that God really has anything good planned for us. We simply tell ourselves, "This will soon be over. I'm a survivor." We never receive what God has planned for us if we stay here.

(3) *Acceptance with joy.* This is the response God seeks from us. When we accept adversity with joy, we rest in God's love and trust that He knows best. We realize that nothing can happen to us without His permission. If there is pain in our lives, we know it's because God deems it necessary for our growth or that He wishes to use our pain to minister to others.

God revealed to the prophet Habakkuk that Israel was to be invaded by the Babylonians. Habakkuk knew that Israel was about to suffer intense adversity as part of God's loving discipline of His people, and he faced the looming national tragedy with an attitude of acceptance and joy.

If Habakkuk could be joyful in the face of a national calamity, then we can rejoice in the Lord no matter what comes our way.

JACOB'S DEFINING MOMENT

*So Jacob called the place Peniel, saying, "It is because I saw God
face to face, and yet my life was spared."*
GENESIS 32:30

Every believer in Jesus Christ must have a defining moment in his or her life. Jacob's moment occurred when he was about to meet his brother, Esau, in the desert after years of separation. The last time he had seen Esau was when he manipulated Esau's birthright years ago. Jacob assumed that when they met, Esau was going to try to kill him, so he sent gifts ahead as a peace offering. And he spent a restless night in prayer asking God to spare his and his family's life.

Jacob lived a life of control and manipulation. Yet, there was something in Jacob that God found worthy of redemption. Jacob had a heart that genuinely wanted to serve and be used of God. But God had to do something in him to chisel away the bad traits in his life.

God chose to combat Jacob's flaws by sending an angel in the form of a man to wrestle away the striving in Jacob. The only way to remove this characteristic from Jacob was to injure his physical abilities. "When the man saw that he could not overpower him, he touched the socket of Jacob's hip so that his hip was wrenched as he wrestled with the man" (Genesis 32:25-26).

Jacob's natural abilities were so great that God literally had to *make Jacob a weaker man physically in order for God's power to be manifested in his life.* This marked a turning point for Jacob. A new nature was birthed in him that required a total trust in God. In recognition of this defining moment, his name was changed. In Genesis it is written, "Then the man said, 'Your name will no longer be Jacob, but Israel, because you have struggled with God and with men and have overcome'" (Genesis 32:28).

My friend Bob Mumford once said, "Beware of any Christian leader who does not walk with a limp." If a leader has not wrestled with God over his or her natural abilities and come to a place of total dependence on God, that leader will live a life of striving and manipulation.

Let go and let God do the work needed in you. When this happens, even your enemies will be at peace with you.

THE SUCCESS TEST

But remember the LORD your God, for it is he who gives you the ability to produce wealth, and so confirms his covenant, which he swore to your forefathers, as it is today.
DEUTERONOMY 8:18

Muhammad Ali is considered the greatest heavyweight boxer of all time. He won 56 of his 61 professional fights and knocked out 37 opponents. His most famous catchphrase was "I am the greatest!"

One day, Ali was seated in an airplane when the flight attendant came up the aisle to make sure that all the passengers had their seatbelts fastened. Reaching Ali's seat, she asked him to buckle up.

"Hmph!" the champ sneered. "Superman don't need no seatbelt!"

The flight attendant smiled sweetly and replied, "Superman don't need no airplane, either." Ali fastened his seatbelt.

The greater our success, the greater the risk of us thinking too highly of ourselves. Scottish historian Thomas Carlyle observed, "Adversity is sometimes hard upon a man; but for one man who can stand prosperity there are a hundred that will stand adversity." And Oswald Chambers wrote, "Sudden elevation frequently leads to pride and a fall. The most exacting test of all to survive is prosperity."

Each of us must view success as a gift from God, not a result of our own achievement. The Lord is the source of all success, all elevation and all blessing. If you have a good mind and a healthy body, if you live in a land of opportunity, if you have a good education, if you've had a few breaks go your way, then you have much to be grateful for—and no cause for arrogance. You didn't *achieve* success; you *received* it as a gift.

Each of us must voluntarily humble ourselves before God—or God will have to humble us Himself. I have learned that it is better to learn humility voluntarily than involuntarily! Paul tells us, "For by the grace given me I say to every one of you: Do not think of yourself more highly than you ought, but rather think of yourself with sober judgment, in accordance with the measure of faith God has given you" (Romans 12:3).

TESTING FOR OBEDIENCE

Test me, O LORD, and try me, examine my heart and my mind.
PSALM 26:2

Throughout the Old Testament, we see many situations in which God tests His people in order to determine if they will follow Him or follow the systems of this world.

The nation of Israel was tested many times during the 40-year sojourn in the wilderness: "Remember how the LORD your God led you all the way in the desert these forty years, to humble you and to test you in order to know what was in your heart, whether or not you would keep his commands" (Deuteronomy 8:2).

You might ask, "Why does God need to test us? Doesn't He know everything, including what we would do in every situation?" Yes, God knows—but we don't know ourselves! God doesn't test us in order to find out something He doesn't already know. He tests us so that we can learn about ourselves and His love, power and faithfulness.

In Genesis 22, God tested Abraham by commanding him to sacrifice his son Isaac on a mountain in the land of Moriah. Isaac was Abraham's only son by his wife Sarah—the son God had promised to Abraham. By demanding that Isaac be sacrificed, God seemed to nullify His covenant of making a great nation of Abraham. How could God's promise be fulfilled if Isaac was dead?

God tested Abraham to reveal whether or not Abraham truly trusted His promise. Yes, God knew what Abraham would do, but He wanted Abraham to know as well. So God put Abraham to the test—and Abraham passed. As Abraham raised the knife to sacrifice his own son, God stopped him and provided a sacrificial ram instead.

Every test involves obedience in one way or another. When God tests us, He reveals the true state of our hearts. Are we obedient to His will, or are we self-willed? We might *think* we know the answer, but we would never *truly* know unless we were tested.

BEING LED BY GOD

For my thoughts are not your thoughts, neither are your ways my ways, declares the LORD. As the heavens are higher than the earth, so are my ways higher than your ways and my thoughts than your thoughts.

ISAIAH 55:8-9

How do you know what thoughts are your thoughts versus God's thoughts? One of the great paradoxes of walking with God is discerning the difference between a "natural idea" versus a "God idea." One of my mentors challenged me one day to make sure that my ideas and the actions I take are directed by God and not my own reasoning. But being in a marketing profession, there is a constant rub between the "natural" and the "spiritual."

There are three places from which a thought or idea originate: (1) our natural man, (2) Satan, or (3) the Holy Spirit. There are a few ways to discern from which place a thought is coming. If a thought comes into your mind that you would never have thought of, and if it might be something you would not normally consider doing, this is likely God speaking.

I once participated in a conference when an offering was being taken to make up for a poorly organized event that left the organizers very short on funds. It was clearly a case of poor management. Nevertheless, I prayed. I assumed I would give a token gift. However, the figure that suddenly came into my mind was $1,000. I argued with God and struggled with my attitude. I thought He must have two zeros out of place! But I obeyed—as I knew that the amount I had thought of was not my idea.

In order to be obedient, we must not make advance decisions about a particular matter. Each of our decisions must be submitted to the Lord for His counsel to us; they must not just be based on our reasoning.

GIDEON'S STAFF

With the tip of the staff that was in his hand, the angel of the LORD
touched the meat and the unleavened bread.

JUDGES 6:21

Gideon was a farmer who threshed wheat for a living, using a staff. He was busy doing his work when an angel of God appeared to him. The angel told him that he was going to be used to deliver the people of Israel from the Midianites who had been ravaging their land and crops for seven years. God was calling Gideon to do a new type of threshing. Instead of threshing wheat, he was being called to thresh the Midianites.

God often calls men and women when they are in the middle of their workplace activities. Like Moses, Gideon received this word from God with reluctance and feelings of insecurity, citing that his family was of no stature to accomplish such a task. Nevertheless, God addressed Gideon as a "mighty warrior" (Judges 6:12).

God often sees us for what we will become, not what we think we are. Once Gideon determined through a series of fleeces that it truly was God speaking to him, he did an interesting thing: He prepared an offering to the Lord of meat and bread. Once this offering was prepared, the angel used the *tip of Gideon's staff* to ignite the fire that consumed the offering. Here, God used the symbol of Gideon's work to consummate their partnership. Gideon was officially going to accomplish one of God's purposes in the nation of Israel.

Be watchful for times when God orchestrates events during the commonplace activity of work. He may be orchestrating something through you for His purposes.

DISSOLVING A PARTNERSHIP

*So Lot chose for himself the whole plain of the Jordan and set out
toward the east. The two men parted company.*

GENESIS 13:11

Several years ago, my friend Danny was in a teaching session I was giving about Abraham being a great example of dissolving a partnership. When Abraham and Lot realized their families and livestock could no longer live off the same land, there had to be a separation. In the natural, it would be logical that Abraham, the senior partner, would make the decision and get first choice of the land options. However, Abraham told Lot to choose where he wanted to live. He set himself at Lot's mercy. Sodom seemed to be the most fertile and logical place to locate. So Lot chose Sodom and Abraham moved to a place called Mamre.

Danny had come to a decision that the Lord desired him to dissolve a partnership in which he was involved. The partner questioned Danny, "How are we going to divide our accounts?"

"That's easy. I want you to choose the accounts you want and I will take what you don't want." This was quite a step of faith for Danny, but he felt the Lord leading him to make this offer.

Sure enough, the partner chose the very best clients they had and left Danny with accounts that generated less than 20 percent of the revenue. Danny was surprised but did not challenge his partner. However, the two men did have a conversation as they parted ways.

Danny said to his partner, "I can see the decision you have made. I can tell you that you have made a very poor decision that God will not bless. You should know that because of your decision, you can be assured that the value of your clients will go down in the coming months." Danny had no basis to make this assumption other than the story of Abraham and the Holy Spirit's prompting inside of him.

Time passed and Danny had some lean months. However, over time those small accounts gradually increased in value and the accounts his former partner had decreased. It was a profound lesson to Danny and to his former partner.

Sometimes, faith requires total trust in a future outcome you cannot see.

RESURRECTED FAITH

Then he reached out his hand and took the knife to slay his son.
GENESIS 22:10

There are times in our lives when God tests us to see if we are ready to put to death the very things that He promised we would have. Such was the case in the life of Abraham with Isaac. Isaac was the promised son. Yet, God said to raise the knife to sacrifice Isaac in obedience. When Abraham proved his obedience and was about to kill his son, God honored him, spared Isaac and ignited Abraham's ministry.

When God brings such a test into our lives, we have a choice. One choice is to salvage some aspect of the vision God has promised. The other choice is to kill the vision, from our perspective, in complete faith and obedience. Neither choice is attractive. However, the second choice is the faith decision. From God's perspective, the second choice is the only choice.

If we choose the faith decision that kills the vision, God will resurrect the vision to fulfill His promise in an even greater way than before. Our own faith will be launched into a whole new dimension if we choose to faithfully kill the vision. Because of our obedience, God will raise us up in order to speak through our lives out of that experience. God often brings those who sacrifice in obedience to Him into very public ministries.

However, if we choose to spare the vision, we will reside in a lesser walk with God. God will accept our decision but not without consequences to our faith journey. When we are not willing to make a sacrifice, God cannot trust us with a bigger vision, because He sees that our obedience is based on our perceived consequences.

If we choose to trust our perception and spare the initial vision, God will often orchestrate other events (usually unpleasant events) in our lives that are designed to develop our faith to a level that will allow us to make the right decision the next time.

Do you have resurrection faith that will trust God to raise your situation from the dead?

ARE YOU HORIZONTAL OR VERTICAL?

Woe to those who are wise in their own eyes and clever in their own sight.
ISAIAH 5:21

Many of us have been trained to make decisions and respond to problems in a *horizontal* way instead of a *vertical* way. Operating from a horizontal basis means that we try to fix problems through our own efforts, through our reasoning or our natural skills. Operating from a vertical position, on the other hand, means that we seek God for answers and wait for Him to impact the problem.

God knows the solution to our problems before they ever exist. Our responsibility is to ask Him for help in solving our problems and to rely on Him for the outcome. The minute we take on the responsibility, God quietly stands by to let us experience failure until we decide to seek Him for the answer.

One of the best examples of the contrast between a *vertical* and *horizontal* dimension in Scripture is that of King Saul and David (see 1 Samuel 25). King Saul thought the way to preserve his kingdom was to kill David. While in pursuit of him there were several occasions when, instead, David had the opportunity to kill Saul, but David chose to wait upon God's timing and to await his own deliverance. He understood authority. David had such respect for those who had been put in authority by God over him that he would not take matters into his own hands.

Saul represents the exact opposite of this principle. He thought David was the problem and sought to get rid of him through force. As a result, he lost his kingdom because he chose to rule horizontally, by his own power, instead of vertically, under God's rule in his life.

No matter what problem you face today, stay vertical with God.

MOVING AHEAD OF GOD

The LORD has kept me from having children. Go, sleep with my maidservant;
perhaps I can build a family through her.
GENESIS 16:2

Do you ever feel that you are supposed to receive something from God that just hasn't materialized? You wait and wait until finally you decide that maybe God wants you to help out the situation. This is exactly what happened in the case of Abraham and Sarah.

God had promised them a son, but as years passed by they were still without a child. Eventually, they took their eyes off the One who had made the promise and decided to take matters into their own hands. So Abraham lay with Sarah's maidservant, Hagar, and she bore a son, Ishmael (see Genesis 16). The son of promise, Isaac, came later through Sarah, just like God had promised. (Many believe that the modern-day conflict between the Arabs and Israelis is the fruit of their act of disobedience centuries ago.)

I recall a time when I launched a business enterprise only to fall on my face. It had all the hallmarks of a godly venture, but I was premature and guilty of presumption instead of faith. The resulting financial losses are lasting reminders to me of a decision that I based on a horizontal choice instead of a vertical dependence that required patience until God said, "Go."

The way to avoid making "Ishmael" decisions is to seek God fully on every matter in prayer, to be in an accountable relationship with your spouse and close associates who know you well, and to gain support and affirmation from two or more people. The Bible says, "The heart is deceitful above all things and beyond cure. Who can understand it?" (Jeremiah 17:9).

Whenever we want something strongly, we are in a dangerous place because we no longer look at the matter objectively with a willingness to change our viewpoint. We have to approach a matter in partnership with God and wait for Him to give the command to go.

MAKING DECISIONS BY HEARING GOD

"For my thoughts are not your thoughts, neither are your ways my ways,"
declares the Lord. "As the heavens are higher than the earth,
so are my ways higher than your ways."
ISAIAH 55:8-9

God speaks to His children in many varied ways. God has said that His ways are not our ways. If left to our reasoning, we will fail to walk in the full counsel of God, which leads to poor decisions.

Thus, our goal is to avoid being deceived and to develop a listening ear that hears the voice of God with confidence. Our goal is to have such intimacy with God that we can walk in the full blessing of our decisions and be assured that they are not based on our own reasoning alone.

A. W. Tozer said that the man or woman who is wholly and joyously surrendered to Christ can't make a wrong choice—any choice will be the right one. J. Oswald Sanders explains his method of receiving guidance from God for decisions: "I try to gather all the information and all the facts that are involved in a decision, and then weigh them up and pray over them in the Lord's presence, and trust the Holy Spirit to sway my mind in the direction of God's will. And God generally guides by presenting reasons to my mind for acting in a certain way."

The apostle Paul said, "For it is God who works in you to will and to act according to his good purpose" (Philippians 2:13). God has equipped us with everything we need to make good decisions. Hearing His voice is the first step toward making right choices in life.

Do you have a decision to make? Submit that decision to the Lord, ask God for clarity. Ask Him to make the desires of your heart the same desires that He has for you. Await His perfect timing on the matter. Then you can be assured of making the right decisions.

REMOVING HINDRANCES

But perfect love drives out fear, because fear has to do with punishment. The one who fears is not made perfect in love. We love because he first loved us.

1 JOHN 4:18-19

I was in another country and had just completed a teaching on how spiritual strongholds can hinder us from fulfilling our destinies (see 2 Corinthians 10:4). A woman approached me at the end of the meeting and asked me if I could join her and her friend for lunch so that they could learn more. I just happened to be available, so I agree to join them.

At lunch I noticed that one of the women was slightly overweight, exhibited extremely high energy and was aggressive. Before she began to ask me questions, I asked her to tell me about her relationship with her father. "Why in the world would you ask me such a question? What does that have to do with spiritual strongholds?" she asked.

I pressed her for the answer to my question. She responded, "I have an awful relationship with my father. He says I'm fat and that I'll never amount to anything."

I replied gently, "Jennifer, you have a generational stronghold of rejection. You try to mask it with your success in business. Your aggressive nature is rooted in a fear of failure because you've lived your whole life trying to win the approval of your father through performance. But I want you to know that you are totally loved and accepted by your Heavenly Father. You can stop trying to win His favor."

Immediately, she began to weep in the middle of the restaurant. Her friend was intrigued by what was I was saying. "No one has ever told me this, but what you say is true," she said through her tears. Then we prayed for God to destroy the stronghold of fear and rejection in her life through the blood of Jesus Christ.

She walked out of the restaurant that day with a new sense of love and acceptance.

HEBRAIC THOUGHT

The fear of the LORD is the beginning of wisdom;
all who follow his precepts have good understanding.
PSALM 111:10

Education is a high priority in any society that wants to advance. Education should also be a priority for every believer in Jesus Christ in order to better understand God's ways. However, education that is not mixed with faith and obedience will result in programmatic religion.

In the Early Church, which was largely Jewish, wisdom was gained by obedience. Hebrews learned that wisdom was gained by knowing and doing the will of God and that it often did not line up with logic. However, as the Church became impacted by the Greek culture through the influence of scholars like Socrates and Aristotle, knowledge-based systems became more influential in the way education was taught and applied.

When Joshua walked around the city of Jericho seven times blowing his trumpets, he was exhibiting a Hebraic model of decision-making—pure obedience. Logic and reason played no part in this decision. When Elisha instructed the army general to go wash in a lake in order to be healed of leprosy, it confronted his intellect. This was Hebraic thought rooted in obedience.

The Church today has moved into a more knowledge-based and pro-grammatic system of operation over the centuries, rather than obedience-based methods that are motivated by a heart fully devoted to following God. We've replaced obedience with reason, logic and slick marketing for attrac-tive programs to entice people into our churches.

Ultimately, God desires us to take the Hebraic approach when making decisions. He wants us to make decisions based on our heart's desire to follow Him.

PAUL'S DISAGREEMENT WITH THE PROPHET

Coming over to us, he took Paul's belt, tied his own hands and feet with it and said, "The Holy Spirit says, 'In this way the Jews of Jerusalem will bind the owner of this belt and will hand him over to the Gentiles.'"

ACTS 21:11

In Acts 21, we find an interesting scene involving Paul, the disciples and a prophet named Agabus. Agabus tied Paul's hands and feet in a prophetic act to dramatize a word of prophecy that revealed that Paul would be bound and persecuted in Jerusalem. The leaders concluded from this that Paul was not to go to Jerusalem. However, Paul disagreed:

> When we heard this, we and the people there pleaded with Paul not to go up to Jerusalem. Then Paul answered, "Why are you weeping and breaking my heart? I am ready not only to be bound, but also to die in Jerusalem for the name of the Lord Jesus" (Acts 21:12).

Was Paul acting in disobedience to the counsel of others and even the Holy Spirit's confirmation by other believers? If so, does that mean that Paul was not to go? By his response, Paul seemed to know something the others didn't. He didn't disagree with the prophecy, he disagreed with the interpretation.

It is always the individual's responsibility to interpret the meaning and action required from the counsel of others. Interpretation is not the role of the prophet. He is the messenger and the recipient is the one who needs to determine the action required from the message.

There is no reason to think that Paul went to Jerusalem in violation of the will of God. The prophetic forecasts were not prohibitions from the Holy Spirit but forewarnings of what lay ahead. Paul's friends tried to dissuade him from risking his life; but the apostle remained steadfast in accomplishing his mission, which he believed was from God in spite of personal danger.

The important lesson for us to understand is that doing the will of God does not always have a positive personal outcome, but the eternal consequences are always great. After all, Jesus' death on the cross was a personal hardship but an eternal glory.

THE *RHEMA* WORD

Your word is a lamp to my feet and a light for my path.
PSALM 119:105

Rhema is a Greek word that means "living." The Bible is often spoken of as the "living" Word of God, which means that God will speak to you directly and personally through the Scriptures. There have been many times in my and my wife's life when God gave us specific direction or confirmation of a decision through His *rhema* Word.

My wife, Angie, had only been a Christian for about six months when she began to read the Bible for the first time. She had heard people talk about how God spoke to them through the Bible, and she thought they were crazy—until one day it happened to her. She was in the midst of a Bible study and read in Matthew 7 that you could ask and receive. Immediately she thought, "I'll ask God to bring me a husband or someone to fill the gap." The very next verse she went to in her Bible study was "Be still and know that I am God" (Psalm 46:10). She knew that God was telling her through His "living" Word that she was to wait.

Two years later, the Lord had done a mighty work in her life, and she asked for a husband a second time. Days later, she got a note that had "Psalm 27:14" written at the bottom of it. With great anticipation she opened her Bible to read the psalm, only to be greatly disappointed—the verse read, "Wait for the Lord, be strong and take heart and wait for the Lord." Again, God had spoken to her personally through His Word. After that, the Lord taught Angie to fall in love with Him, and she did not date for seven years.

Then, one day the Lord spoke to Angie in a still voice during her quite time. He said, "I'm about to bring you your husband, and it will be the best thing that ever happened to you." She was shocked and refused to write it down. However, 30 days later she and I met. Nine months after that we were married.

Just as God spoke to Angie through the Bible, you also can fully expect Him to speak through His living Word regarding specific situations in your life. As you read your Bible, be aware of the *rhema* Word of God. The Lord may speak to you in specific ways you never thought possible.

FASTING AND PRAYER

*So, after they had fasted and prayed, they placed their
hands on them and sent them off.*

Acts 13:3

There are times in our lives when major decisions require concerted effort on our part to press into the heart of God. Fasting is one of the best ways to align our hearts with God's.

The practice of fasting is recorded in Acts 13. The disciples had undertaken a strategic time of worship and fasting because Barnabas and Saul were being set apart for the work to which God had called them. During this time, God spoke to them with some specific instructions. Fasting was an important aspect of hearing from God in the Early Church, and God continues to speak to His people through fasting today.

Angie and I have often set aside times of fasting whenever a major decision has to be made. We fast because it is a physical demonstration to God that we are serious about wanting an answer. It allows us to be totally focused on the issue at hand. The physical aspects of fasting contribute to our mind being more in tune with the spiritual dimensions of life.

In 1997, before I was married to Angie, I was troubled over where I was in my life. It seemed as though nothing was moving forward. I was struggling with whether to rebuild my advertising agency or focus on the new calling for ministry that God seemed to be raising up in me. I decided to fast and assumed that I would do so for only a few days. However, as each day went by I did not feel as though I was getting direction. By my fourteenth day of fasting I decided to extend the fast for 40 days.

It just so happened that the last day of my 40-day fast was the first day of a conference I had planned to attend months earlier. That night an intercessor from South Africa came forward with a word of prophecy for someone in the audience. The minute he read his words, I knew they were directed at me because the Scripture verse he used had been a passage that God has used consistently in my life. I had finally received direction from God.

The next time you have an important decision to make, consider setting aside a time of fasting and prayer to gain clarity on your decision.

THREE THINGS

I pray also that the eyes of your heart may be enlightened in order that you may know the hope to which he has called you, the riches of his glorious inheritance in the saints, and his incomparably great power for us who believe.
EPHESIANS 1:18-19

Paul's letter to the Ephesians exhorts believers to experience three important things in their spiritual lives, each of which he experienced personally. As a good mentor, he desired those he was leading to follow his example.

First, Paul shared that God wants us to have the eyes of our hearts enlightened in order to know the hope to which He has called us. God has called each of us to a future and a hope. Some do not ever realize the dreams they envision for their lives. Paul prayed that those of us who do not ever realize the dreams we envision for our lives would experience hope in Christ.

Second, Paul declared that God wants us to know that there is an inheritance for each believer in Jesus Christ. There are riches to be had—not financial riches—but spiritual riches that are laid up for every saint. As we are faithful to His calling in our lives, we will be rewarded.

Third, Paul shared that God desires us to tap into the power that is available to every believer. Paul often exhorted believers not to look at his persuasive words but at the demonstration of the power of God in his life. Paul wanted us to know that this same power is available to us. After all, Jesus said we would do even greater works than He did after He sent the Holy Spirit to us (see John 14:12).

Pray that God reveals the hope that exists inside of you, be encouraged that there is an inheritance awaiting you, and know that you have power residing in you that awaits those who exercise their faith to release it.

COMING OUT OF EGYPT

But thanks be to God that, though you used to be slaves to sin, you wholeheartedly
obeyed the form of teaching to which you were entrusted. You have been set free
from sin and have become slaves to righteousness.

ROMANS 6:17-18

Becoming a new person in Christ is part of a life-long journey that begins at conversion. Before coming to Christ, we were living (in a metaphorical sense) in Egypt, in the land of bondage. Just as the people of Israel toiled as slaves in Egypt, we also were slaves to sin and worldly ambition.

Before we came to Christ, we sweated and toiled to build our career and acquire material possessions. Work was our idol. Greed was our taskmaster. We may have had all the trappings of power in the business world—a corner office, a staff of our own, a key to the executive washroom—but we were living as a slave in the land of Egypt. We didn't run our career; our career ran us.

Jesus once said, "No servant can serve two masters . . . You cannot serve both God and money" (Luke 16:13). In the original language, the word translated "money" was an Aramaic word, *Mammon*. This does not refer merely to money as a medium of exchange but also to a demonic spirit designed to promote a mind-set of ambition for riches, power and worldly gain. The word is capitalized in the original text because the people of Jesus' day thought of Mammon as a false god. Jesus made this connection when He said that those who spend their lives seeking worldly gain are idolaters. No one can serve two masters. No one can worship both the true God and a false god.

We often cannot experience the grace that God gives to His children because we are too busy striving for riches and are enslaved to Mammon. The only way we can be free is to turn away from Mammon and allow the one true God to transform us into a different person.

Ask yourself today if your life is best represented as Egypt or the Promised Land.

BAPTISM AT THE RED SEA

*We were therefore buried with him through baptism into death in order that,
just as Christ was raised from the dead through the glory of the Father,
we too may live a new life.*

ROMANS 6:4

When Moses led the people of Israel out of Egypt, he took them to the edge of the Red Sea. The people saw the sea before them and heard the chariots of the Egyptians behind them. They knew they were trapped—and they lost their faith in God. They thought God was no longer at work in their lives. In panic and despair, they turned on Moses and said, "Why did you bring us out into the desert to die? When we were slaves in Egypt, didn't we tell you, 'Just leave us alone and let us continue serving the Egyptians.' Better to live as slaves than to die out here!"

They couldn't imagine that God's path to freedom actually led straight into and *through* the deep waters! The waters of the Red Sea, like the New Testament sacrament of baptism, are a symbol of death. When Moses parted the Red Sea, the people of Israel walked upon the dry seabed with walls of water on either side. They descended into the depths of the sea, metaphorically dying to their old selves and rising to a new life that led to the Promised Land.

Like the people of Israel during their journey, we panic and cry out to God, "Did You bring me out into this desert of adversity to die?" We would rather live as slaves than die to self and yield control of our lives to God. But God takes us through the depths so that we can emerge as new people, ready to enter the Promised Land.

In general, I've observed that *the greater and higher the calling, the more intense the adversity.* I'm not saying one person's call is more important, but I am saying that one person may have a farther-reaching impact on others. This kind of impact, though, often requires greater, more difficult preparation.

If you find yourself in deep water, thank God today that He is preparing you for a life that is designed to impact many.

SHEDDING FORMER THINGS

Then the LORD said to Joshua, "Today I have rolled away the reproach of Egypt from you."
JOSHUA 5:9

God is calling thousands of people out of Egypt, out of their old lives of bondage. He's calling them to become new people, living out His plan for their lives in the Promised Land, a land flowing with milk and honey. God wants Christians to take their places in the financial marketplace, the corridors of commerce, the capitals of information and entertainment, and the halls of the government.

When the people of Israel crossed over the Jordan River and set foot upon the land of promise, God told Joshua to make flint knives and revive a ritual that had fallen into disuse: circumcision.

The rite of circumcision, of course, is the surgical removal of the foreskin (prepuce) of the penis. This rite was established as a sign of God's covenant with Abraham in Genesis 17, but it had not been practiced during the 40 years that Israel wandered in the wilderness before reaching the Promised Land. Joshua obeyed God's command and had all the Israelite men circumcised at a place they called Gibeath Haaraloth (a rather graphic name that means "hill of foreskins").

The rite of circumcision is painful, bloody and personal, and the Israelite men were incapacitated until their wounds had healed. With the removal of the foreskins, the men of Israel both literally and metaphorically became a new and different people. They were no longer slaves of the past; they were free people with a future. It was time to put aside the old way of life, to put Egypt behind them and to enter the Promised Land with confidence and power.

The people of Israel did just that. They went on to fight 39 major battles before the Promised Land came under their control. They refused to compromise with the evil and idolatry that was in the land. God told them to destroy it, and they did. As believers, we will always be in a battle against evil until the war is won. God has designed a bright future for us—and it's ours if we accept His calling and cling to Him as He reshapes and remakes us.

JOSIAH, GOD'S LEADER

Neither before nor after Josiah was there a king like him who turned to the LORD as he did—with all his heart and with all his soul and with all his strength, in accordance with all the Law of Moses.

2 KINGS 23:25

What type of person did God raise up when the nation of Israel became synonymous with idol worship and sin? God raised up a leader who had the courage to destroy the evil and bring the nation back to God. His name was Josiah: "Manasseh was twelve years old when he became king, and he reigned in Jerusalem fifty-five years . . . He did evil in the eyes of the LORD, following the detestable practices of the nations the LORD had driven out before the Israelites" (2 Kings 21:1-2).

Manasseh's son, Amon, reigned for 22 years after him and was also wicked. However, Amon's son, Josiah, became king at eight years old, after his father was assassinated.

Josiah was a courageous leader and "did what was right in the eyes of the LORD and walked in all the ways of his father David, not turning aside to the right or to the left . . . Nevertheless, the LORD did not turn away from the heat of his fierce anger, which burned against Judah because of all that Manasseh had done to provoke him to anger. So the LORD said, 'I will remove Judah also from my presence as I removed Israel, and I will reject Jerusalem, the city I chose, and this temple, about which I said, 'There shall my Name be'" (2 Kings 22:2; 23:26).

God responded to the godly reforms that Josiah brought to his nation: "Because your heart was responsive and you humbled yourself before the LORD . . . Therefore I will gather you to your fathers, and you will be buried in peace. Your eyes will not see all the disaster I am going to bring on this place" (2 Kings 22:19-20).

Judgment always follows the sin of a nation. If there were ever a time we needed God to raise up Josiahs in our cities and nations, it is now. Pray that God brings forth Godly leaders in your city and nation.

DESERT TRAINING

O God, you are my God, earnestly I seek you; my soul thirsts for you, my body longs for you, in a dry and weary land where there is no water.

PSALM 63:1

The desert holds a special place in God's Word. The Scriptures portray the desert as a place of inspiration and exaltation—a place where people met God in a powerful new way.

For Joseph, a deep pit in the desert was the first stop on a 13-year journey through desolation and despair that happened to be a deep pit in the desert. Joseph's 13-year desert experience served to break his self-will and self-confidence. It taught him that he could not control anything and that he needed to rely on God to manage the events in his life. Joseph's desert trial prepared him by scorching the youthful pride and arrogance out of his young life so that when he was 30 years old he could rule Egypt at Pharaoh's side in a spirit of humility and servanthood.

King David wrote the sixty-third Psalm while in exile in the Desert of Judah. He was hiding there from his son Absalom, who wanted to replace him as king of Israel. Before becoming king of Israel, David was a shepherd. Part of his training for leadership involved hand-to-claw combat with the beasts of the wilderness, including the lion and the bear.

Elijah, too, learned the principles of spiritual leadership while in the wilderness of Gilead, and Jesus was tempted and tested for 40 days in the desert before He began to preach.

Perhaps God has given you a dream that seems to have withered and died under the scorching desert sun. Maybe it seems that God has gone away and is not listening to your prayers. But I want you to know that your dream still lives. God is with you, even if you can't see Him, hear Him or sense His presence. He is preparing you in the desert.

In His good time, He will bring you to a place of refreshment and restoration.

HEARING GOD

My sheep listen to my voice; I know them, and they follow me.
JOHN 10:27

I have discovered a pattern in the way God speaks to me when I'm faced with *major* decisions. Generally, I spend a great deal of time seeking direction from Him and asking Him to speak to me regarding my decision. Then I spend time in prayer and Bible study. Many times somewhere during this process I suddenly feel an overwhelming feeling of His presence rushing over me. The feeling is usually so intense that I begin to cry, sometimes uncontrollably. (Thank God this doesn't happen too often, because it is rather embarrassing in a public setting.)

I recall one time when I was praying about whether I should make a one-year commitment to work for a ministry. It seemed like the right thing, but I was still awaiting confirmation. That morning during my quiet time, I felt the rush of the Spirit come over me. At that moment, Angie walked into the room to find me crying. (She always laughs when this happens and says there's nothing like seeing a grown man cry.) I told her that God was telling me to enter into a working relationship with a ministry. Hearing from God was a great release in my spirit and a confirmation of what I was to do. Two years later, I was able to look back and see that God had led my decision to join a ministry and that He had used it to produce much fruit.

The famous Bible teacher F. B. Meyer also has insight about hearing from God and determining His will. One night as Meyer stood on the deck of a ship approaching land, he wondered how the crew knew when and how to safely steer to the dock. It was a stormy night and visibility was low. Meyer, standing on the bridge and peering through the window, asked the captain, "How do you know when to turn this ship into that narrow harbor?"

"That's an art," replied the captain. "Do you see those three red lights on the shore? When they're all in a straight line I go right in!"

Later Meyer said, "When we want to know God's will, there are three things which always occur: the inward impulse, the Word of God and the trend of circumstances. Never act until these three things agree."

THE ROLE OF SPOUSES IN MAKING DECISIONS

The way of a fool seems right to him, but a wise man listens to advice.
PROVERBS 12:15

When John Benson decided to make some financial investments in a new business venture, he was very excited about the possibilities for a handsome financial return. His business and financial background had served him well. John felt strongly that his wife, Jenny, would not understand the complexity of his investment, so he casually mentioned it to her. When she asked a few simple questions, John became defensive and justified his plans for investing in the venture.

A year later, after investing a large sum of money, John received a phone call from the investment company. All the investors who had put money in the company were going to lose their investment with no ability to recoup it.

Similar instances have occurred repeatedly across the world. God's principles for making decisions require input from both spouses, regardless of their level of expertise. I learned this lesson the hard way after making many independent decisions outside the counsel of my wife. Today, whenever I am faced with a major decision, I first consult the Lord, and then I consult my wife. She may disagree totally with something that seems very straightforward to me, but I have learned not to move forward if we are not in agreement.

God has called married couples to be one. If we seek to make decisions independently, then we benefit from only 50 percent of the intended resource God has placed within our grasp. In marriage, this stewardship of decisions requires two people. God blesses this union when we make decisions with the motive of glorifying God and relying on His Spirit to lead in our decision-making process.

Before you make a major decision, get confirmation for your decision from your spouse.

TIME MANAGEMENT

Show me, O LORD, my life's end and the number of my days;
let me know how fleeting is my life.
PSALM 39:4

David accomplished a great deal in his lifetime. Psalm 39 shows that he understood that life had an end to it, and that he wanted to make the most of the time he had been given. He learned to use his time wisely, and so should we.

Peter Drucker is a renowned management consultant to major corporations and has authored many best-selling business books. He suggests three activities that might help busy executives better manage their time.

First, do not start with the task. Start with your time. Determine where your time is going. Then, attempt to manage that time and cut back unproductive demands on your time. Consolidate your "discretionary" time into the largest possible continuing time units.

Drucker refers to the second step as time management. After listing the activities to which we devote our time, he suggests that we ask three questions about each of these activities to help us minimize the amount of time we waste: "What would happen if this were not done at all?" And if the answer is, "Nothing would happen," then obviously the conclusion is to stop doing it. Next, "Which of the activities on my time log could be done by somebody else just as well, if not better? What do I do that wastes my time without contributing to my effectiveness?"

Drucker closes by saying "Know Thyself," this old prescription for wisdom is impossibly difficult for mortal men. But everyone can follow the injunction "Know Thy Time" if you want to, and be well on the road toward contribution and effectiveness.[41]

Why not evaluate how you are spending your time, and ask God how to better use the time you have.

HOW'S YOUR "JOY" QUOTIENT?

Do not grieve, for the joy of the LORD is your strength.
NEHEMIAH 8:10

One of the overriding evidences that someone has a genuine relationship with our living Savior is his or her consistent attitude of joy and positive outlook on life. A follower of Jesus should not be a person who always considers the glass half full. Instead, he or she should be one of the most positive people on Earth. That person should see opportunity in the midst of challenges.

The light that resides in us should be like the beam of a lighthouse to a ship that is seeking direction. Our lives should have the fragrance of Christ. People should be attracted to our lives, just as the bee is attracted to the nectar in the colorful flower.

The apostle Paul understood this when he said:

But thanks be to God, who always leads us in triumphal procession in Christ and through us spreads everywhere the fragrance of the knowledge of him. For we are to God the aroma of Christ among those who are being saved and those who are perishing. To the one we are the smell of death; to the other, the fragrance of life (2 Corinthians 2:14-16).

No matter what circumstance you may find yourself in, the joy of the Lord must be your strength. Paul learned this truth even in the midst of his adversities. He said, "I have learned the secret of being content in any and every situation, whether well fed or hungry, whether living in plenty or in want. I can do everything through him who gives me strength" (Philippians 4:12-13).

How would others describe your joy quotient? On a scale of 1 to 10, where would they rank you? Today, make a commitment to greet every circumstance knowing that the joy of the Lord is your strength.

SERVANT-LEADERSHIP

Instead, whoever wants to become great among you must be your servant, and whoever wants to be first must be your slave—just as the Son of Man did not come to be served, but to serve, and to give his life as a ransom for many.
MATTHEW 20:26-28

A rider on horseback, many years ago, came upon a squad of soldiers who were trying to move a heavy piece of timber. A corporal stood by, giving lordly orders to "heave." But the piece of timber was a trifle too heavy for the squad.

"Why don't you help them?" asked the quiet man on the horse, addressing the important corporal.

"Me? Why, I'm a corporal, sir!" Dismounting, the stranger carefully took his place with the soldiers.

"Now, all together boys—heave!" he said. And the big piece of timber slid into place. The stranger mounted his horse and addressed the corporal.

"The next time you have a piece of timber for your men to handle, corporal, send for the commander-in-chief."

The horseman was George Washington, the first American president.

Whenever someone mentions your name, does the word "servant" come to his or her mind? Jesus modeled servanthood to 12 young men and changed the world. If you want to see others become servants, you must model it yourself.

George Washington was a great example of a Christian leader, soldier and servant to those he led. No wonder God used him to establish a new nation.

Moses was also a great leader of men. The Bible says that Moses was the most humble man on Earth. God used him to lead hundreds of thousands out of slavery into the Promised Land.

Pray that God makes you a great and humble servant-leader of others.

ONE BODY

The body is a unit, though it is made up of many parts; and though
all its parts are many, they form one body. So it is with Christ.
1 CORINTHIANS 12:12

Imagine with me for a moment that you have won a very expensive car. However, in order to receive your prize, you must agree to an unusual requirement. You must remove one major component in that car in order to receive the gift. Which component will you remove?

Will it be the steering wheel? Perhaps it will be the left front tire or the front seat or the two headlights. My illustration may seem ridiculous, but you get the point. Unless you have the complete car and have the ability to use all of its components, your ability to benefit from that car is severely limited.

The Bible says you and I are part of a larger Body—the Body of Christ. We each have our own body, but we are also part of the larger Body and we each have a unique function. When you are not functioning as God intended, the entire Body suffers because you are not fulfilling your prescribed purpose. When you function in a way that is not directly connected to the larger Body, you are only fulfilling a small portion of what the Manufacturer made you to do.

Today, the Body of Christ is fragmented. Our individual church "silos" stand alone—often as monuments to man, instead of to the greater mission of reaching the city.

Jesus knew the key to fulfilling His mission was getting His larger Body to work as one. He said, "I pray also for those who will believe in me through their message, that all of them may be one, Father, just as you are in me and I am in you. May they also be in us so that the world may believe that you have sent me" (John 17:20-21).

What is your part in the overall mission? Are you fulfilling your prescribed function as designed by the Manufacturer?

IS PERCEPTION REALITY?

*The Israelites have rejected your covenant, broken down your altars,
and put your prophets to death with the sword. I am the only one left,
and now they are trying to kill me too.*

1 KINGS 19:14

The CEO walked into his manufacturing plant only to observe an employee standing by idly, not working. Angrily, he walked over to him, peeled off a $100 bill and gave it to the man: "Here, go spend your time elsewhere!" The man looked at the CEO somewhat puzzled, but left with the $100.

"How long has that man worked for us?" said the CEO to another worker.

"Well, sir, he doesn't work for us; he is only the delivery man" was the reply.

Perception is not always reality. Elijah was in a crisis. Jezebel wanted to kill him. The nation was falling to Baal worship. From Elijah's vantage point, it was all over. He was the only prophet remaining in all the land who had not bent his knee to the idol of Baal. He wanted to die.

Then the Lord sent His angel to correct Elijah's perception. The angel said, "Yet I reserve seven thousand in Israel—all whose knees have not bowed down to Baal and all whose mouths have not kissed him" (1 Kings 19:18). There were 7,000 like him that Elijah knew nothing about!

Whenever things are going poorly, there is a temptation to believe that God is not working in the situation. We may even believe that our life is over. Everything from our vantage point is dark. We see no future. However, even in these times, God is orchestrating His plan behind the scenes. He is accomplishing His purposes. But we need a fresh perspective on our situation.

Do you need a reality check on your situation? Ask God to show you the truth. It may be very different than your perception.

"THE LORD IS NOT IN IT"

*The LORD said, "Go out and stand on the mountain in the
presence of the LORD, for the LORD is about to pass by."*
1 KINGS 19:11

Elijah was in a crisis in his ministry. God had just corrected his perspective
of his situation. If any man needed a touch from God, it was Elijah. He was
in such distress that he wanted to die.

The Lord intervened and told Elijah that He was coming to talk to him.
But God did not tell Elijah how He was going to reveal Himself. It was up to
Elijah to tell whether God was in the situations about to take place:

> Then a great and powerful wind tore the mountains apart and shat-
> tered the rocks before the LORD, but the LORD was not in the wind.
> After the wind there was an earthquake, but the LORD was not in the
> earthquake. After the earthquake came a fire, but the LORD was not
> in the fire. And after the fire came a gentle whisper. When Elijah
> heard it, he pulled his cloak over his face and went out and stood at
> the mouth of the cave (1 Kings 19:11-13).

We often think that God is in our grand projects only to discover that
He is not. We may also assume that because of the success or visibility of a
situation God is in it. And He may actually be in the project. However, God's
ways are not always highly visible. In fact, He often shows Himself in subtle
ways. Sometimes He chooses to come in a soft, gentle whisper.

We need to be able to discern God's involvement in our situations. Ask
Him today for wisdom to know when He is involved.

HE HAD SUCH GREAT POTENTIAL

Then Jacob gave Esau some bread and some lentil stew. He ate and drank, and then got up and left. So Esau despised his birthright.
GENESIS 25:34

Have you ever heard someone say, "Oh, he had such great potential, but he never lived up to it"?

Esau was Jacob's brother. He was a man who had great potential. He was skilled in almost everything he did. He was a hunter. He was a leader. He came from a godly patriarch family. He could do just about anything to which he put his mind. The problem was that he put his energies in all the wrong places. The Bible says that he was a lady's man. He was promiscuous and married outside the tribe. His parents were greatly saddened by the direction his life was taking.

During a moment of weakness, Esau made the greatest mistake of his life when he traded away his birthright for a simple meal. He had just returned from hunting and he was hungry. His brother was making stew but would not give him any. Esau was angered by this and negotiated for what he wanted by agreeing to give Jacob his family inheritance. It seems almost unbelievable that Esau would do such a thing.

Esau had not understood the value of his birthright or his future in God. He could only see the immediate pleasures available to him. His appetites were driven by his flesh, and his choices led him to live a life that even God said He despised.

Every day, there are Esaus living in the same way. They see the fruits that their professional life can give them. They make choices based on what seems right at the moment, for immediate gratification.

God has a future and a plan for every person, but not every person will choose to follow this plan. Pray for those you encounter today who are still living as Esaus, and ask God to move on their behalf in order that they may fulfill their Godly heritage.

ALLOWING GOD TO PROMOTE

So David's fame spread throughout every land, and the LORD
made all the nations fear him.

1 CHRONICLES 14:17

We live in a day of self-promotion. Marketing firms are hired today to persuade others to view a person or situation in the way they want you to. There are millions of dollars spent annually by sports companies, personality agents, and marketing firms to create fame for their clients and products. They negotiate sponsorship deals and try to get the most money for the most exposure. The ultimate goal is fame and notoriety.

There is great danger in self-promotion. Self-promotion is trying to move from the place you are to a place ahead of where God may want you. It is not wrong to become famous, popular or desired by others as long as it happens as a fruit of your calling. However, when you begin to orchestrate things in an effort to inflate who you are for the sake of gain, you have crossed the line.

David's fame was a result of his fulfilling his mission in life. When he failed, he repented. When he was successful, he acknowledged the Lord. Never do you see David exalt himself over the Lord. Yes, he made some selfish decisions that led to sin. But David could not be criticized for self-promotion.

We all must carefully balance the difference between marketing designed to inform and educate versus promote and manipulate. Describing the true attributes of a product, service or person is good marketing communications. However, persuasion designed to inflate reality is witchcraft.

Proverbs says, "Let another praise you, and not your own mouth; someone else, and not your own lips" (27:2). Following this principle will keep you from moving beyond God's method of promotion.

STRONGHOLDS OVER INDUSTRIES

*Then the LORD said to Joshua, "Today I have rolled away
the reproach of Egypt from you."*

JOSHUA 5:9

Brett, a long-time *TGIF* subscriber, called and asked for my help. I met him in Lake Tahoe and, over a three-hour lunch, he confided to me some of his struggles in his industry. He said that he'd often been lied to and exploited by others in his business. The Holy Spirit prompted me to say, "That's because the ruling spirit in this industry is mammon and deceit. I believe that God has called you to play a part in cleaning up your industry."

"But how?" he said. "I've got a federal lawsuit on my back. I'm being driven out of business."

"Brett," I said, "God has put you in a season of preparation in order to remove the 'Egypt' from your working life in order to bring His kingdom into your industry."

God desires to bring His kingdom into every sphere of life. When Jesus wanted to bring His kingdom into the corrupt tax system in Jerusalem, the first thing He did was recruit Matthew, the tax collector. He began investing in his life.

The same was true of Zachaeus. Jesus entered Jericho and was passing through. When Jesus reached the tree, He looked up and said to him, "'Zacchaeus, come down immediately. I must stay at your house today.' So he came down at once and welcomed him gladly. All the people saw this and began to mutter, 'He has gone to be the guest of a sinner.' But Zacchaeus stood up and said to the Lord, 'Look, Lord! Here and now I give half of my possessions to the poor, and if I have cheated anybody out of anything, I will pay back four times the amount'" (Luke 19:2,6-8). Jesus' presence brought conviction to anyone who was operating in an ungodly manner.

Do you need the presence of Jesus in your industry? Invite Him in today.

TEACHING VERSUS IMPARTING

The people were amazed at his teaching, because he taught them
as one who had authority, not as the teachers of the law.
MARK 1:22

"It is not enough to simply teach; you must also impart to others," said my mentor one day. One of the spiritual gifts God has given to me is the gift of teaching (see Romans 12:7). However, the Lord does not desire that teachers only impart knowledge to others. Knowledge alone will not empower others to be mature disciples of Christ.

The people recognized there was something different about Jesus. He was a teacher of the law as a rabbi. However, whenever He taught there was an authority that went beyond the conveying of information. He was imparting truth through the authority of His life. His words impacted others profoundly.

A Bible teacher who wants to have the greatest impact on those he or she teaches should teach transferable life application from the Scriptures that he or she has lived out personally. This is what gives you your authority to teach. I rarely teach a concept that I have not personally lived out and have an accompanying testimony. Paul believed and lived this principle as well: "When I came to you, brothers, I did not come with eloquence or superior wisdom as I proclaimed to you the testimony about God" (1 Corinthians 2:1).

Each of us has been given an authority to impart the message of the Kingdom to others. Some of us have a particular anointing that God uses in the lives of others. Ask God to reveal your anointing so that you can impart it to others.

When you study under a teacher, make sure your teacher not only teaches but also imparts the life-giving power of the anointing in his or her life!

WHO SHOULD BE IN CHARGE?

When the righteous are in authority, the people rejoice;
But when a wicked man rules, the people groan.
PROVERBS 29:2, *NKJV*

We hear a lot these days about being politically correct. It seems we must be sensitive to every group, no matter how that group might negatively impact our lives or violate ethical or moral laws. When God created the earth, He did not care what people thought of His policies. His policy was *the* way!

But His primary motive was not to control but to bless mankind, His creation. His nature was only good. In Jeremiah 9:24, we find God's nature described: "'I am the LORD, who exercises kindness, justice and righteousness on earth, for in these I delight,' declares the LORD."

He laid down rules in the Garden of Eden for Adam and Eve to follow. As long as they followed the rules, they would reign over every living creature. They were representing the Creator in all aspects. God's government was being expressed through His creation in humans, nature and animals. He was and is the ultimate righteous ruler.

God's desire was to extend this mandate across the earth through godly leaders who could represent and legislate His kingdom in all spheres of life. This is why He said in Deuteronomy 28:13, "The LORD will make you the head, not the tail. If you pay attention to the commands of the LORD your God that I give you this day and carefully follow them, you will always be at the top, never at the bottom."

God desires to raise up godly leaders who can represent His interest on the earth. He has called you and me to be one of His representatives.

FROM ADVERSITY TO DESTINY

The brother in humble circumstances ought to take pride in his high position.
James 1:9

Although God takes no pleasure in our pain, we have to acknowledge that He sometimes allows painful circumstances to occur in our lives in order to shape us and make us more like Christ. Sometimes our times of despair turn out to be a much-needed light into our soul.

I once came across the following poem written by an anonymous Confederate soldier, a devout young man who fought in the American Civil War. The lines of this poem express the soul of a man who has learned to view his times of adversity from a different perspective:

I asked God for strength, that I might achieve;
I was made weak, that I might learn humbly to obey.
I asked God for health, that I might do greater things;
I was given infirmity, that I might do better things.
I asked for riches, that I might be happy;
I was given poverty, that I might be wise.
I asked for power, that I might have the praise of men;
I was given weakness, that I might feel the need of God.
I asked for all things, that I might enjoy life;
I was given life, that I might enjoy all things.
I got nothing that I asked for but everything I had hoped for.
Almost despite myself, my unspoken prayers were answered.
I am among men, most richly blessed.[42]

Do we trust God to lead us even though we can't see the pathway in front of us? Do we trust Him to be all-knowing, all-loving and all-powerful? Do we believe He does all things well? As Paul wrote, "Everything that does not come from faith is sin" (Romans 14:23). That's why God leads us through the dark places.

Only in the darkness do we learn to walk by faith.

HIGHER EDUCATION

To one there is given through the Spirit the message of wisdom, to another
the message of knowledge by means of the same Spirit.
1 CORINTHIANS 12:8

I walked out of the church parking lot after participating in a training class on hearing the voice of God. As I was talking to a friend, I looked over at a woman who was talking to her friend. The words "higher education" popped into my mind.

We had just learned that whenever something pops into our mind that seems foreign to our normal thinking, it is often the Holy Spirit speaking to us. We must connect the thought to an action that the Holy Spirit may desire us to take.

I decided to be bold and walked over to the woman. "Pardon me, can I ask you if you have, by chance, had a good bit of education in your life?"

The woman responded immediately, "Why, yes. I have two MBAs." I was encouraged to proceed.

"I believe the Lord wants to encourage you that He has directed you in your education and although you cannot see the results of that investment in time and money, He is going to use it for His purposes. He wants you to be encouraged to know this."

The woman was very encouraged by the words I spoke to her. I walked away feeling good about being obedient to His prompting.

Every believer has been wired to hear the Holy Spirit's promptings in our lives. One of the primary ways He encourages believers is through other believers. However, many of us have been duped into thinking we cannot hear God's voice.

Today, be especially sensitive to that still, small voice inside of you. Whenever a thought or picture pops into your mind that seems out of character for you, consider that it might be the Holy Spirit speaking to you.

DEFINING MOMENTS

Then Moses stretched out his hand over the sea, and all that night the LORD drove the sea back with a strong east wind and turned it into dry land. The waters were divided, and the Israelites went through the sea on dry ground, with a wall of water on their right and on their left.

EXODUS 14:21-22

History often remembers people because of a defining moment that took place in their life. There are good defining moments and bad defining moments. September 11, 2001, was a bad defining moment for the United States of America. Many people's lives were changed as a result. Israel had a defining moment when they crossed the Jordan River and stepped onto the Promised Land. Moses had a defining moment when he parted the Red Sea with his staff. We could go on.

How would you like to be remembered? Is there a defining moment in your life that others will associate your name with? Thomas, one of the disciples of Jesus, is remembered as "Doubting Thomas." What a shame. I wonder what other good things Thomas did. However, because Thomas doubted that Jesus had truly come back from the dead and needed Jesus to show the nail marks in His hands and side, he will forever be associated with this question posed to the Savior when he saw Him after He was resurrected.

For most of us we can still define our moments for the future. God may yet have a defining moment when you will discover something new or see the work of God in your life in a unique way. I think God likes defining moments. He wants you to have an experience with Him that is memorable.

Make a commitment to the Lord today to allow your defining moment to be one that has a positive faith experience, not a regret.

GETTING REFUELED

Very early in the morning, while it was still dark, Jesus got up, left the house and went off to a solitary place, where he prayed.

MARK 1:35

How do you get refueled? When our cars run low on fuel, we simply drop by the local filling station to get more fuel. When our bodies are hungry, we feed them. How do we refuel our spiritual lives? We can learn from the example Jesus modeled in His life.

In the New Testament we see that Jesus had a very demanding schedule. He traveled from town to town, often walking many miles between the towns. He spent a lot of time with people. As a speaker and teacher, I can tell you that it is very draining to minister for extended periods. Your body and your spirit become fatigued.

The day before the above Scripture was recorded, Jesus had a full day of ministry healing the sick, delivering people from demons and walking to different cities (see Mark 1:29-37). The following day it says Jesus got up before the sun rose and went to pray. The disciples were wondering where He was.

When Jesus was on Earth, He was fully man. Everything He did was based upon receiving specific directions and power from His father to do them. He was not operating as God, but as a human being with the same limitations you and I have. So, Jesus knew one of the key ways to refuel His mind, body and spirit was by spending time in prayer to His heavenly Father.

This is a critical discipline for every follower of Jesus if you expect to have power and victory in your Christian walk. We each need to find a solitary place to focus upon the Lord, His Word and His input for our lives.

If this is not a part of your daily experience, why not start tomorrow with a few minutes of focused time of reading and prayer. You will be encouraged with the new spiritual focus you will have by making this a priority.

DEFINING YOUR SELF-WORTH

I praise you because I am fearfully and wonderfully made;
your works are wonderful, I know that full well.

PSALM 139:14

What measurements do you use to define your self-worth? Do you define it based on your financial assets? Is it based on what you have achieved professionally? Perhaps you define your value based on the number of children you have.

There are many things we can use to define our self-worth. However, the Scriptures tell us there is only one measure for our self-worth. Each of us has self-worth because we are made in the image of God. And because we are made in the image of God, we are valuable. Whenever you and I place a value on ourselves that is based on some other performance criteria, we have moved beyond God's view of our worth as human beings. You are never more valuable to God than you were the day you were born.

Many of us have sought to determine our self-worth based on the amount of money we have. This is a dangerous trap. Paul warns us against seeking to build wealth in order to gain greater value. Paul came to understand that the greatest riches could not compare with knowing Christ. In fact, he considered all other material things to be mere rubbish in comparison: "I consider everything a loss compared to the surpassing greatness of knowing Christ Jesus my Lord" (Philippians 3:8).

Basing our self-worth on how much money we have or on our achievements is an easy trap. We are bombarded with messages that say we are defined by what we drive, where we live, how many toys we own, and the size of our investment account. The media message is designed to create dissatisfaction and lust for what we don't have.

Paul said the purpose for his existence was "to know Christ and the power of his resurrection and the fellowship of sharing in his sufferings, becoming like him in his death" (Philippians 3:10). In what terms do you define yourself? Is it based on knowing Christ alone?

OBEDIENCE TESTS

They were left to test the Israelites to see whether they would obey the Lord's commands, which he had given their forefathers through Moses.

Judges 3:4

There is a spiritual truth God revealed in the conquest of the Promised Land recorded in Judges 3: "These are the nations the Lord left to test all those Israelites who had not experienced any of the wars in Canaan" (v. 1).

They didn't pass the test: "The Israelites did evil in the eyes of the Lord; they forgot the Lord their God and served the Baals and the Asherahs" (v. 7).

Martin Luther said there are three things necessary to create a successful minister of God: prayer, meditation and temptation. You'll really never know the strength and reality of your faith until you experience difficulty in life. You'll never know for sure whether God can be trusted or if you'll fall to temptation.

The apostle Peter thought his faith in Christ was solid until the temptation came to deny Him. Jesus knew Peter was not mature yet and that he would deny Jesus three times in one day. Peter didn't believe it. Sure enough, Peter denied Jesus three times. Peter could not believe he could do such a terrible thing. In order to discover this about himself, he needed to be placed in a situation to reveal his true condition.

God allows circumstances to develop around your life to give your faith opportunity to be proven. It is only when we are tested in battle that we become skilled warriors. You can be confident God will allow trials to come your way through situations like an unreasonable boss, a client who refuses to pay, a false assault on your character, or a difficult relationship that requires unconditional love. These battles are sent your way to test what you know in the mind in order that they might become part of your heart.

If you fail the test, do not be overly concerned. It, too, is part of the maturing process. Learn from it and grow through the experience just as Peter did.

CRYING OUT TO THE LORD

But when they cried out to the LORD, he raised up for them a deliverer.

JUDGES 3:9

I often receive requests to help someone whose life is in a difficult place. After a few questions I am able to discern if the Lord has called me to get involved. More often than not, I am not to be involved. Many times I find this person has not experienced enough pain to want to do anything about his or her situation. Until the person is really ready to cry out to the Lord for a solution to the situation, he or she will simply talk about desiring change but will never take the necessary steps needed for change.

If you invest time into someone who has not yet come to the place of wanting a spiritual solution to his or her problem, you will become emotionally exhausted. The apostle Paul understood this principle when he actually "turned such people over to Satan for the destruction of their flesh" (see 1 Corinthians 5:5).

The people of Israel were finally in enough pain to cry out to God for relief from their oppression. Like so many times throughout the Scriptures, God answered by raising up a deliverer. "But when they cried out to the LORD, he raised up for them a deliverer, Othniel son of Kenaz, Caleb's younger brother, who saved them. The Spirit of the LORD came upon him, so that he became Israel's judge and went to war. The LORD gave Cushan-Rishathaim king of Aram into the hands of Othniel, who overpowered him. So the land had peace for forty years, until Othniel son of Kenaz died" (Judges 3:9-11).

Are you in a difficult place in your life? Are you only talking about changing or are you really ready to cry out to the Lord for a solution? Start now the process of changing your situation for the better and asking for help if needed.

GOD DELAYS

Yet when he heard that Lazarus was sick, he stayed where he was two more days.
JOHN 11:6

"Why doesn't God heal me? I have prayed and prayed and I am still sick. Do I not have enough faith? I am so tired of this," said my wife who had gone more than three years battling her illness.

Lazarus, Mary and Martha's brother, had become terminally ill. Jesus, who considered the three siblings His dear friends, was two miles away in Jerusalem during the time of Lazarus's illness. After Jesus heard the news that Lazarus was ill, instead of running to the aid of Mary and Martha, Jesus waited several days. Meanwhile, Lazarus died and was placed in a tomb. But, Jesus' response to the news was that "This sickness will not end in death. No, it is for God's glory so that God's Son may be glorified through it" (John 11:4). Jesus had to look beyond Mary and Martha's current grief in order to fulfill God's purpose for Lazarus's sickness.

Mary was in deep mourning over the death of her brother. When she ran to meet Jesus when He finally came, she immediately cried out to Him, "Lord, if you had been here, my brother would not have died." But there was a preordained purpose behind Lazarus's death. Only Jesus knew about the plan. He healed Lazarus that day.

When we experience sickness and do not see a breakthrough, we can only seek Jesus for our healing and leave the outcome to Him. We must trust that He knows the answer to our need and the timing for its solution.

There are times when we experience supernatural healing and other times that we simply do not get a breakthrough. In either case, our devotion to Jesus must not change.

God-delays are always pre-ordained for a greater purpose. If you find yourself in this place, bring your concerns to Jesus and leave them there. A day will come when Jesus will reveal His purposes in your situation.

GAINING DIRECTION THROUGH A LACK OF PROVISION

You will drink from the brook, and I have ordered the ravens to feed you there.

1 KINGS 17:4

The prophet Elijah pronounced a drought upon the land because of the sin of Ahab and the nation of Israel. There was only one problem. Elijah had to live in the same land as Ahab:

> Now Elijah the Tishbite, from Tishbe in Gilead, said to Ahab, "As the LORD, the God of Israel, lives, whom I serve, there will be neither dew nor rain in the next few years except at my word." Then the word of the LORD came to Elijah: "Leave here, turn eastward and hide in the Kerith Ravine, east of the Jordan. You will drink from the brook, and I have ordered the ravens to feed you there" (1 Kings 17:1-4).

God provided for Elijah in a supernatural way. The ravens brought bread in the morning and meat in the evening. His water came from the brook.

God often uses money to confirm His direction for our lives. Many times God uses a lack of provision to move us into new directions; it is often a catalyst to encourage new ideas and strategies. Many times a loss of job becomes the greatest blessing to our lives because it provides the catalyst to do things we simply would never do without taking the step to get out of our comfort zone.

Friend, if you are fully following the Lord in your life, and if you are seeking direction from Him and have no un-confessed sin in your life, there is no way He will allow you to miss His provision for you. He has 1,000 ways to get the provision you need at the time you need it. Provision follows obedience.

Today, consider that God can even send a raven to feed you if that is His plan.

FINISH THE JOB

When Israel became strong, they pressed the Canaanites into
forced labor but never drove them out completely.
JUDGES 1:28

Have you ever hired a contractor to do some work and ended up having to spend time and energy to get him back to finish the job? Do small, unfinished projects simply irritate you and create ill will between you and your contractor? If you have been involved in a building project, you have surely had a similar experience.

Likewise, God wanted His people to finish the job. He often told the Israelites to remove their enemies from the Promised Land. However, many times they would not finish the job, and the remnant that was left would come back and create difficulties. In most cases, the people of Israel would intermarry, which enticed them into their enemy's way of living. Other times they had to enslave their enemies, which took time away from their mission.

Whenever we fail to complete a job, it creates ill will from those we are serving. It also violates a basic biblical mandate for every believer to do his or her work with excellence. The Bible gives the example of Daniel and his friends, who did their work 10 times better than anyone else. They were known for their excellence.

It is often said of American football that the hardest place to score from is the one-yard line. That is because the defenses are greatest where there is the most resistance. Sometimes completing a job is like this.

Whenever you have a project to do, make sure you complete the job fully. Go the extra distance to make sure your boss or your client is totally satisfied with your work. You may complete 95 percent of your work, but if it is not completed you will be known for what you did not finish, rather than for what you did finish.

YOU WERE MADE TO FLY

Naked I came from my mother's womb, and naked I will depart. The LORD gave and the LORD has taken away; may the name of the LORD be praised.

JOB 1:21

Can a caterpillar fly? If you said no, you would be partially correct. Actually, a caterpillar can fly, but it must have a transformation first.

The butterfly begins life as a caterpillar, a wormlike larva that spins a cocoon for itself. For weeks, the larva remains hidden within the cocoon as it undergoes metamorphosis. When it's time for the butterfly to emerge, it must struggle and fight its way out of the cocoon.

We might be tempted to help this process by tearing open the cocoon—but that's the worst thing we could do. The struggle makes the new butterfly strong and enables it to fly. Butterflies need adversity to become what God intended them to be. So do we.

The book of Job is the story of a wealthy and successful community leader named Job. He was a successful and righteous businessman with huge holdings of livestock and real estate. One day, Satan came before God, and God asked him, "Where have you come from?" Satan replied, "From roaming through the earth and going back and forth in it."

God said to Satan, "Have you considered my servant Job? He is blameless and upright, a man who fears God and shuns evil." Although God did not directly bring this calamity on Job, He did *point Job out* to Satan!

God gave Satan permission to put Job through a trial of adversity. Job's herds were stolen, his servants were murdered and all of Job's children were killed by a sudden tornado. But through his trial of adversity, he grew in strength, wisdom and faith. His entire perspective on God was transformed by his suffering.

The most difficult faith barrier human beings wrestle with is why bad things happen to good people. We must get beyond the immature notion that God is only interested in making us healthy, wealthy and happy. More than anything, He wants us to be like Christ. And the road to becoming like Christ often leads through the wilderness of adversity.

TO KNOW MY WAYS

That is why I was angry with that generation, and I said, "Their hearts are always going astray, and they have not known my ways." So I declared on oath in my anger, "They shall never enter my rest."
HEBREWS 3:10-11

Technology is supposed to make our ability to accomplish things easier and make us more productive. I love the technology gadgets available to us today. But in 20 years, these will seem as old and archaic as the 8-track player (see, some of you don't know what that is).

Research reveals that the average person is working much longer hours today because we can literally work from anywhere. Our technology allows us to stay in constant contact with others, which means that we are always on call. Unless we intentionally set boundaries, we will never rest from our work.

God got angry with the people of Israel because they did not know His ways. They failed to recognize the boundaries He had set for them that would ensure a spiritual and physically successful life. Because they chose to disregard His ways, their disobedience led to their inability to enter God's rest.

God's rest means that we can actually do our work and still be refreshed through His Spirit in our inner self. It is the opposite of sweat and toil. It means that the fruit of our work comes as a result of abiding in the vine of His grace and power. Jesus said we can do nothing (worthwhile) unless we are connected to the vine.

In order to do this, you and I must do two things. We must understand His ways, and we must do His ways. When we follow these two things, we will begin to experience His supernatural rest in all of our endeavors.

PEACE: OUR WEAPON AGAINST FEAR

For God has not given us a spirit of fear, but of power
and of love and of a sound mind.
2 TIMOTHY 1:6-7, *NKJV*

Fear is the enemy of faith. Fear is bondage. Satan wants us to live in bondage to the past and even the future, but God wants us to live in the freedom of His love and power in the present. As Paul wrote, "For you did not receive a spirit that makes you a slave again to fear, but you received the Spirit of sonship. And by him we cry, 'Abba, Father'" (Romans 8:15).

In order to be the leaders God calls us to be, we must conquer our fear and put it to death. This is a spiritual battle, and it can only be won with spiritual weapons. We must replace our fear with the peace that surpasses understanding. As Jesus told His followers, "I have told you these things, so that in me you may have peace. In this world you will have trouble. But take heart! I have overcome the world" (John 16:33).

As the apostle Paul told the persecuted Christians in Rome, "The God of peace will soon crush Satan under your feet" (Romans 16:20). The God of peace is our conquering King; the peace of God is our weapon against fear and Satan.

Before going to the cross, Jesus told His disciples, "Peace I leave with you; my peace I give you. I do not give to you as the world gives. Do not let your hearts be troubled and do not be afraid" (John 14:27).

Fear is a *natural* response to obstacles, adversity and failure, but peace is the *supernatural* response that God gives us by His grace. Just as Jesus had authority over the wind and waves, He has authority over the storms in our lives. He has authority over our doubts, fears and shame.

Doubts, fear and shame are the weapons of Satan, but Jesus stands against Satan's fury and says with authority, "Peace, be still." The peace of God shatters the weapons of Satan and sends our enemy fleeing.

Appropriate the peace God has already provided for you today.

PRESUMING UPON THE FUTURE

The rich rule over the poor, and the borrower is servant to the lender.
PROVERBS 22:7

"Do you think I should pay off my mortgage?" I said to the investment counselor. "Oh, absolutely not; you can use that money to invest and make more than what you are paying in mortgage interest. Plus, you will get an interest deduction from your mortgage."

This was the advice I got from a Christian investment counselor years ago when I had the chance to pay off all my debts—including my home mortgage. I chose to follow his advice and lived to regret it.

It was not long after our meeting that I was thrust into a seven-year adversity that took all the financial assets I had available that could have paid that mortgage. Through a series of unusual circumstances, my money was gone.

The world's wisdom presumes upon the future. Debt is one of those instruments that has the ability to make one a servant to money. I don't believe the Bible speaks totally against debt, but it gives a strong warning that debt can be an evil taskmaster and that if we choose to use debt inappropriately, we will have to live with the consequences.

After that experience I decided to commit myself to becoming debt free. And if I ever had the opportunity to pay off my mortgage again, I promised myself I would do it. Several years later, the time came again for this opportunity. The same financial counsel was given to me, but I chose to disregard it and paid off my mortgage.

Now, many years later I can tell you that I am a free man. I am no longer servant to the lender. God is free to move in greater ways in my life because of my lack of bondage to debt. I am free to sow more into God's kingdom!

Ask God to bring you into the Promised Land of debt-free living. You will find a peace that surpasses all understanding.

LITTLE BY LITTLE

All hard work brings a profit, but mere talk leads only to poverty.
PROVERBS 14:23

Is there something you would like to accomplish in life but simply cannot find the hours in the day to get started? Many of us suffer from procrastination. We justify putting our dreams aside because we don't believe we have the time or resources to accomplish the task.

Many times people tell me they believe they are called to write a book. I tell them, "Great, if God has called you to write a book, begin to write it." Sometimes the response is: "But I don't have a publisher."

"That has nothing to do with it," I say. "That is not your problem. If God calls you to write a book, you are to begin to write. You may not be writing to get published. You may be writing for other purposes."

"The LORD your God will drive out those nations before you, little by little" (Deuteronomy 7:22). If God has given you a vision to do something, begin by taking baby steps toward that project. Begin to focus on the vision, and take action steps toward your goal.

Many times people ask me, "How in the world do you have time to write? You travel so much and seem to have such a full schedule." My answer to them is that I have a specific time of day in which I commit to writing. It is usually between 5 A.M. and 8 A.M. I have found this to be my most creative and productive time. Very little can get in the way of this time if I believe God has given me a project to do.

You will be amazed at what God can do with a little each day. Do not let procrastination prevent you from accomplishing what God may want to do through your life.

Make plans today to take baby steps toward the vision that is in your heart.

HOW SHARP IS YOUR AX?

If the ax is dull and its edge unsharpened, more strength
is needed but skill will bring success.
ECCLESIASTES 10:10

Manufacturing companies live and die by the ability of their designers, engineers and staff to bring new products to market quickly. Yet for many organizations, a team's capacity to turn promising ideas into new revenue is diminished because of fragmented business processes, a geographically dispersed workforce and a lack of technology innovation standards across the supply chain.

We live in an information age where the level of knowledge is increasing at warp speed. The way you did things two years ago may not be the same way you do things today. The knowledge you had two years ago may not be adequate to compete in the global marketplace today. Businesses have gone bankrupt because they were not willing to change with the times. Have you seen a Polaroid camera lately? Do you know someone over 60 years old who chose not to learn about computers? The world passes by such people because they are unwilling to "sharpen their ax."

God calls every workplace believer to model four key attributes: (1) excellence, (2) ethics and integrity, (3) extravagant love and service, and (4) signs and wonders.

Let's focus on the first quality of a Christian worker: excellence. Excellence does not just mean the way we do our jobs but it also means staying abreast of *how* we do our jobs. God desires to reveal His innovations in His creation. You will not compete in the marketplace today unless you make a commitment to stay abreast of innovation. This too is good stewardship.

How is your workplace ax? Does it need sharpening? What are the areas in your working life that need to be sharpened? What innovation is needed to ensure that you will be the head, not the tail, in your workplace calling? Begin today to evaluate action steps you may need to take to have a very sharp ax.

KNOWING WHEN TO QUIT

Then the LORD opened Balaam's eyes, and he saw the angel of the LORD standing in the road with his sword drawn. So he bowed low and fell facedown.

NUMBERS 22:31

Have you ever wanted something so badly that your perception of the situation became distorted? We can force situations so much that we lose perspective.

The Israelites were defeating all their enemies in the Promised Land. Balak, the king of Moab, feared that his people would be defeated by the Israelites. Balaam was a prophet of the Lord whom Balak knew had the power to bless or curse a nation. So he sent a delegation to get Balaam to curse the nation of Israel. Balaam wanted to do this for a nice fee that would come with his cooperation. However, God was not pleased. "But God said to Balaam, 'Do not go with them. You must not put a curse on those people, because they are blessed' " (Numbers 22:12).

Despite hearing from the Lord, Balaam was not obedient. Balaam instead proceeded with his original plan. This displeased the Lord. God sent an angel to stop Balaam. Were it not for his "talking donkey" sent to warn him, the angel would have killed Balaam.

In the workplace, we can become driven to achieve. Corporate pressure drives executives to make decisions that can impact many people. We become deceived by the need to succeed at any cost in our venture.

In order to achieve godly success, we must be sensitive to those around us who can give input to the direction we may be taking. God will confirm His direction in our lives if we are willing to accept input from those around us. It can come through a spouse, a coworker, a boss, a secretary or even a donkey! Be aware of situations that encourage you to press too hard for a particular outcome.

Achieving goals should be a result of following the actions you believe God leads you to take. Let results become a fruit of your strategic and obedient actions.

YOUR POSITION IS A RESULT OF YOUR ACTIONS

Even a child is known by his actions, by whether his conduct is pure and right.
PROVERBS 20:11

In the workplace, companies and products are known by their position in the industry they represent. Lexus and Mercedes hold the top position among luxury automobiles. They are known for their high quality. Nike is a sports merchandise company known for products that serve those who play sports—they own the number one position in their industry. Coca-Cola is a soft drink company that currently has the number one position in the world among soft drinks. Companies spend millions trying to gain the number one position.

You also are called to achieve a certain position in what and how you represent yourself. Your position is often a result of actions taken over several years. Usually, when your name is mentioned, your position is revealed. It is the most distinguishing attribute of your life and work, and people associate you with your perceived position.

In the workplace you are known by what you do and what you achieve. Your reputation is often built around productivity or the lack thereof. Years of productivity in an industry can allow you to own the number one position in your industry.

Do your actions line up with the position God desires for your life? Are you modeling the fruits of the Holy Spirit in all aspects of your life? Paul prayed that you would "live a life worthy of the Lord and may please him in every way: bearing fruit in every good work, growing in the knowledge of God" (Colossians 1:10-11). Paul desired that we all have a position from which we bear fruit from our knowledge of God.

Today, strive to have an excellent *position* for the benefit of the kingdom of God.

"GIVE ME YOUR LAST MEAL"

I am gathering a few sticks to take home and make a meal for myself
and my son, that we may eat it—and die.
1 Kings 17:12

Imagine telling a widow who was about to eat her last meal with her only son to give you a portion of that meal. That would seem like a cruel and unusually selfish thing to do. Imagine that you have a need for provision and God tells you to go to the most desperate person in the land to get your provision.

God led Elijah to a poor widow who was on her last meal of flour. Why would God lead Elijah from one desperate situation into another? It was because He wished to perform yet another miracle and show His faithfulness to those who needed it most.

Elijah proceeded to tell the widow, "But first make a small cake of bread for me from what you have and bring it to me, and then make something for yourself and your son. For this is what the LORD, the God of Israel, says: 'The jar of flour will not be used up and the jug of oil will not run dry until the day the LORD gives rain on the land'" (1 Kings 17:13-14).

Would you have questioned such logic in the face of a life-threatening situation? The woman demonstrated her faith in God and Elijah by giving him her last meal. This act of faith ensured that her provision would be there day after day. God multiplied her flour and her jug of oil. Provision followed obedience: "For the jar of flour was not used up and the jug of oil did not run dry, in keeping with the word of the LORD spoken by Elijah" (1 Kings 17:16).

God often multiplies what we already have in our hand in a miraculous way when we yield it to Him. God took the widow's only resource, just like He took the loaves and fishes, and multiplied it for those who were in need.

God has placed skills and resources in our hands already. We need to apply faith to that which He has placed in our hands in order to see His provision manifested through us.

GOD VERSUS MAMMON

No one can serve two masters; for either he will hate the one and love the other, or else he will be loyal to the one and despise the other. You cannot serve God and mammon.

MATTHEW 6:24, *NKJV*

The New Testament contains 2,084 verses dealing with money and finance. Sixteen of Jesus' 38 parables deal with money. I believe the reason Jesus spoke so much about money was because He was always trying to see where a person's loyalty resided. He said a person could not serve two masters. Instead, he will love one but hate the other. "For where your treasure is, there your heart will be also" (Matthew 6:21, *NKJV*).

Many people believe money is synonymous with mammon. This is incorrect. Mammon is an Aramaic demonic spirit that was worshiped as a false god by the Philistines. Mammon desires to be worshiped, have influence and control peoples' lives through the love of money. Money is the instrument by which mammon seeks to have power.

Any spirit that opposes God seeks to influence people through deception. It wants to gain loyalty and love without you knowing it has done so. The primary lie behind the spirit of mammon is that money contains power. It encourages people to place disproportionate value on money because of the power it has to influence and control others.

The symptoms of being controlled by the spirit of mammon are revealed when we allow our activities to be governed by the amount of money we have instead of by God alone. It makes us believe that our provision is our employer, spouse, investments or other money source. When we allow money to rule the choices in our lives, we have yielded to the spirit of mammon.

Mammon also leads to other problems, as Paul writes to Timothy: "For the love of money is a root of all kinds of evil. Some people, eager for money, have wandered from the faith and pierced themselves with many griefs" (1 Timothy 6:10).

Today, ask God if you have been influenced by the spirit of mammon. If so, renounce it, and place your total trust in Christ as your source for all provision.

WHEN OTHERS DISAPPOINT YOU

Do your best to come to me quickly, for Demas, because he loved this world, has deserted me and has gone to Thessalonica.

2 TIMOTHY 4:9-10

Adversity molded the apostle Paul into the greatest warrior for Christ the world has ever known. But there were times when adversity and disappointment took their toll on this rugged warrior. We can sense Paul's hurt and discouragement near the end of his second letter to Timothy: "Do your best to come to me quickly, for Demas, because he loved this world, has deserted me and has gone to Thessalonica . . . At my first defense, no one came to my support, but everyone deserted me . . . Do your best to get here before winter" (4:9-10,16,21).

Do you hear the pain in those words? Twice he urges Timothy to come to him. Do you feel his anguish when he twice speaks of being deserted by his friends?

In most of his letters, Paul seems to have an invincible spirit, yet he was a man who suffered, felt betrayed and was at times very lonely. But in spite of his circumstances, Paul chose to look at life from a heavenly perspective. That's why he could write, "We are hard pressed on every side, but not crushed; perplexed, but not in despair; persecuted, but not abandoned; struck down, but not destroyed. We always carry around in our body the death of Jesus, so that the life of Jesus may also be revealed in our body" (2 Corinthians 4:8-10).

Paul experienced a level of opposition and suffering that you and I can scarcely imagine. Yet he was not crushed, and he refused to give in to despair. His goal was to live in such a way that the life of Jesus would be revealed in his response to adversity.

Beware of placing too much expectation on others. Realize that people will let you down from time to time, but do not let that impact your faith. Trust God to work even through these disappointments.

HOW SOLID IS YOUR FOUNDATION?

At the king's command they removed from the quarry large blocks of quality stone to provide a foundation of dressed stone for the temple.

1 KINGS 5:17

Several years ago I visited Jerusalem, the ancient city in Israel where Jesus walked. It was an incredible experience. One of the most memorable things I saw was the actual stones used to build the foundation of the Temple. These stones lie beneath the ground and can be accessed only by going into an underground tunnel.

The stones are massive, and they are perfectly rectangular in shape. The Bible says the stones were moved to the Temple area in a quiet manner in respect of the Holy site:

> All these structures, from the outside to the great courtyard and from foundation to eaves, were made of blocks of high-grade stone cut to size and trimmed with a saw on their inner and outer faces. The foundations were laid with large stones of good quality, some measuring ten cubits and some eight. Above were high-grade stones, cut to size, and cedar beams. The great courtyard was surrounded by a wall of three courses of dressed stone and one course of trimmed cedar beams, as was the inner courtyard of the temple of the LORD with its portico (1 Kings 7:9-12).

Do you see the effort put into the type and quality of stone that would be used to build the Temple of God? In order to achieve anything worthwhile in life, you must lay a quality foundation. Everything else is going to be impacted if that foundation is not laid with the best materials and the finest craftsmanship.

The Bible says that Jesus must be the foundation from which we build everything in our lives (see 1 Corinthians 3:11). Anything else will result in a weak foundation. Are you building on a solid foundation that will last? If not, begin today to shore up your foundation.

MAKING JUDGMENTS

*Do not judge, and you will not be judged. Do not condemn, and you will not
be condemned. Forgive, and you will be forgiven.*

LUKE 6:37

Have you ever made a judgment about a person or situation only to discover
how wrong you were in your assessment? Such was the case in a story told by Os
Guinness in his book *The Call*:

> Arthur F. Burns, the chairman of the United States Federal Reserve System
> and ambassador to West Germany, was a man of considerable gravity . . .
> [He] was also Jewish, so when he began attending an informational White
> House group for prayer and fellowship in the 1970s, he was accorded spe-
> cial respect. In fact, no one knew quite how to involve him in the group
> and, week after week when different people took turns to end the meeting
> in prayer, Burns was passed by—out of a mixture of respect and reticence.
>
> One week, however, the group was led by a newcomer who did not
> know of Burns' status. As the meeting ended, the newcomer turned to
> Arthur Burns and asked him to close the time with a prayer. Some of
> the old-timers glanced at each other in surprise and wondered what
> would happen. But without missing a beat, Burns reached out, held
> hands with others in the circle, and prayed this prayer: "Lord, I pray that
> you would bring Jews to know Jesus Christ. I pray that you would bring
> Muslims to know Jesus Christ. Finally, Lord, I pray that you would
> bring Christians to know Jesus Christ. Amen."
>
> Burns' prayer has become legendary in Washington. Not only did he
> startle those present with refreshing directness, but he also underscored
> a point about "Christians" and "Christianity" that needs repeating regu-
> larly. It highlights another important aspect of the truth of calling:
> Calling reminds Christians ceaselessly that, far from having arrived, a
> Christian is someone who in this life is always on the road as "a follow-
> er of Christ" and a follower of "the Way."[43]

Before you judge a situation, consider that your judgment might not be an
accurate assessment. Perception is not always reality.

INTIMACY WITH THE UPRIGHT

For the devious are an abomination to the LORD;
But He is intimate with the upright.
PROVERBS 3:32, *NASB*

It is human nature to want to be included in the inner circle. It means that you are qualified to hear things, experience things and be privy to information that the masses are not allowed to see.

Jesus had an inner circle of friends made up of Peter, James and John. John in particular had a very special relationship with Jesus. He was considered to be Jesus' best friend. It was John who first recognized Jesus after the crucifixion, when He came to them on the seashore. "Then the disciple whom Jesus loved, said to Peter, 'It is the Lord!'" (John 21:7).

The Bible tells us that John's friendship was such that he could even lay his head upon Jesus' shoulder at the last supper when he inquired about the betrayer: "So lying thus, close to the breast of Jesus, he said to him, 'Lord, who is it?'" (John 13:25-26, *RSV*). Almost 40 years after the Last Supper, John wrote the final book of Revelation in A.D. 90. He was chosen by God to receive the vision and record it.

It was Peter, James and John who had the privilege to see the transfiguration. "After six days Jesus took Peter, James and John with him and led them up a high mountain, where they were all alone. There he was transfigured before them. His clothes became dazzling white, whiter than anyone in the world could bleach them. And there appeared before them Elijah and Moses, who were talking with Jesus" (Mark 9:2-4).

Do you long to have an intimate relationship with your Creator? The Lord desires to have the same with you. He does not want you to have a mere form of religion but a relationship whereby you experience His presence and power—where you can see Him perform His acts of power and love among others.

One of the keys to intimacy is uprightness. Uprightness means we are living a life of obedience and submission to His will in our lives. When we live at this place, we enter His inner circle.

STEPHEN: A MARKETPLACE MINISTER

Now Stephen, a man full of God's grace and power,
did great wonders and miraculous signs among the people.
ACTS 6:8

In the beginnings of the Early Church, the disciples saw God move in mighty ways. The disciples found themselves preaching the word of God all over the region. Eventually, however, practical needs arose among the people and, due to their focus on preaching, those needs were not being met adequately.

One of these needs involved food distribution to widows. This brought pressure upon the disciples, who felt that their primary focus must be to preach the gospel. They realized that they could not do both ministries adequately. This led the disciples to appoint seven men whose lives qualified for service as leaders to serve the "non-spiritual" needs of the people.

The first man named to fill this responsibility was Stephen, described as a man full of faith and the Holy Ghost, with a strong faith in Christ. He was full of courage, gifts and graces. He was an extraordinary man and excelled in everything that was good.

After appointing Stephen, the Church began to mobilize other workplace believers for ministry in the community. "So the word of God spread. The number of disciples in Jerusalem increased rapidly, and a large number of priests became obedient to the faith" (Acts 6:7). It is as though the Lord took the cap off and everything started happening. Even a large number of priests came into the faith.

Take an inventory of your life today, and determine if someone could describe you as a person full of faith and of the Holy Spirit, full of grace and power, and one who does great wonders and miraculous things. If not, begin asking God today to accomplish this in your life.

OUR STAFF AS OUR PROTECTOR

The Amalekites came and attacked the Israelites at Rephidim. Moses said to Joshua, "Choose some of our men and go out to fight the Amalekites. Tomorrow I will stand on top of the hill with the staff of God in my hands."

EXODUS 17:8-9

Moses' staff represented his vocation as a shepherd. When God first met Moses in the desert at the burning bush, He told Moses that He was going to use his staff to perform miracles and to bring a people out of slavery.

Moses later faced one of his enemies in the new land, the Amalekites. God told him to go to the top of the mountain and to hold his staff up to heaven. As long as his staff was outstretched to heaven, Israel would win the battle. But if it was not uplifted, they would suffer defeat:

> So Joshua fought the Amalekites as Moses had ordered, and Moses, Aaron and Hur went to the top of the hill. As long as Moses held up his hands, the Israelites were winning, but whenever he lowered his hands, the Amalekites were winning (Exodus 17:10-11).

When God told Moses He was going to use his staff to bring a people out of bondage, Moses first had to lay his staff down on the ground. God changed it into a snake, and then God told Moses to pick it up by the tail. Many interpret this as God telling Moses to take authority over Satan, the serpent, in this prophetic act. When Moses picked up the staff, the Scripture tells us that it was no longer Moses' staff, but now the staff of God.

Friend, the lesson for you is to continually offer up your work lives, or your "staff," to the Lord and see His protection and blessing on you as you continually raise your work to the Lord for His use. God wants to perform miracles through your *staff*.

THE WORSHIP SERVICE

This is why I weep and my eyes overflow with tears. No one is near to comfort me, no one to restore my spirit. My children are destitute because the enemy has prevailed.
LAMENTATIONS 1:16

Angie and I walked into the worship service. I pushed my mom's wheelchair into the room among many, many others. This was no ordinary worship service. This wasn't our first time, and the organizer recognized us and asked if we would assist in handing out the songbooks. Only about 20 percent of the participants could actually use them. *Why does life have to be reduced to this?* I questioned, and prayed silently to the Lord, *If You walked through this room, how many would You restore?* You see, Angie and I were in a dementia and Alzheimer's nursing home unit where my mom resided.

A few chairs over sat the father of my older sisters' longtime best friend. Next to him was my brother-in-law's grandmother. They were all once successful people—doctors, lawyers, business leaders or stay-at-home moms. They had, at one time, lived in fine Southern homes. But now, they lived in one-half of a single room. Some patients could recognize their loved ones; others could not.

The service began with singing. Only a few voices could be heard among the patients. A simple message followed. Then something remarkable happened. The speaker said they would close with a well-known song. It began this way: "Jesus loves me, this I know, for the Bible tells me so." Suddenly, the voices in the room got louder. Patients who were not singing before were now singing. I looked over at my mom. She was whistling the tune. I looked over at Angie; tears were streaming down her face.

Yes, the presence of Jesus was walking through the room. But it wasn't in the way I thought He would come. Sometimes the presence of God can show up in the smallest and simplest acts.

LIVING UNDER AUTHORITY

Submit yourselves to every ordinance of man for the Lord's sake: whether it be to the king, as supreme: or unto governors, as unto them that are sent by him for the punishment of evildoers, and for the praise of them that do well.
1 PETER 2:13,14

God used government authority in the lives of many people in the Bible to accomplish His purposes in their lives. Scripture tells us that even the king's heart is in the hand of God (see Proverbs 21:1). God uses political authorities to continue the work that He has started in us, and He will continue to manifest His character in us through governmental authorities.

Moses and Pharaoh, Joseph and Potiphar, Daniel and Nebuchadnezzar, Esther and the king, Jesus and Pilate and many others throughout the Bible became great men and women of God because they gave those in authority their rightful honor.

If we find it difficult to live under the authorities in our life, we'll usually find it difficult to submit to the will of God in our lives, too. Rebellion is reflected in our unwillingness to live under the authority placed over us. We may not have respect for the *person* who is the president of our nation, but we are still to honor and respect the *position* the presidency represents, and we are to recognize that God has placed that person in authority over us. As long as we are not asked to violate a biblical commandment, we must recognize those in authority as God-given and working on our behalf.

We must not obey the government when it calls us to compromise God's Word. Issues that violate the Word of God may require civil disobedience. However, each person must evaluate these situations in light of what God's Word says and be true to their own conscience.

Today, pray for those in authority over you.

GOD'S TIMING

Immediately the leprosy left him and he was cured. Jesus sent him away at once with a strong warning: "See that you don't tell this to anyone."

MARK 1:42-43

Have you ever had a problem keeping a secret—especially if that secret involves good news? My wife can't keep a secret like this. She is sure to blurt it out to the wrong person at the wrong time.

There is a timing that is ideal for releasing information or moving forward with a project. Jesus understood the importance of timing. When He performed His first healing miracle, He instructed the man He healed not to tell anyone. Now that would be difficult—not to share being healed from leprosy! He could not keep the secret.

As a result, Jesus could no longer enter a town openly but stayed outside in lonely places. Yet the people still came to Him from everywhere. Jesus desired to do more things in that city, but because the man could not keep quiet, Jesus' ministry there was limited.

How often has Jesus not been able to move in your situation because you have failed to honor His timing? Perhaps you have moved ahead when you were not supposed to move.

Early in my writing career, I wrote a book before I should have. I was called to write it, but my enthusiasm and passion kept me from releasing it in the right timing. The premature release resulted in not having a complete understanding of the topic. Had I waited on His timing for release, I would have had a greater understanding and would have written a better, more thorough book.

In the Old Testament, David was fighting the Philistines. He won the first battle, but when they were coming against him again, he inquired of God and God told him to go to battle, but not until he heard the marching in the balsam trees (see 2 Samuel 5:23). There was a strategic timing associated with his actions.

"There is a time for everything, and a season for every activity under heaven" (Ecclesiastes 3:1). Ask God for His timing in your projects to be released.

HOW WOULD JESUS IMPACT YOUR WEDDING PARTY?

"Dear woman, why do you involve me?" Jesus replied, "My time has not yet come." His mother said to the servants, "Do whatever he tells you."

JOHN 2:4-5

In Bible times, a Jewish wedding was a special celebration that could last seven days or more. It was a time of joy and celebration on behalf of the couple. Wine was an integral part of these festivities.

Jesus, the disciples and Mary, Jesus' mother, were invited guests to such a wedding. At some point during the celebration there was no more wine. Mary became concerned and turned to Jesus to solve the problem. Jesus had not yet performed any miracles; however, His mother must have known that He was capable of doing so.

When she proposed to Jesus that He solve this problem, He answered, "My time has not yet come." You can almost hear that motherly Jewish tone— "Yes, it has, son. Please handle this emergency for me." Then Mary instructed the servants to do whatever Jesus told them to do, seeming to know that He was going to solve the problem, but not really knowing how. In the end, Jesus accomplished His mother's request.

The quality of the wine that Jesus made was exceptional and would have cost a fortune. Imagine, 180 gallons of fine wine! As in most miracles Jesus performed, He involved the faith and obedience of others. In this case, the servants were an important part of the miracle—they did just what Jesus told them to do.

My Western mind can only imagine what the headline would be the day after this wedding, in the politically incorrect *Cana's Daily News*: "Son of Mary turns water into alcoholic drink—180 gallons!" What a way to begin a ministry! Thankfully, there was no negative press.

Have you ever asked Jesus to get involved in an unusual problem? No matter what problem you have, Jesus invites you to seek Him as the solution.

GOD SPEAKS THROUGH CIRCUMSTANCES

As you do not know the path of the wind, or how the body is formed in a mother's womb, so you cannot understand the work of God, the Maker of all things.
ECCLESIASTES 11:5

God will often use circumstances in our lives to direct us in making and confirming decisions. I have often discovered this to be the case—but only after a situation has occurred. I later look back and see how God worked in the situation.

Years ago, I launched a magazine designed for Christians in the workplace. I was having lunch with a Christian leader named Larry who headed a ministry that helps men and women apply biblical principles to managing money. During our lunch, I explained to Larry that I had noticed that there were many grassroots workplace ministries cropping up all over the country.

I asked Larry if he was familiar with some of the groups, because he had taught a course and wrote a book on operating a business on biblical principles. But he said he was not. He then asked, "It would be nice to know what all these groups are doing so we don't duplicate efforts. Do you think you could invite some of these groups for a roundtable discussion?" I told him I would, and I proceeded to invite four main workplace ministries that I had worked with in the past.

Then something unexpected began to happen. I began to get requests to attend the roundtable from ministries all around the country that had heard about the gathering. By the time the event actually took place, 54 people showed up representing 45 organizations from around the country! Unfortunately, Larry had a last minute conflict and was not able to attend. He informed me that I would have to host the meeting myself.

That was the birth of Marketplace Leaders, the ministry I now lead full time. I often joke that God tricked me into starting this ministry because He knew I never would have done that on my own at that time.

God often confirms His direction through circumstances. Be on alert that when God sets up situations that are out of your control, He may be giving you direction.

CONFIRMING DECISIONS

Plans fail for lack of counsel, but with many advisers they succeed.
PROVERBS 15:22

Confirming major decisions through the counsel of others is one way God protects us from poor decisions. This process is designed to confirm direction for which we are seeking confirmation. Paul was sensitive not to get too heavy-handed in the confirmation process, though. He offered advice to others but was not the enforcer of their decisions.

The requirement for efficient administration frequently requires single points of decision-making. Where there is willingness and trust to receive input, there is also humility, faith and grace for God to work His pleasure in His servant. Where there is unwillingness, the opposite is true.

There have been times in my life when I have felt strongly about a certain issue only to receive feedback from those close to me that revealed that I was not accurate in my assessment of the situation. I have learned to yield in such situations, trusting that God is working through those to whom I am accountable.

The Scriptures encourage us to seek advice and counsel from godly people who share our same values and goals. "Listen to advice and accept instruction, and in the end you will be wise" (Proverbs 19:20). "Make plans by seeking advice; if you wage war, obtain guidance" (Proverbs 20:18).

Peace of mind is another important requirement for making decisions. If you do not have peace about a decision, you should wait until God gives you peace. This does not mean your decision may not have some tension due to the faith aspect of it, but deep down you should have a peace that it is the right decision. "Do not be anxious about anything, but in everything, by prayer and petition, with thanksgiving, present your requests to God. And the peace of God, which transcends all understanding, will guard your hearts and your minds in Christ Jesus" (Philippians 4:6-7).

Do you need to make a major decision? Ask God to give you confirmation through others.

ARE YOU A THREAT?

But I will tarry in Ephesus until Pentecost. For a great and effective
door has opened to me, and there are many adversaries.
1 CORINTHIANS 16:8-9, *NKJV*

Angie and I entered the airport when suddenly she began to feel sick. "Honey, I don't think I can go. I feel awful. I was fine driving down here," she said. We stopped and prayed. She didn't feel any better. She decided she would not go. Sadly, we said goodbye to one another.

About 30 minutes later I was sitting at the gate when Angie came running up to me. "I am coming with you," she said.

"What happened?" I responded.

"I asked the Lord if I was to go and He said yes. So I am coming, despite the way I feel."

We got onto the airplane and it was only a few minutes into the flight when she turned to me and said, "I feel fine now. I can't believe how much better I feel."

Angie and I began to recognize that this happens consistently whenever we go on our ministry trips. We have become increasingly aware of Paul's admonition in Ephesians 6:12: "For our struggle is not against flesh and blood, but against the rulers, against the authorities, against the powers of this dark world and against the spiritual forces of evil in the heavenly realms."

How big of a threat are you to the kingdom of God? If you are pushing back the kingdom of darkness, chances are, you will have opposition in your life. The apostle Paul realized that as doors became open to him, so the adversaries in the spiritual realm were determined to thwart his activities.

Today, realize that you are in a physical and spiritual battle, and put on the armor of God. "Submit yourselves, then, to God. Resist the devil, and he will flee from you. Come near to God and he will come near to you" (James 4:7-8).

MIRACULOUS SIGNS

The apostles performed many miraculous signs and wonders among the people.
And all the believers used to meet together in Solomon's Colonnade.

ACTS 5:12

When is the last time you saw a miracle in your workplace? Perhaps you prayed for a coworker, and he or she was instantly healed. Perhaps you prayed for a coworker's financial problem, and it was resolved. Perhaps you led a coworker to Christ. Or maybe God gave you an answer to a major problem at work that benefited your organization.

The disciples were working people. They turned the world upside down not because of their knowledge of Jesus but because of their outflow of the power of Jesus. And they did so in the public square, where all could see.

Workplace Bible and prayer groups are great, but you must transition to public action if you want to change the spiritual climate in an organization. The only risk is that God might actually show up in a powerful way.

A number of years ago, I taught a lunchtime Bible study in an insurance company for two years. God moved powerfully in the meetings. People came to Christ. Some experienced healing. Word got out and nonbelievers came to check out what we did.

When is the last time someone saw something happen that could not be explained other than that it was God working through you? When you begin to see this happen, you will be modeling ministry as Jesus modeled it. You will be bringing the Church to the people, not the people to church.

Pray that God makes you a vessel of His power, not simply a vessel of words.

SEEING THORNS AS BLESSINGS

To keep me from becoming conceited because of these surpassingly great revelations,
there was given me a thorn in my flesh, a messenger of Satan, to torment me.
2 CORINTHIANS 12:7

Have you ever had something in your life you wish was not there? If God gave you one wish, perhaps it would be to change that one thing. Perhaps it is the source of pain or challenge in your life. You seek God continually for relief from it, but He seems strangely silent.

Paul also experienced an ongoing burden that he called a "thorn in [his] flesh." Bible scholars have speculated as to what this thorn might have been, but no one knows for sure. We do know that it was so hurtful to Paul that he asked God on three different occasions to remove it from his life:

> To keep me from becoming conceited because of these surpassingly great revelations, there was given me a thorn in my flesh, a messenger of Satan, to torment me. Three times I pleaded with the Lord to take it away from me. But he said to me, "My grace is sufficient for you, for my power is made perfect in weakness." Therefore I will boast all the more gladly about my weaknesses, so that Christ's power may rest on me. That is why, for Christ's sake, I delight in weaknesses, in insults, in hardships, in persecutions, in difficulties. For when I am weak, then I am strong (2 Corinthians 12:7-10).

Paul had a great calling on his life. The revelations and faith experiences that God gave him would have been too much for any man's humility, so God, in order to ensure His investment in Paul's life, gave Paul a thorn in his flesh to help him maintain a humble, godly perspective.

Perhaps God has given you a thorn designed to allow you to place greater trust and reliance upon Him. Ask God to reveal to you the blessing of the thorn He has placed in your life.

Thorns hurt us, but they also humble us. They allow His power to be made perfect in weakness.

VESTED INTERESTS

When Sanballat heard that we were rebuilding the wall,
he became angry and was greatly incensed.
NEHEMIAH 4:1

Leaders who attempt something greater than themselves almost always get attacked by those who have a vested interest in what the leader is changing.

Nehemiah was rebuilding the ancient wall of Jerusalem. It was a major undertaking. Not everyone was pleased with this initiative. In particular, Sanballat, another government worker, did not want this to happen.

Similarly, when Jesus began to confront the Pharisees about religious traditions, the religious establishment attacked Him because they had a vested interest that would be negatively impacted by His teaching. The apostle Paul also confronted a religious tradition that generated income for those in the trade. Opposition arose because he was impacting a vested interest:

About that time there arose a great disturbance about the Way. A silversmith named Demetrius, who made silver shrines of Artemis, brought in no little business for the craftsmen. He called them together, along with the workmen in related trades, and said: "Men, you know we receive a good income from this business. And you see and hear how this fellow Paul has convinced and led astray large numbers of people here in Ephesus and in practically the whole province of Asia. He says that man-made gods are no gods at all. There is danger not only that our trade will lose its good name, but also that the temple of the great goddess Artemis will be discredited" (Acts 19:23-27).

Whenever you introduce a new product into the market, expect opposition from competitive products that have a vested interest. If God leads you to initiate a cause greater than yourself, expect opposition. But also expect God to walk with you through the challenges your opposition sends your way.

STOPLIGHT FAITH

And he did not do many miracles there because of their lack of faith.
MATTHEW 13:58

You can learn a lot sitting in traffic.

Imagine side-by-side left-hand turn lanes. One lane has three cars waiting to turn left, while the other has 20. The people in the longer line want to make sure that they will be able to make their next turn after the light. The people in the shorter line, on the other hand, want to make it through the light faster and will worry about making their next turn later. The long-line people and the short-line people have different tolerances for risk—or perhaps different levels of faith.

No matter which person you are in this situation, faith is often spelled R-I-S-K. When the priests carried the Ark into the Jordan River at flood stage, there was a risk they could lose the Ark to the Jordan River. However, that is not what happened. "And as soon as the priests who carry the ark of the LORD—the Lord of all the earth—set foot in the Jordan, its waters flowing downstream will be cut off and stand up in a heap" (Joshua 3:13). God changed the entire environment and made it possible to walk across the Jordan without the pressure of wading through the powerful water—*but only after they took the first step.*

Risk means there is a potential for loss. However, when God leads us to take a risk, He is there with us whether we succeed or fail—He is there in the success and He is there in the failure. If He leads you to take a risk, you may not always succeed in the way you think. In fact, you may even fail.

The only true failure, though, is when we fail to take the risks God is leading us to. Sometimes, the fear of failure is the greater obstacle than the risk itself.

Has God called you to step out in an area that requires risk? This could be the place He wants you to move. Ask Jesus to give you the courage to step out.

PRIDE THAT LEADS TO ARGUMENTS

Warn a divisive person once, and then warn him a second time.
After that, have nothing to do with him. You may be sure that
such a man is warped and sinful; he is self-condemned.

TITUS 3:10-11

Have you ever had to deal with a person who just wanted to argue with you, no matter which position you took? This person usually has a strong opinion and draws conclusions quickly, rarely giving credence to other's viewpoints. The apostle Paul knew how to deal with such people. Once he saw this pattern, he confronted the person. If the person continued, he cut off fellowship.

However, if this person happens to be your boss, you will not be able to avoid him or her! The root strongholds of a person who is argumentative are pride and fear. Argumentative people are insecure in who they are as a person. They mask their inadequacies through a need to always be right.

I had a business partner once who was deeply hurt by lawyers in a corporate takeover. After that bad experience, he was argumentative with every lawyer he had to deal with. One time I had to confront him and tell him what was behind his behavior. Thankfully, he had the grace and humility to repent and renounce his stronghold of pride, insecurity and fear. We proceeded to finish our project peacefully.

When you run into this in the workplace, pray for understanding. Negative behavior is like the warning light on your car dashboard: It's telling you that there is something going on under the hood. Realize that those afflicted with negativity are in a prison guarded by a root stronghold that has been a part of his or her life for a long time. Unfortunately, it usually takes a significant crisis for negative people to examine themselves and become free.

Pray that God gives you grace to work with such people, and pray that God will deliver them.

FROM PAIN TO DESTINY

*Consider it pure joy, my brothers, whenever you face trials of many kinds,
because you know that the testing of your faith develops perseverance.
Perseverance must finish its work so that you may be mature and complete,
not lacking anything.*

JAMES 1:2-4

God often allows pain to ignite destiny in our lives. Without motivation, many of us would never fulfill the purposes for which God created us. Oftentimes a measured assault invades our life and creates a depth of pain so that all we know to do is press into God with all our being.

At first, our motivation is to alleviate the pain. Then, after a season of extreme emotional and sometimes physical pain, a second phase begins. This phase moves us to discover a new and deeper relationship with God. We begin to discover things about ourselves and about God that we never would have discovered without the motivation of pain.

Gradually, our heart changes our motivation from pain avoidance to loving obedience. No longer do we seek God for deliverance from the pain—we seek God because He is God. We seek His face and not His hand.

When we move to the second phase, we often find ourselves moving into a new destiny and calling for our lives because God often separates us from the old life in this process. Like Joseph, after our crises have passed, we are able to say to Satan, "You meant it for evil, but God meant it for good."

Today, let God move you from the place of pain to the place of destiny. Let God show you the secret things He has reserved for you as a result of the crisis you may find yourself in.

THE HANDKERCHIEF

For the foolishness of God is wiser than man's wisdom,
and the weakness of God is stronger than man's strength.
1 CORINTHIANS 1:25

Frank had just completed a long trip and settled into his seat for a quiet return home when the man next to him started up a conversation. Frank politely conversed with the man, hoping it would be a brief conversation so that he could rest.

However, as time went on, the man began to ask more and more questions. Strangely, he seemed to be looking for something, by the nature of his questions. Finally, the conversation turned to family, and the subject of babies came up. Frank confided in the man that his daughter had been seeking to become pregnant for years without success.

The man turned to Frank and said, "That's it! I knew there was something the Lord wanted me to press in on with you, but until you said that, I was searching and searching." Frank did not even realize the man was a believer until that moment. "This may sound strange to you, but God has given me a strange kind of gift to help barren women become pregnant. Whenever I pray for women, they get pregnant. May I ask you to do something rather unusual?" Frank continued to listen before committing to anything.

"I would like us to pray over this handkerchief. When you get back to your daughter, I would like you to lay this handkerchief on your daughter's belly and pray over it." Frank was a bit taken aback by the thought, but he had seen more unusual things than this in his international travels.

Frank returned to the States, and a short time later arranged a time for his daughter and her husband to come by the house. Frank felt very awkward, as he knew his son-in-law would think this was foolishness. Nevertheless, Frank proceeded to explain what had happened, and they laid the handkerchief on his daughter's belly and prayed.

A few weeks passed and Frank received a phone call from his daughter. "Dad, you will never guess what has happened! I am pregnant!" she exclaimed.

"But God chose the foolish things of the world to shame the wise" (1 Corinthians 1:27).

GIDEON'S SUCCESS TEST

All Israel prostituted themselves by worshiping [the idol] there,
and it became a snare to Gideon and his family.

JUDGES 8:27

Israel was at war with the Midianites and the Amalekites. So God chose a humble young man, Gideon, to deliver Israel by cleansing the land of idols. After determining that it was truly God who was calling him, Gideon obeyed the Lord and destroyed the pagan idols in the region. Then he summoned a large army—more than 30,000 men—to fight the Midianites and Amalekites. But God said the army was too large, so He first reduced Gideon's army to 10,000 men, and then to a mere 300 men. When God gave Israel the victory with an army of only 300 men, all of Israel knew that it was the power of God, not the strength of Gideon's army, that had won the battle.

If the story had ended there, all would have been well. But at the moment of Israel's triumph, Gideon stumbled. He told the people, "I do have one request, that each of you give me an earring from your share of the plunder." The Israelites took the gold from the bodies of the enemy dead, and Gideon melted it and fashioned it into an idol. The Bible calls this idol an *ephod*, a word that refers to a ceremonial breastplate—Gideon probably depicted the Lord God as a warrior with an ephod of gold.

But God does not allow Himself to be represented by an idol. This idol was an offense against God and a trap for the people. After Gideon's death, the Israelites again worshiped the pagan god Baal. They forgot the Lord God who had rescued them from their enemies.

The story of Gideon has a great beginning but a tragic ending. This is an instructive lesson for us all. As the apostle Paul tells us, "If you think you are standing firm, be careful that you don't fall!" (1 Corinthians 10:12).

If we fail the Success Test, we must go back to God without fear. We can ask Him to help us learn the lessons of our failure and to strengthen us for another effort. The God of second chances is able to accomplish His purpose through us even if we have failed Him many times before.

FAITH PROVED GENUINE

Even one of their own prophets has said, "Cretans are always liars, evil brutes,
lazy gluttons." This testimony is true. Therefore, rebuke them sharply, so that
they will be sound in the faith and will pay no attention to Jewish myths
or to the commands of those who reject the truth.
TITUS 1:12-14

In December 1983, the Princeton Religion Research Center published a land-mark survey conducted for the *Wall Street Journal* by the Gallup Organization. The researchers measured a wide range of moral and ethical behaviors, such as calling in sick when not sick, cheating on income tax and pilfering company supplies for personal use. The results were disappointing, to say the least.

What the researchers found most startling was that there was no significant difference between the churched and the unchurched with regard to ethics and values on the job. In other words, despite the fact that more and more people were attending churches, churches seemed to be having less and less of an impact on the moral fiber of their people, at least in the workplace.

To quote the researchers: "These findings will come as a shock to the religious leaders and underscore the need for religious leaders to channel the new religious interest in America not simply into religious involvement but in deep spiritual commitment."[44]

"Either these are not the gospels, or we're not Christians," said Thomas Linacre, Henry VIII's doctor and Renaissance thinker, after he was given the four Gospels in Greek. Linacre recognized a great disparity between those who proclaimed Christ and how those people lived their lives.

If our faith life is not validated through our behavior, then one must question if we have a genuine relationship with Christ.

Pray that your faith is "proved genuine and may result in praise, glory and honor when Jesus Christ is revealed" (1 Peter 1:7).

AUGUST 24

JUDAH'S INTEGRITY TEST

I made a covenant with my eyes not to look lustfully at a girl.
JOB 31:1

In Genesis 38, we read how Judah, one of Joseph's brothers, allowed both his purity and the staff that represented his stature and position in the community to be taken from him.

Against the customs of the times and the memory of Tamar's deceased husband, Judah deprived his daughter-in-law Tamar of her right to have children. Under the law, Judah did a great injustice to her. Although Tamar lived in Judah's house, Judah withheld his son from her.

So Tamar devised a plan. Hearing that Judah planned to go to the town of Timnah, she disguised herself with a veil and hurried to the village of Enaim. She posed as a Canaanite prostitute and waited for Judah to pass by. Soon, Judah came up, saw a prostitute sitting at the gate, propositioned her and promised a goat for payment.

Tamar asked for a pledge—the personal seal and the staff in his hand. The staff was the symbol of Judah's position in the community. Judah gave her the staff and the seal with its cord. He slept with Tamar, and she became pregnant.

Time passed and Judah discovered that Tamar was pregnant. He knew that there was only one way this could have happened—she had prostituted herself! Enraged, Judah said, "Bring her out and have her burned to death!" (Genesis 38:24).

As the people brought Tamar out to be executed, she cried out, "I am pregnant by the man who owns these!" (v. 25). She held in her hands the seal and staff of Judah. Seeing them, Judah knew he stood convicted. He broke down and confessed, "She is more righteous than I" (v. 26).

Sexual sin can take everything away from a man or woman: reputation, career and even family. No matter how strong we think we are, no one is immune from temptation. Be intentional about setting boundaries around your life to keep you morally pure. And pray that God's grace keeps you pure.

WHEN HIS WORK EXCEEDS HIS PRESENCE

If your presence does not go with us, do not send us up from here.
EXODUS 33:15

One of the great dangers in Christian service is to move from presence-based work to operating purely on our natural skill. Once we become established in something, the daily maintenance can lead us into complacency until a crisis arises that forces us back to our knees to appeal to the Lord for His presence to return.

Things were going well for Moses as he led the people out of Egypt. God was calling him to Mt. Horeb, the mountain of God, to receive the Ten Commandments. While he was there, the people fell away from the Lord by returning to the ways of Egypt—they built and worshiped a golden calf on Aaron's watch.

This revealed that the spiritual foundation of the people and the leadership of Aaron were not yet grounded enough for Moses to have an extended absence. God's presence had left the people.

If you are in management, you must know the condition of your team to know how long you can be away from hands-on leadership.

When Moses came back and saw what had happened, he recognized the solution right away. The return of God's presence was the only way they could proceed and have success:

How will anyone know that you are pleased with me and with your people unless you go with us? What else will distinguish me and your people from all the other people on the face of the earth? (Exodus 33:16).

Moses also realized a weakness in his own ability to lead. He pleaded to God to mentor him. "If you are pleased with me, teach me your ways so I may know you and continue to find favor with you" (Exodus 33:13).

Is the presence of God in your current activities? Are the people you lead mature enough in their faith that you can be off site? Ask for God's help on both counts.

HAVING A GREAT "NUMBER TWO" MAN

*Then Moses would return to the camp, but his young aide
Joshua son of Nun did not leave the tent.*

Exodus 33:11

An organization cannot grow without a trusted and skilled second in command or "number two" man or woman. Joshua was Moses' number two man. He could trust Joshua explicitly in all matters.

Joshua came to Moses as a young man and demonstrated his devotion to Moses early. Then one day a situation arose in the camp in which Joshua felt others were seeking to usurp Moses' leadership:

Joshua son of Nun, who had been Moses' aide since youth, spoke up and said, "Moses, my lord, stop them!" But Moses replied, "Are you jealous for my sake? I wish that all the LORD's people were prophets and that the LORD would put his Spirit on them!" Then Moses and the elders of Israel returned to the camp (Numbers 11:28-30).

Joshua's loyalty is an example of what is required of a number two man. Joshua never sought to elevate himself. He served Moses until the day came when God promoted him to be the leader. He was a model of servanthood.

When our ministry began to expand, God sent me a great number two man named Joey. He was living in Florida with his wife and their three small children. He learned of our need through our prayer letter—God spoke to him and his wife before we ever talked.

We could not pay Joey what he was worth, but he came anyway, by faith. God honored Joey's faith and enabled our work to grow, and he has now benefited from our growth as well. God honored his faith. His support allows me to be away from the office to minister around the world.

Do you need a number two man? Ask God to bring him or her to you.

SHARING YOUR FAITH WITH OTHERS

*I pray that you may be active in sharing your faith, so that you will have
a full understanding of every good thing we have in Christ.*

PHILEMON 1:6

There is a strong correlation between those who publicly share their faith with others and an increase in spiritual growth for the individual. In my own journey I've discovered that when I stop sharing my faith with non-believers I begin to see a dryness in my walk with God.

Sometimes we justify our lack of verbal witness by saying we don't have the spiritual gift of evangelism. Or we conclude that because we have an introverted personality, we leave witnessing to others who we deem more qualified. As an introvert myself, I've often wanted to use that excuse. Then the Holy Spirit reminds me of a few instructions Jesus said to everyone: "But whoever disowns me before men, I will disown him before my Father in heaven" (Matthew 10:33). "He said to them, 'Go into all the world and preach the good news to all creation'" (Mark 16:15). What Jesus is saying in these verses is very clear—and it relates to all of us.

When we share Christ with others, God allows us to gain a deeper and greater understanding of every good thing in Christ. Do you see the direct correlation between sharing your faith and your own spiritual growth? Paul says sharing with others is actually a prerequisite to spiritual growth.

One of the great ways to turn a conversation to faith is by asking someone if there is anything you can pray about for him or her. You will be surprised how easily this will transition you into a conversation about his or her faith condition.

Ask God for boldness to offer to pray for someone today.

KNOW YOUR CUSTOMER

Be sure you know the condition of your flocks,
give careful attention to your herds.
PROVERBS 27:23

Identifying and meeting the needs of customers is key to any successful marketing venture. Many years ago, Coca-Cola decided to introduce a new Coke. The company executives conducted research among loyal customers to determine if their customers would embrace the new taste. The evidence proved that the new Coke would be successful, as people liked the taste of new Coke.

However, what Coke did not realize was the emotional attachment Coke users had to their existing Coke product. Once the new product hit the stores, there was a massive outpouring of negative publicity when Coke users rebelled against the new Coke. Loyal Coke drinkers may have liked the taste of the new Coke, but they did not want it as a replacement for what they were accustomed to.

The man responsible for the change was fired. It became one of the most famous marketing blunders ever. However, the story does not end there. The company eventually turned a bad situation into a positive one. Coke ended up having two versions of Coke—"new" and "classic." The man responsible for the new product was rehired and went on to be successful in the company.

Jesus sought to meet the needs of His customers by ministering to their needs as His heavenly Father revealed them to Him. He also showed His customers their most important need—the need for salvation—when He fulfilled God's need for a physical sacrifice, on the cross.

Some of your customers have a perceived need for your product. But they also have a spiritual need that they may not realize they have. God wants to use you to meet both needs. That's why it is important for you to know your customer.

GIVING AND RECEIVING

Not that I am looking for a gift, but I am looking for what
may be credited to your account.

PHILEMON 4:17

The apostle Paul had a tent-making business. Over time, it was evident that more and more of his time was being given to vocational ministry activities. It became increasingly difficult for him to run a business and travel and minister. Doing so required him to receive income from those in whom he invested his life.

His letter to the Philippians gives us a perspective on giving. Although Paul appreciated the support financially, his real joy came from the fact that their gift was being credited to their heavenly account:

Yet it was good of you to share in my troubles. Moreover, as you Philippians know, in the early days of your acquaintance with the gospel, when I set out from Macedonia, not one church shared with me in the matter of giving and receiving, except you only; for even when I was in Thessalonica, you sent me aid again and again when I was in need. *Not that I am looking for a gift, but I am looking for what may be credited to your account.* I have received full payment and even more; I am amply supplied, now that I have received from Epaphroditus the gifts you sent. They are a fragrant offering, an acceptable sacrifice, pleasing to God. And my God will meet all your needs according to his glorious riches in Christ Jesus (Philippians 4:14-19, emphasis added).

Paul had a confidence that God would always provide what he needed. Sometimes it came from his business. Sometimes it came through others. He was not overly concerned with where his provision would come from. His confidence was in God.

Paul learned that it wasn't a church or a business that was his provider. It was God. The funds he received were merely tools that God used to support him.

CONFRONTING YOUR INDUSTRY CULTURE

Jesus entered the temple area and drove out all who were buying and selling there. He overturned the tables of the money changers and the benches of those selling doves. "It is written," he said to them, "My house will be called a house of prayer, but you are making it a 'den of robbers.'"

MATTHEW 21:12-13

Sometimes, a corporate culture dictates the way business is conducted because the corporation was established years ago. We simply inherit whatever the accepted practice is. But some of these practices violate a biblical principle. For instance, some businesses withhold payment on invoices for 60, 90 or 120 days as a form of cash management, which places a heavy burden on suppliers. Some government custom's employees require a bribe in order to get products into their country. One nation thinks nothing about their practice of software piracy because it has simply become a part of their culture.

God never allows for situational ethics. There are absolutes in the kingdom of God. The Word of God does not change because of culture or accepted practice.

It was an "industry practice" to sell doves in the Temple. But Jesus never accepted the practice because He knew it was turning a holy place of prayer into a commercial enterprise. It did not matter that it was an accepted practice.

God calls each of us to operate from a plumb line of righteousness in our work life, no matter the consequence. Zerubbabel, for example, led the first band of Jews to return from Babylonian captivity in the first year of Cyrus, King of Persia (see the book of Ezra). He is noted for laying the foundation of the second temple in Jerusalem the next year. He was a leader who managed with integrity and righteousness, a man who God and others wanted in charge. "Men will rejoice when they see the plumb line in the hand of Zerubbabel" (Zechariah 4:10).

Evaluate your industry practices and make sure you are not violating God's Word. Let your plumb line be measured by His precepts.

CONCEALING A MATTER

*He who conceals his sins does not prosper, but whoever confesses
and renounces them finds mercy.*

PROVERBS 28:13

None of us is immune from making poor choices in our lives. David made a number of poor choices that snowballed into an avalanche of suffering, shame and tragedy. It started when he chose to stay at home in Jerusalem instead of going out to lead his troops into battle, as was his duty. David had too much time on his hands, which ultimately led to him committing adultery with Bathsheba and trying to cover up that sin with murder.

God sent the prophet Nathan to tell King David a story. He began by telling David that there were two men in a town: one rich and one poor. The rich man had many sheep and cattle. The poor man had nothing but one little ewe lamb, which he raised like one of the family. The ewe lamb shared the man's food, drank from his cup and slept in his arms. One day when the rich man had a guest to entertain, he didn't want to slaughter any of his own sheep or cattle, so he took the poor man's lamb, killed it, and prepared it as a feast for his guest (see 2 Samuel 12:1-4).

David responded, "As surely as the LORD lives, the man who did this deserves to die! He must pay for that lamb four times over, because he did such a thing and had not pity" (v. 5).

Then Nathan turned to King David and said, "You are the man! . . . Why did you despise the word of the LORD by doing what is evil in His eyes? You struck down Uriah the Hittite with the sword and took his wife to be your own!" (vv. 7,9). To his credit, David confessed and repented of his sins, and God forgave him.

God's forgiveness restores the broken relationship between Himself and the sinner, but forgiveness can't make everything exactly as it was. Sin has consequences that forgiveness cannot change. David had consequences he had to live with for the rest of his life.

Every good or bad act begins as a thought with an underlying motive. Today, ask God to take every thought captive and make every motive pure before Him.

ACCEPTING GOD'S DESIGN

Does not the potter have the right to make out of the same lump of clay
some pottery for noble purposes and some for common use?
ROMANS 9:21

Angie and I had just started dating. One night at a restaurant, she brushed her hair behind her ears and said, "Check out my ear. See how much bigger the left one is than the right?" I was shocked. How was I supposed to respond to that?

I began to stammer and said that her ear really wasn't that much bigger . . . but honestly, it was. I had never seen anything quite like it. Angie often jokes and says that when God was putting her together He must have dropped one of her ears on the floor and picked up the wrong one and put that on instead.

Have you ever wished that God made you differently? Perhaps you wished you were more athletic or could have a totally different career. Or perhaps you wished you were prettier or taller or even had a different nose. Or, as in Angie's case, had a smaller ear.

God made every person different and for different purposes. It is important to know and be at peace with how and why God made you. Paul tells us in Romans that we are all crafted out of the same clay. There is no one molded and shaped like you. No one has the exact personality. Your DNA is one of a kind.

God uses the common to produce the uncommon. No matter how inferior you may feel, you are in a particular area in which God desires to use you for His purposes. Your unique qualities are made to fit with the way He plans to use you for His purposes. This is why we must accept our uniqueness. We want God's power to be manifested in our individuality.

One day when Angie and her friend were getting their nails done, the manicurist remarked that God did not make mistakes. Angie was quick to point out her big ear. Without missing a beat, the manicurist said, "I bet you hear better out of that ear!" In a flash of revelation, Angie realized that she did, and they all burst all laughing.

God does not make mistakes. Thank Him today for the way He made you!

BEWARE OF MIXTURE

Then they said, "These are your gods, O Israel,
who brought you up out of Egypt."
EXODUS 32:4

Moses went up to Mount Sinai to meet with God and to receive the Ten Commandments. While he was gone, he left his brother, Aaron, in charge. Moses had mentored Aaron, but we learn that Aaron still had vestiges of Egypt residing in him. He had not yet had a complete conversion from the ways of Egypt to the ways of God. His leadership was not strong enough to thwart a rebellion in the camp, and he allowed the people to make an idol of gold. Later, he tried to justify his actions by saying that the idol was a God of Israel.

Today, we see similar mixtures in the Body of Christ. We promote guaranteed prosperity without the cross. We call adversity a sign of a lack of faith. We promote New Age philosophies mixed with the Scriptures and call it a new freedom in Christ. This is not only mixture—it is an abomination to the Lord.

Because Aaron had a mixture in his own life, he was unable to be truthful to Moses when confronted with his actions. "He said to Aaron, 'What did these people do to you, that you led them into such great sin?' . . . So I told them, 'Whoever has any gold jewelry, take it off.' Then they gave me the gold, and I threw it into the fire, and out came this calf!" (Exodus 32:21-24).

Did you notice Aaron's explanation? "Out came this calf"—all by itself! Aaron attempted to deceive Moses. He failed to fulfill his role as a strong, godly leader. He allowed mixture to have power over the people of God.

Today, we live in a time in which tolerance is encouraged at the expense of truth. Pray that you will be faithful to the Word of God and not allow new philosophies to distort Scripture's ageless truths.

ARE YOU USEFUL?

*Formerly he was useless to you, but now he has
become useful both to you and to me.*

PHILEMON 1:11

Onesimus was the slave of a man named Philemon. In Paul's letter, he reveals that Philemon viewed Onesimus as useless. But while Paul was in chains, Onesimus came and helped him greatly during his time of need. Paul wanted to show in his letter to Philemon that Onesimus was useful instead of useless.

When Jesus met Peter, He saw an impetuous man who drew quick conclusions and who was very opinionated. I'm sure others had doubts about the wisdom of using Peter for future leadership, but Jesus saw something in Peter that would be useful once the rough edges were removed.

Both Peter and Paul were simple fools in the kingdom of God—and I don't mean this as an insult! A *simple* fool, or *peti*, is a person who makes mistakes but quickly rights them and is restored to fellowship with God and others. King David was a *simple* fool. He made mistakes, but he always kept a repentant heart toward God. This is why God did not turn away from him for his many sins.

On the other hand, the hardened fool, *kesil* and *ewil*, makes mistakes, never learns from them, is not repentant and will not listen to others. These people can expect God's reproof to continue in their lives and will eat the fruit of their own way (see Proverbs 1:31-32). King Saul was a hardened fool. He made mistakes and continued to do so even after realizing that he was wrong.

We are going to err in our ways. The question is, once we know we have made a mistake before God, will we make the necessary adjustments that will allow Him to intervene on our behalf? Will we avoid the same course of action in the future? God says, "If you had responded to my rebuke, I would have poured out my heart to you and made my thoughts known to you" (Proverbs 1:23).

When you work with people who have strong personalities but may be immature in their faith, you must discern if they are simple fools or hardened fools. This will tell you whether or not to invest time and resources into them.

THE PERFECTIONIST

Moses said to the LORD, "O Lord, I have never been eloquent, neither in the past nor since you have spoken to your servant. I am slow of speech and tongue."
EXODUS 4:10

One of the greatest affronts you can commit against God is to refuse the calling that He has placed upon you. Imagine arguing with your Creator and telling Him that you know better than Him.

That is exactly what Moses did when God called him to be His spokesperson to Pharaoh. God and Moses got into an "I know best" competition: "The Lord said to him, 'Who gave man his mouth? Who makes him deaf or mute? Who gives him sight or makes him blind? Is it not I, the Lord? Now go; I will help you speak and will teach you what to say.' But Moses said, 'O Lord, please send someone else to do it'" (Exodus 4:11-13).

God actually relented in the argument. Can you imagine that? But He was not happy about it. "Then the LORD's anger burned against Moses and he said, 'What about your brother, Aaron the Levite?'" (Exodus 4:14). Because of Moses' defiance, God had to use Aaron as Moses' mouthpiece.

Have you ever not pursued something because it had to be perfect? There is a fine line between doing things with excellence and being a perfectionist. Perfectionists become argumentative with God. They refuse to step out in faith and obedience because they care too much about what others think if the results don't turn out perfectly.

I battled these same demons when God led me into a writing and speaking ministry. I prayed, *Lord, I am weak in grammar, and You know I'm an introvert.* Then He reminded me that His "power is made perfect in weakness" (2 Corinthians 12:9).

When God places His anointing on you, He uses whatever level of skill you have to fulfill His purposes in your life. This is why you need not fear moving into an unfamiliar area if He calls you there.

What is God waiting for you to do? It may be time to step out. He specializes in "cliff-catching."

CALLED TO THE MINISTRY

Usually a person should keep on with the work he was doing when God called him.
1 CORINTHIANS 7:20, *TLB*

We've all heard stories of men or women in the workplace who left their jobs for the ministry. Certainly, God does call people into vocational ministry. However, many times this move is more rooted in dissatisfaction with a career in combination with a spiritual renewal or first time commitment to the Lord. The idea of a higher call can also appeal to our sense of a greater and nobler destiny.

We have incorrectly elevated the role of the Christian worker that serves within the Church or a traditional ministry as more holy and committed than the person who is serving in a secular environment. Yet the call to the secular workplace is as important as any other calling. God has to have His people in every sphere of life to meet the needs of His creation. Also, without Christians in the workplace, many would never come to know Jesus, because believers would be separated from society.

I learned this lesson personally when I sought to go into full-time service as a pastor in my late 20s, only to have God thrust me back into the workplace unwillingly. This turned out to be the best thing He could have done for me, because it was never His will for me to be a pastor. He knew I was more suited for the workplace.

We are all in missions. Some are called to foreign lands. Some are called to the jungles of the workplace. Wherever you are called, serve the Lord in that place. Let Him demonstrate His power through your life so that others might experience Him through you today. View your vocation as means to worship Him.

Paul said it right: In most cases we are going to remain in the place where He first called us.

CREATING YOUR NICHE

*Sixty queens there may be, and eighty concubines, and virgins
beyond number; but my dove, my perfect one, is unique.*
SONG OF SOLOMON 6:8-9

Your business must have a unique niche if you wish to separate yourself from others to compete in the marketplace. This is especially true if you are competing in an industry crowded with competition in which low price is a driving incentive for the customer.

It used to be that a cup of coffee was just a cup of coffee. Then a company came along and completely changed the rules. They violated every marketing rule: They overpriced their product, they changed the language—a small is a "tall," a medium is "grande." You get the idea.

Starbucks, the specialty coffee retailer, is one of the great twenty-first-century American success stories. Considered one of the most successful and admired companies today, Starbucks has grown from a single store begun by a Jewish man in Seattle 33 years ago to now having more than 12,000 stores. Of those stores, almost 4,000 are located in countries outside of the United States. In 2006, the company posted revenues of more than $8 billion.[45] Cup by cup, Starbucks has changed the way people drink coffee.

More remarkably, the company successfully transformed a pedestrian commodity into a high-end accessory, creating a "Starbucks lifestyle" that more people continue to embrace in the United States and abroad.

If you're thinking about starting a business or making an existing business better, ask yourself this question: "What's unique about my business or product?"

God created each of us to be unique. Define this uniqueness in your work life, promote it with integrity and you'll have a good chance for success.

WHEN SERVICE EXCEEDS DEVOTION

*She had a sister called Mary, who sat at the Lord's feet
listening to what he said.*

LUKE 10:39

There is a story of a Western missionary group that was sitting with a for-eign visitor, planning strategy for an upcoming evangelistic trip to his coun-try. One man led in prayer, asking for God's help in planning their activities. The visitor was surprised at how the meeting quickly moved to the planning phase after only a few minutes of focused prayer.

He turned to the leader and said, "You have taught us the Scriptures well in our country. However, I've noticed that when it comes to prayer, you spend so little time in listening and much time in planning." The Western believers were convicted by his words.

In the Bible, there is a similar message about listening versus doing. Martha was Mary's older sister. Older sisters always think they know best. They tend to mother the younger siblings. When Jesus came over to spend an evening at their home, Martha wanted Mary to help her to pre-pare a special meal, but Mary was spending all her time in the living room listening to Jesus. Finally, Martha felt compelled to appeal to Jesus about the situation:

> She came to him and asked, "Lord, don't you care that my sister has left me to do the work by myself? Tell her to help me!" "Martha, Martha," the Lord answered, "you are worried and upset about many things, but only one thing is needed. Mary has chosen what is better, and it will not be taken away from her" (Luke 10:40-42).

Jesus reveals a danger in this story that each of us must be aware of. When our concern for *serving* Jesus exceeds our need to *be with* Jesus, we are in danger of focusing on the lesser thing. The hardest thing for most work-place believers is to sit and listen. It is easier to do.

Today, begin to spend more time listening before you begin doing.

SEEING THE ORDINARY AS EXTRAORDINARY

Whether you eat or drink or whatever you do, do it all for the glory of God.
1 CORINTHIANS 10:31

Our Lord never saw mundane activities as ordinary. Whether He healed the sick or sat around the fire with the disciples, He did not see one activity as spiritual and another as non-spiritual. Instead, He lived all of life as a holy service to His heavenly Father.

Many times, we fall prey to a spiritual hierarchy mentality. We believe certain activities are more blessed by God because they are done under a spiritual guise. We conduct our Christian meetings and conclude that God's blessing is equated to the level of attendance. We work to give money to ministry but fail to recognize that the very work we *do* is ministry.

God's glory can be expressed in the most common task, whether washing the dishes, changing diapers or driving to the grocery store. Every activity should be rooted in the motive of our heart. When we recognize that everything we do can have spiritual value, we avoid the trap of placing certain activities into a spiritual hierarchy.

Philip was in the midst of a major crusade when the Holy Spirit abruptly instructed him to stop and go to a desert road. He went down to a city in Samaria and proclaimed the Christ there. When the crowds heard Philip and saw the miraculous signs he did, they all paid close attention to what he said: "Now an angel of the Lord said to Philip, 'Go south to the road—the desert road—that goes down from Jerusalem to Gaza.' So he started out, and on his way he met an Ethiopian eunuch, an important official in charge of all the treasury of Candace, queen of the Ethiopians. This man had gone to Jerusalem to worship, and on his way home was sitting in his chariot reading the book of Isaiah the prophet. The Spirit told Philip, 'Go to that chariot and stay near it'" (Acts 8:26-29).

We see in this story that neither activity was more important than the other. Philip's job was to live in communion with the Holy Spirit and be obedient to His promptings.

Today, view every activity you do with an attitude of worship and communion with Jesus.

HIGH POSITIONS

*The brother in humble circumstances ought to
take pride in his high position.*
JAMES 1:9

Whenever God brings a saint to a very lowly state, it is to accomplish something only that condition can do. Job's trials allowed him to learn things about God, himself and his friends that we all need to know as well. He assumed things about God that he had to recant: "Surely I spoke of things I did not understand, things too wonderful for me to know" (Job 42:3).

God reveals things in the dark places of our circumstances that will be used to reveal something He wants you and others to know. He has sent you ahead to learn these things so that you and others will benefit from your unique experience. God views this place of humility, where you receive these truths, as a high position. The world views it as a place to be despised.

Joseph was led to this high position:

He called down a famine on the land and destroyed all their supplies of food; and he sent a man before them—Joseph, sold as a slave. They bruised his feet with shackles, his neck was put in irons, till what he foretold came to pass, till the word of the LORD proved him true (Psalms 105:16-19).

It was here, as a 30-year-old, that Joseph was prepared to be the most powerful man in the world. He learned many things about God during his captivity that he used later as a ruler over a nation.

If you find yourself in a lowly state, realize that God considers your lowly state to be a high position. He is using adversity in your life as preparation for revealing deep things that He desires you to learn from the dark places.

He will use these experiences to frame your life for the message He has for you to share with others.

SEPTEMBER 10

ROAD CONSTRUCTION

The crooked places shall be made straight and the rough places smooth;
The glory of the LORD shall be revealed, and all flesh shall see it together.
ISAIAH 40:4-5, NKJV

I don't know about you, but I hate road construction. I live in a growing city, and it seems like there has been ongoing road construction for years. Everything is a mess and I can never plan my trips because of delays. Sometimes I get caught off guard when traffic signs are placed in unusual places and the natural flow of traffic takes me off the main road onto bumpy surfaces.

Recently, one of our main local roads developed a sinkhole. The road was closed for more than a year. We had to take alternative routes that were inconvenient, and it took longer to get places.

Sometimes God takes us through our own reconstruction project. Our lives get disrupted, we can no longer depend on the things we did before and we don't have control over our circumstances or timetable. God is doing major reconstruction.

However, even in the midst of the reconstruction, the glory of the Lord is revealed in that place. For some of us, it is the first time we've ever seen the hand of the Lord move at such a degree. Reconstruction is a process we would never choose to go through voluntarily, but it is an experience we value for the rest of our lives, because the glory of the Lord was revealed in the process.

Once the process is complete, things begin to flow better. Just as the new roads allow us to drive on a smooth and more spacious area, God paves a way for us to move into an expanded place with Him. Isaiah tells us, "He will also send you rain for the seed you sow in the ground, and the food that comes from the land will be rich and plentiful. In that day your cattle will graze in broad meadows" (Isaiah 30:23).

Be patient with God's reconstruction project. You will like the finished project.

TURNING TRAGEDY INTO TRIUMPH

So then, death is at work in us, but life is at work in you.
2 CORINTHIANS 4:12

On September 11, 2001, New York City firefighter Stephen Siller had just completed his shift when he heard on his truck's scanner that a plane had hit one of the World Trade Center towers. Siller quickly turned his truck around and attempted to drive back to Manhattan via the Brooklyn Battery Tunnel but found the entrance blocked by abandoned vehicles. Desperate to join his elite Squad One brothers, Siller donned 75 pounds of fire gear and ran a mile and a half through the tunnel before an emergency vehicle picked him up and dropped him off at Tower Two.

Siller had been orphaned at the age of 10 and was raised by his much older brothers and sisters. Siller died that day trying to save others. He left behind a wife and five children. His story proved so inspirational that it became a legend in the newsrooms and firehouses of New York City. His six siblings—who in many ways viewed Siller as a son as well as a brother—found themselves grappling with a dilemma: Should they allow the tragic circumstances of their brother's death to paralyze and embitter them or use it as a catalyst to help others and preserve his memory?

The Siller family chose the latter. Once they made that decision, armed with no extraordinary wealth or political clout, the siblings combined forces to convince New York officials to close down the Brooklyn Battery Tunnel the last Sunday morning of each September to stage the "Tunnel to Towers Run" in honor of their brother's heroic last run.

Each year since 9/11, tens of thousands of runners have retraced the steps of a hero. As part of the event, 343 New York City firefighters, each representing a fallen comrade and holding an American flag, stand throughout the length of the tunnel. They are joined by firefighters from across the United States, each holding a poster-size picture of a firefighter who perished on 9/11. The Siller family has raised more than $1 million and has donated the money to charities that benefit families of those affected by the 9/11 attacks.[46]

This is a tribute to one heartbroken family who opted to turn their tragedy into triumph.

THE WIZARD OF OZ

I am the LORD, the God of Israel, who summons you by name.
ISAIAH 45:3

During a workplace conference I met Ed, a small business owner of a marketing communications company. We struck up a conversation, and I immediately felt a kindred spirit between us. I appreciated his obvious talent and began an exchange by email about providing services to our organization. At a later conference Ed came up to me and shared a wonderful supernatural story of how God had led him to connect with me:

> Driving to church one evening, a license plate on a car in front of me grabbed my attention. I don't recall the numbers on the plate, but the last three letters were OZZ. I felt that God caused me to focus on this and it kept coming to mind as I continued to drive to the service. During the service, a friend who has prophetic gifts came up to me and began to speak to me concerning things the Lord was doing in my work life. She finished by saying that "God had not given me the scarecrow, the tin man or the lion, but He had given me OZ."
>
> Needless to say that got my attention and I continually asked the Lord what He meant. Several months later, after attending a LifeWorks conference at our church, I was writing an email to Os Hillman about some work I was doing for him. As I began to type the salutation, "Dear Os," I felt a rush that Os Hillman was the OZ of the prophecy and the OZZ from the license plate! When I called my friend to tell her about this, she became so excited about the connection.
>
> My connection to Os and Marketplace Leaders has proven to be an incredible blessing to me personally as well as professionally. While at the conference, the Lord continually affirmed my call in the workplace and fulfilled a significant dream I had nine years ago.

Friend, God knows you by name. There are people and circumstances that God will orchestrate to bring you into the place He has for you. Be aware of the divine appointments He may bring into your life today.

AFFIRMING NEW LEADERSHIP

But Moses replied, "Are you jealous for my sake? I wish that all the LORD's people were prophets and that the LORD would put his Spirit on them!"

NUMBERS 11:29

One of the attributes of a Kingdom leader is the ability to recognize when God is raising new leadership and affirming and encouraging up-and-coming leaders. Kingdom leaders also model a level of humility that God blesses, while leaders who are insecure about their leadership will put down new leadership in order to maintain their own status.

The Bible says that Moses was the most humble man on the face of the earth. That is why God used him as a leader to bring an entire nation out of bondage.

Joshua, Moses' second in command, was concerned about two young men who had prophesied in the camp. He considered their actions an affront to Moses' leadership. But Moses viewed the situation very differently. He viewed it from the perspective of a Kingdom leader and modeled humility and a Kingdom focus. Moses was secure in his own leadership and did not need to put down others who he might construe as usurping his leadership.

King Saul represented the opposite of this principle. The people began to see that God was raising David into leadership. However, because Saul had a stronghold of insecurity in his life, he was not able to affirm God's new leader. This ultimately led to Saul's removal from the kingship. God rejected Saul because of his inability to humble himself before an upcoming leader.

The Body of Christ is in great need of leaders who are secure in their leadership. If God has called you to be a leader, look for opportunities to encourage new leaders. As you do, God will ensure that you will fulfill the purpose for which He called you.

OPPOSING GOD'S LEADERSHIP

The anger of the LORD burned against them, and he left them.
NUMBERS 12:9

Beware of trying to depose a leader that God has raised up in your midst. God places leaders in business, government, churches—everywhere leaders are required. When God places a person in a position of authority, it is a grievous sin to go against that leadership. God Himself opposes those who come against His leaders.

God's leaders are not perfect. They make mistakes. That is why following a leader can require a faith that goes beyond faith in the leader. Our faith must lie in the God who has elevated the leader to his or her position.

Miriam and Aaron, the older brother and sister of Moses, had a family dispute about Moses' wife, who was an Ethiopian and Cushite. We do not know the nature of the dispute, but we can assume that it was a typical family conflict.

The "typical" family conflict began to impact God's agenda for a nation. Miriam and Aaron were meddling in God's business—they were calling Moses' judgment into question, and God did not like that in the least. As a consequence for rebelling against His appointed leader, God brought Aaron and Miriam into the "switching house." He judged both Miriam and Aaron for their rebellion against His ordained leader.

Miriam was stricken with leprosy, and had it not been for Moses' appeal on her behalf, she would have been cast out for good. God gave her a second chance, but it required that she first be cast away from the camp for seven days. Miriam and Aaron repented for their rebellion.

If you struggle with a leader that God has over you, pray for that leader. If God wants to remove that leader, He can do it. But you should think twice about conspiring to remove a leader whom God has not chosen to remove.

THE MERCY GIFT

Here I am! I stand at the door and knock. If anyone hears my voice and opens the door, I will come in and eat with him, and he with me.

R E V E L A T I O N 3:20

I am constantly amazed that the Creator of the universe wants to have an intimate relationship with us. While we frantically search for that certain something to make us happy, God stands there the entire time, saying, "Here I am!" The Scripture in Revelation says that He stands at our door and knocks. If only we would take the time to listen and invite Him in! My neighbor Gerry told my wife and me a story that gave us the perfect picture of this concept.

Gerry is single, an attorney by vocation and works from his home. He has an amazing gift of mercy, an incredible love for animals and a malfunctioning front door. His door doesn't shut properly, and the only way to keep the door closed is to lock it, which Gerry rarely does. One day while working at home, he heard his front door open. When he investigated the noise, he discovered that Buddy, one of the neighborhood dogs, had let himself in by pushing on the front door.

Gerry gave him a treat and day after day, Buddy would come and visit. Each day it was the same routine. Buddy would push the door open, stand in the foyer and patiently wait for Gerry to come and give him a treat. He never forced his way in or begged for food—he always waited for Gerry to come to him. And Gerry always came. A few weeks later, Buddy started bringing his friends—other dogs in the neighborhood—and soon the dogs started hanging out for days before they would go back home.

Angie and I laugh as we often drive by Gerry's house and see his front door wide open. We know that inside he is enjoying the fellowship of the neighborhood dogs.

We can have that same fellowship with Jesus when we open the doors of our hearts to Him. He is standing at the door, waiting for you to invite Him in.

VICTORIA'S FRIENDS

*If we confess our sins, he is faithful and just and will forgive us
our sins and purify us from all unrighteousness.*

1 JOHN 1:9

Victoria grew up like many middle-income families. She loved school and was in homecoming court all four years in high school. However, after some tragic family deaths during her teen years, she began to experiment with alcohol and drugs. She was raped, underwent multiple abortions and worked for more than four years as a dancer at a local nude dancing club.

After suffering nosebleeds from her cocaine addition, Victoria became very involved with the New Age movement, nearly had a nervous breakdown and eventually became suicidal. By the age of 28 she was homeless, stranded and fired from her job as a strip-club dancer. At barely 100 pounds, she was no longer profitable to the industry.

It was then that a Christian gave her a Bible. The first book she read was Job, and something in his story gripped her heart. Soon a church family took her into their home. They surrounded her with love and pointed her to who she was in Christ.

Now, years later, Victoria's compassionate heart is focused on reaching other lives on the brink of life and death. She testifies that "Jesus is the only healer of deep, deep wounds." Because of her salvation experience, she founded a ministry called Victoria's Friends, which goes into the heart of the darkest places of the city, in the strip clubs. Trained women ministry volunteers bring baskets to the dancers in their dressing rooms with no motive other than to show that they care. Men stay outside the clubs and pray for the women going inside.

It is the ultimate rescue mission. It is the love of Christ expressed in a simple but powerful way. Hundreds of young women have come out of this lifestyle because one woman decided to do what others had done for her—rescue her from the pit of darkness.

What type of rescue mission might God call you to lead?

COMPLETING THE WORK

*I have brought you glory on earth by completing
the work you gave me to do.*

JOHN 17:4

Have you ever had a big project to do? Did you feel great when you finished the job and it was a big success? Angie worked on a big project during the 1996 Olympics that involved placing 2,000 family members of foreign athletes into Christian homes. It was a massive project, but it was a rewarding experience to see the job completed.

The Lord has revealed to us that the number one thing we are to do is to love the Lord our God with all our heart and to love our neighbors as ourselves. His desire is for us to know Him and the power of His resurrection. These mandates deal with our relationship with Him. The fruit of this relationship must then result in our glorifying Him by completing the work He has given each of us to do. Work will become a by-product of this relationship, not an end in itself.

What is the work God has called you to do? Jesus never did anything the Father had not instructed Him to do. He lived in such communion with the Father that He knew when to turn to the left and when to turn to the right. Is it possible for us to have such a relationship with our heavenly Father? I think that if it weren't, He would not have given us such an example.

The Lord says, "Call to me and I will answer you and tell you great and unsearchable things you do not know" (Jeremiah 33:3). What has He called you to do? Perhaps you are called to be the best lawyer in your city, or the best advertising executive, or the best office worker or assembly line person in your company. Whatever work He has called you to, He will use you as His instrument to accomplish something that He has uniquely prepared you to do.

When our life is complete, what a glorious day it will be if we can each say, "I have completed the work you gave me to do." This will have brought great glory to Him.

RECEIVING BAD NEWS

Also our enemies said, "Before they know it or see us, we will be right there among them and will kill them and put an end to the work."
NEHEMIAH 4:11

I opened the letter from the attorney and began to read the contents. The more I read, the more I could not believe the words. I literally felt sick with fear. Perhaps you've had a similar experience. Maybe you got news that you've got cancer or that someone has had an accident or that you are being sued.

Nehemiah was rebuilding the wall in Jerusalem. The going was tough. As if things were not tough enough, he got a letter from another corrupt government official threatening to kill anyone involved in rebuilding the wall:

> But when Sanballat, Tobiah, the Arabs, the Ammonites and the men of Ashdod heard that the repairs to Jerusalem's walls had gone ahead and that the gaps were being closed, they were very angry. They all plotted together to come and fight against Jerusalem and stir up trouble against it. But we prayed to our God and posted a guard day and night to meet this threat (Nehemiah 4:7-9).

There is only one response we should have to bad news: We should pray to our God and take the necessary steps to defend ourselves against the threat. This was Nehemiah's response. Once you begin to take these actions, avoid projecting what might happen to you in the future. This is a surefire first step toward depression. Ask God's grace for one day at a time:

> Consider the ravens: They do not sow or reap, they have no storeroom or barn; yet God feeds them. And how much more valuable you are than birds! Who of you by worrying can add a single hour to his life? Since you cannot do this very little thing, why do you worry about the rest? (Luke 12:24-26).

Turn your bad news over to the Lord. Allow the God of the storm to bring peace into your situation. He specializes in turning crises into opportunities.

USING OTHERS

So in everything, do to others what you would have them do to you, for this sums up the Law and the Prophets.

MATTHEW 7:12

Have you ever heard the phrase "money talks"? This old cliché has some truth to it. How we handle money speaks very loudly about our values, especially among those in the marketplace.

One of the common business practices today is to extend payment on invoices to extend a company's cash flow. Bigger companies often insist upon even longer times between payments. This delayed payment policy violates a basic biblical principle:

> Give everyone what you owe him: If you owe taxes, pay taxes; if revenue, then revenue; if respect, then respect; if honor, then honor (Romans 13:7).

Because this practice is so prevalent, businesses that honor their vendors with on-time payments stand out from the crowd.

One of our greatest opportunities to show that we are different is through practical matters of being faithful to our obligations. True servanthood is revealed when we have the best interests of others in mind. This means not always seeking to negotiate the lowest price for services but rather making sure the price is fair and honors the vendor for his or her service or product. "For in the same way you judge others, you will be judged, and with the measure you use, it will be measured to you" (Matthew 7:2).

Use money to demonstrate your respect of others by paying others in a timely manner. How you treat others in this area reveals what you *really* believe.

INNOVATION

In the beginning God created the heavens and the earth.
GENESIS 1:1

"The concept is interesting and well-formed, but in order to earn better than a C, the idea must be feasible."

Those were the words of a Yale University management professor in response to Fred Smith's paper in which he proposed a reliable overnight delivery service. Smith went on to found Federal Express, the number one overnight delivery service in the world with 260,000 employees. Founder Fred Smith is synonymous with the word "innovation."

There have been many great innovators who have turned concepts into successful companies. Walt Disney said, "It's kind of fun to do the impossible."

God is the source of all creativity and innovation. He created the world in seven days. He has made you like Him—to create. If God has placed an idea in your heart, ask the Lord for His help in bringing it to reality. He desires to see His people create new things that can serve mankind and bring glory to God.

Faith plays an important role when we are considering stepping out to launch a new endeavor. "Now faith is being sure of what we hope for and certain of what we do not see. This is what the ancients were commended for" (Hebrews 11:1-2).

Perhaps you've failed in the past and you're afraid to step out again. Most successful entrepreneurs failed several times before they were successful. Don't let fear of failure keep you from success. Take the first step toward your dream.

You were made to create. You were made to succeed.

MODELING CHRIST TO YOUR EMPLOYER

*Urge slaves to obey their masters and to try their best to satisfy them. They must
not talk back, nor steal, but must show themselves to be entirely trustworthy.
In this way they will make people want to believe in our Savior and God.*

TITUS 2:9-10, *TLB*

Sometimes I hear people say that they don't see how they can have any significant impact on their workplace because they are low on the totem pole, with little authority to make change. "I'm just a worker," they say. They fail to realize that the authority to impact any workplace comes from God, not man. And each person can have great authority in God.

The apostle Paul instructed Titus about how common workers on the island of Crete could have an impact on their employers. These workers were often no more than slaves, working in deplorable conditions for masters who were likely involved in lawlessness, drunkenness and idolatry. Not the nicest of working conditions! Paul felt that the way to win over these types of employers was to follow several key principles: (1) don't talk back, (2) don't steal, and (3) be trustworthy.

There is a great example in the Bible of a young girl who worked for an army commander named Naaman. Naaman had leprosy and the godly servant girl from Israel told her employer how he could get healed:

Now Naaman was commander of the army of the king of Aram. . . .
He was a valiant soldier, but he had leprosy. Now bands from Aram
had gone out and had taken captive a young girl from Israel, and she
served Naaman's wife. She said to her mistress, "If only my master
would see the prophet who is in Samaria! He would cure him of his
leprosy" (2 Kings 5:1-3).

Naaman followed the advice of the lowly servant girl, and God healed him through Elisha. I can only imagine the conversations between the servant girl and her employers after this healing occurred!

How might God want to use you in your employer's life? Today, be aware of opportunities in which God might want you to be a catalyst for His use.

EMPOWERING OTHERS

I tell you the truth, anyone who has faith in me will do what I have been doing.
He will do even greater things than these, because I am going to the Father.
JOHN 14:12

A CEO was excited that he'd found the right man to be general manager of his growing enterprise. He had all the training, the right skill set and great people skills. The CEO gave him all authority to fulfill his role. However, after six months the CEO had to fire him. The general manager refused to use the authority given him to accomplish his tasks.

Great leaders, mentors and managers must empower others to fulfill the mission of any organization. Jesus invested time and energy developing leaders. Only at the point at which they could properly manage the resource did Jesus empower them. He knew that the teacher who offers authority too early sets up followers for failure. On the other hand, the leader who fails to empower capable people creates frustration.

Good empowerment also involves engaging your follower to use the authority entrusted to him or her to fulfill the mission. Jesus imparted to His followers a proper balance of authority to fulfill the mission He gave to them. They had to learn the freedom and boundaries in exercising that God-given authority.

Peter, for example, was not ready for leadership before the crucifixion. He failed to use the authority given to him by Jesus. It required a failure in Peter's life before he matured in his leadership. However, once Peter began to appropriate what Jesus had imparted to him, he became a powerful and effective leader.

Empowering others is a key attribute of a leader who wants to advance his or her followers' mission.

STAYING THE COURSE

*Then the angel of the LORD ordered Gad to tell David to go up and build an altar
to the LORD on the threshing floor of Araunah the Jebusite. So David went up in
obedience to the word that Gad had spoken in the name of the LORD.*

1 CHRONICLES 21:18-19

In 1857, an American businessman named Jeremiah Lanphier was sent out
by his local church to begin a noonday prayer meeting on Fulton Street, right
around the corner from Wall Street, in New York City. His simple prayer, willing heart and act of obedience resulted in transformation throughout the
United States.

At the very first meeting, no one showed up in the first 35 minutes.
Jeremiah waited. Then six people wandered into the room. Six months later,
10,000 people were meeting for prayer throughout New York City. This led
to one of the greatest spiritual renewals in United States history.

In a small, darkened room, in the back of one of New York City's lesser churches, a man prayed alone. His request of God was simple, but
earth-shattering: "Lord, what wilt Thou have me to do?" He was a
man approaching midlife, without a wife or family, but he had financial means. He had made a decision to reject the "success syndrome"
that drove the city's businessmen and bankers. God used this businessman to turn New York City's commercial empire on its head.
He began a businessmen's prayer meeting on September 23, 1857.

The meetings began slowly, but within a few months 20 noonday meetings were convening daily throughout the city. Thousands
met to pray because one man stepped out. This was an extraordinary move of God through one man.[47]

What would have happened if Lanphier had decided to abandon the
idea after 30 minutes? It only takes one willing and obedient man or woman
to impact a workplace, city or even an entire nation. Simple obedience to the
small assignments can lead to things you cannot imagine.

THE CHURCH

*Five of you will chase a hundred, and a hundred of you will chase ten thousand,
and your enemies will fall by the sword before you.*

The Church of Jesus Christ is called to impact the world. The Greek word for "church" in the New Testament (*ekklesia*) does not denote an institution or building—it simply means "the people of God." Jesus said that wherever two or more meet together, He is there in the midst of them.

The New Testament uses the word "church" in two different ways. Sometimes it refers to the people of God gathered together in congregations—that is, our traditional idea of the local church. But other times, it means believers in general, wherever they might find themselves.

God calls the Church to be transformers of society through their collective influence. Jesus prayed that His Church would be unified *in order for the world to respond to Him*. He prayed:

May they be brought to complete unity to let the world know that you sent me and have loved them even as you have loved me (John 17:23).

When local congregations fail to come together as a collective voice and operate instead as individual silos in their community, a door is opened for society to be given over to the evil known as secularism—a religion that says there is no God. Conversely, when the Body of Christ—the Church—puts its collective resources together to solve societal issues, our enemies of crime, poverty, sexual perversion and such will fall.

God is birthing coalitions of His Church among congregations in cities across the world in order to fulfill the prophecy of John 17:23. Are you willing to be a catalyst in your community to see His Church take back your city?

GOD IS THE GOD OF SUCCESS

If you fully obey the LORD your God and carefully follow all his commands I give you today, the LORD your God will set you high above all the nations on earth.
DEUTERONOMY 28:1

Our God is a God of success. God created you to be a success. However, success is rooted in our relationship with God, not in our abilities. When our abilities are separated from our relationship with God, success is short-lived:

All these blessings will come upon you and accompany you if you obey the LORD your God: You will be blessed in the city and blessed in the country. The fruit of your womb will be blessed, and the crops of your land and the young of your livestock—the calves of your herds and the lambs of your flocks. Your basket and your kneading trough will be blessed. You will be blessed when you come in and blessed when you go out. The LORD will grant that the enemies who rise up against you will be defeated before you. They will come at you from one direction but flee from you in seven. The LORD will send a blessing on your barns and on everything you put your hand to. The LORD your God will bless you in the land he is giving you (Deuteronomy 28:2-8).

Sometimes God allows us to fail in order for us to succeed. Each of us must first experience our own death and resurrection from our old nature. This is for us to learn Who the source of true success is. You will be amazed at how easy success will come when your life is in proper alignment with the purposes of God.

Today, reaffirm your commitment to follow His ways in all that you do. This will ensure that God's purposes will be fulfilled in you.

FORGIVENESS ENSURES FREEDOM

But if you do not forgive men their sins, your Father will not forgive your sins.
MATTHEW 6:15

Corrie ten Boom (1892-1983) was born in Amsterdam and raised in the Dutch Reformed Church. When the Nazis came to power in the late 1930s, Corrie and her family hid Jews in the basement of their home. In 1944, Corrie's family was arrested and sent to Ravensbrück, one of the worst concentration camps in Nazi Germany. There, Corrie's entire family died. Corrie herself was scheduled for execution—but she was released shortly before the end of World War II because of a clerical error.

Corrie concluded that God had saved her for a purpose. She committed her life to preaching the good news of Jesus Christ, speaking in churches, tent meetings and open-air rallies. At one meeting in Germany in 1947, she taught on God's forgiveness. Afterwards, a man came up to her and introduced himself as a former Ravensbrück guard—but Corrie needed no introduction. She remembered him well. He was notorious for his cruelty.

"I've become a Christian since the war," he said. "I know God has forgiven me for the horrible things I did, but I would like to hear it from you. Could you tell me that you've forgiven me, too?" He put out his hand.

Corrie stood there for what seemed like an eternity, unable to think of anything but the horrors this man had committed. Then she remembered the words of Jesus that required her to forgive *any* sin. She silently prayed, *Jesus, help me*—then she took the man's hand and cried out, "I forgive you, brother!" She later recalled, "I had never known God's love so intensely as I did then."

That was the defining moment in Corrie's ministry. Over the years that followed, she took the Christian gospel to more than 60 countries around the world and changed hundreds of thousands of lives through her speaking, writing and the motion picture *The Hiding Place*, based on her autobiography.

If we want to be used in a great way by God, we must be willing to forgive those who may be a great source of pain in our lives. We must be willing to wash the feet of our Judases, just as Jesus did.

Is there someone who needs your forgiveness today?

ADVERSITY: CATALYST TO A CALL

Saul got up from the ground, but when he opened his eyes he could see nothing.
So they led him by the hand into Damascus. For three days he was blind, and did
not eat or drink anything.

Acts 9:8-9

I've said it before and I'll say it again: It's hard to find anyone in Christian history who became a great leader without earning an advanced degree in adversity.

Looking at John Wesley (1703-1791), you wouldn't think of him as a great Christian leader. He was just over five feet tall and skeletally thin. In his early years, he suffered greatly from feelings of guilt, inadequacy and a morbid fear of death. Though he didn't understand the Christian gospel, he devoted himself to doing good works for the poor in an effort to earn his way to heaven. Thus, in his early 30s, he sailed to America to do missionary work among the American Indians.

While crossing the Atlantic, Wesley's ship passed through a violent storm that broke the main mast off its base and nearly sank the ship. As the waves crashed over the ship, Wesley huddled in terror, knowing that he didn't have peace with God. He survived the storm and continued to struggle in his relationship with God for several more years.

Finally, back in London, he attended a meeting on Aldersgate Street, where he heard a preacher say that salvation comes by faith in Christ alone. At that point, he said, "I felt my heart strangely warmed."

Soon after that, Wesley began preaching the gospel. His 52-year preaching ministry became the foundation of the modern evangelical movement. But it never would have happened if John Wesley had not been tossed on the stormy seas of adversity.

Adversity is often God's catalyst for spiritual callings.

YOU HAVE AN ANOINTING

As for you, the anointing you received from him remains in you, and you do not need anyone to teach you. But as his anointing teaches you about all things and as that anointing is real, not counterfeit—just as it has taught you, remain in him.

1 JOHN 2:27

Do you know your anointing? Anointing is the gift that functions in you naturally to benefit others and the kingdom of God. If one has to "work it up," then one has probably gone outside of one's anointing.

One area in which I have a God-given anointing is networking. I have never sought to develop such an anointing. But I know a *lot* of people. Despite being an introvert by nature, God has connected me with people all around the world.

Many times when people call me about something, my natural response is, "Oh, you need to contact so and so. He can help you with that." A mentor once said to me, "Your inheritance is in relationships." He was affirming that my anointing is in relationships and networking.

My wife, on the other hand, has an anointing in the area of disarming people. She can become someone's best friend in five minutes. She disarms people faster than anyone I know. There is no way you can be a shy person around my wife. I have seen people open up to Angie where they would not open up to anyone else. It is her anointing.

Where do you move naturally in your life? What do you do that you don't have to work at? Chances are, that is your anointing. God wants you to walk in the anointing He has given to you.

SELF-DELIVERANCE

Trust in the LORD with all your heart and lean not on your own understanding;
in all your ways acknowledge him, and he will make your paths straight.
Do not be wise in your own eyes; fear the LORD and shun evil.

PROVERBS 3:5-7

Oswald Chambers advised, "Whenever God gives a vision to a saint, he puts the saint in the shadow of His hand, as it were, and the saint's duty is to be still and listen . . . When God gives a vision and darkness follows, waiting on God will bring you into accordance with the vision He has given if you await His timing. Otherwise, you try to do away with the supernatural in God's undertakings. Never try to help God fulfill His word."[48]

In the book of Proverbs, Solomon warns us not to rely on our own fallible wisdom while trying to do God's perfect will. God wants us to wait for His deliverance. His means of bringing us to spiritual maturity requires us to wait through adversity so that we will be able to discern the difference between our own self-deliverance and God's authentic deliverance in our lives.

It's a paradox, but it's true: God often calls us to a ministry—then He deliberately thwarts our efforts to achieve our goals! We see this dynamic in the life of Moses. In obedience to God, Moses told Pharaoh, "Let my people go!" How did Pharaoh respond? He said, "Who is the Lord that I should obey him and let Israel go? I do not know the Lord and I will not let Israel go." Again and again, Moses returned and demanded freedom for his people. Again and again, Pharaoh refused.

God sent plague after plague upon the Egyptians. Pharaoh's heart was hardened, and he persecuted Moses and the people of Israel. So Moses complained to God, "You called me to go to Pharaoh, but You are not freeing the people!" Moses grew discouraged because God had called him to fulfill a vision—a dream of liberation for his people—and the vision seemed to die.

But God was teaching Moses and the people of Israel to persevere, to obey and to wait on the Lord in patient trust for His perfect time for deliverance. So, too, must you wait for God's perfect timing for deliverance.

DELIVERANCE FROM THE BLACK HOLE

As I was with Moses, so I will be with you; I will never leave you nor forsake you.
JOSHUA 1:5

A black hole is a place of total nothingness. It's a time in our life when God removes the resources and supports that we normally rely on—our careers, finances, friends, family, health, and so forth. It is a preparation time.

When you find yourself in a black-hole experience, don't just sit and brood. Take stock of your life. Take a look at your relationship with God.

First, ask God if there are any sins, habits or attitudes that He might be judging in your life. It's important to discern whether the trial you face is the result of God's discipline for sin or if it is preparing you for a future leadership role.

Second, when you enter a black hole, don't trust your feelings. Trust God. Your feelings will tell you, "God has rejected you. Abandon hope. He has left you utterly alone." Feelings change, but God never changes. Feelings come and go, but God is always with us.

Third, remember that your black-hole experience is not only intended to refine and define you, but it's also intended to influence and change the lives of hundreds or even thousands of other people. Often, adversity does not only impact us but also others in our sphere of influence.

Fourth, don't try to hurry the black-hole process along. Remember, when Joseph was in the depths of the pit, there was nothing he could do about it. He couldn't climb out, jump out, levitate out or talk his way out. All he could do was pray and wait upon the Lord.

Fifth, lean on God. Even when you don't feel like praying, pray. Even when you don't feel like reading His Word, read. Even when you don't feel like singing songs of faith, sing. When you pray, don't just talk—*listen*. Be silent before Him and listen for His still, quiet voice.

Sixth, be alert to new truths and new perspectives. During a black-hole experience, God often leads us to amazing new discoveries. A black hole can be a storehouse of unexpected riches for the soul.

STUDYING TO GIVE VERSUS STUDYING TO KNOW

You diligently study the Scriptures because you think that
by them you possess eternal life. These are the Scriptures that testify
about me, yet you refuse to come to me to have life.
JOHN 5:39-40

Sometimes you'd think the Trinity is the *Father, Son* and *Holy Scriptures* instead of the *Holy Spirit*. There can be a tendency in Christianity to focus so much on the Holy Scriptures that we fail to acknowledge the role of the Holy Spirit in our daily activity.

We must be careful not to study the Scriptures for the sake of giving to others rather than desiring more of God for ourselves. This is particularly dangerous for the professional Christian worker who is under continued pressure to feed and teach His people. If we are not careful, this process becomes a religious exercise of production, instead of a time of seeking, learning and experiencing God's presence.

Jesus told His disciples that when He left, He would leave the Holy Spirit, who would help them live victoriously for Him: "All this I have spoken while still with you. But the Counselor, the Holy Spirit, whom the Father will send in my name, will teach you all things and will remind you of everything I have said to you" (John 14:25-26). No longer would converts be baptized just with water, but now they would also be baptized with the Holy Spirit (see Acts 1:5).

It is the Holy Spirit who draws us into intimacy with the Father. He is the One who prompts us with a Scripture verse to share with a friend or coworker. He endues us with the power to live for Him, and not in our own strength. Truly, the Holy Spirit is the third person in the Trinity that must be acknowledged and obeyed as we seek to live for Christ. He is our teacher and guide.

Today, why not ask the Holy Spirit to baptize you afresh with the power to know Him, not just know about Him.

WHEN OTHERS FAIL YOU

Again Jesus said, "Peace be with you!
As the Father has sent me, I am sending you."

JOHN 20:21

Have you ever entrusted someone to carry on a project only to have him or her fail miserably? What was your response?

Many times leaders shame others to make them realize the gravity of their failure. Jesus sets a far different example.

When Jesus was crucified, many of the disciples fled. Peter denied Him three times. He was a leader without followers. Yet after His resurrection, the Lord's words to those who had totally abandoned Him and the mission were, "Peace be with you! As the Father has sent me, I am sending you" (John 20:21). What an incredible greeting the disciples received from Jesus after all they had experienced! No shame, no harsh words, just a reaffirmation of the mission and His commitment to them.

Jesus used grace and total acceptance as motivation for His followers to carry on the mission. He didn't need to remind them of their failure. They already felt bad enough. It was time to recast the vision with new life.

When there is failure in the organization, it is more important to revitalize the team than to focus on the past.

Do you need to rally your team around a mission that has stalled, failed or gotten off-track? Begin by affirming those under your leadership. Be at peace, and send them forth!

GOD LEADS US INTO THE DESERT

*Then Jesus was led by the Spirit into the desert
to be tempted by the devil.*
MATTHEW 4:1

There is a common teaching going around today that says, "If you do all the right things in your Christian life, you will be blessed and will never experience problems." This teaching is heresy. The Bible says that we will encounter many problems during this lifetime. Just read Peter's epistles.

Jesus was led by the Holy Spirit into the desert to be tempted by the devil. Why would God lead His Son into the desert to be tempted? Why would God lead you and me into the desert?

The desert is often the place of silence. However, it can also be a place of temptation where the devil will speak loudly, because in the desert you are in a place of weakness. The desert is also a place where God is often silent, but it can also be a place where God speaks loudly. The word "desert" comes from the Hebrew word *dahbaar,* which means "to speak."

The desert is a place where we can learn something about ourselves. It is the place where we determine if we will truly live by every word of God, not by bread alone. When Satan tempted Jesus in the desert, Jesus responded to every temptation by citing what the Word of God said about that temptation. This is also the way you and I must respond to the temptations that are brought our way. We must have the Word of God written into our hearts in order to know how to respond to any given situation. The Bible says, "the truth will set you free" (John 8:32). It is knowing and doing the will of God that allows us to live free from the temptation of evil.

If God has placed you in the desert, meditate on His Word so that you will withstand the temptation that comes in the desert place.

THE VALLEY OF BACA

Blessed are those whose strength is in you, who have set their hearts on pilgrimage.
As they pass through the Valley of Baca, they make it a place of springs;
the autumn rains also cover it with pools. They go from strength to strength,
till each appears before God in Zion.
PSALM 84:5-7

There is a spiritual law in the kingdom of God that says that every great leader in the Kingdom will pass through the Valley of Baca. In Hebrew, *baca* means "to weep," but it can also mean "a place of springs."

There is nothing better on a hot day, when you're thirsty and weary, than to drink water from a mountain spring. It refreshes. It renews. It gives you a second wind to continue your journey.

Those who commit themselves to a pilgrimage with God will experience the Valley of Baca. But in the midst of Baca they will discover that in this valley they will also drink from a very special spring that refreshes with a different kind of living water.

The Baca spring is the source of "secret things in hidden places," as described by the prophet Isaiah (see Isaiah 45:3). It is reserved only for those willing to journey on the Great Pilgrimage with God. Once you drink from this spring, you will be energized in your spiritual man from strength to strength. Each Valley of Baca will result in a new spiritual spring from which you will drink.

Each spring is handmade just for you by God. But know this—your springs will also be used to provide a refreshing drink for others you will encounter, who are also on their pilgrimage. Ultimately, Baca leads to the presence of God—for us and for those we encounter. There is something about being in a place with God that results in our weeping and crying out to Him.

Do you find yourself in this place with God today? If so, know that His springs are also available to you. Ask Him today to give you a drink from His spring that is only available in the Valley of Baca.

DESTROYING HIGH PLACES

Now it came to pass the same night that the LORD said to him,
"Take your father's young bull, the second bull of seven years old, and tear down
the altar of Baal that your father has, and cut down the wooden image that is
beside it; and build an altar to the LORD your God on top of this rock in the
proper arrangement, and take the second bull and offer a burnt sacrifice
with the wood of the image which you shall cut down."
JUDGES 6:25-26, NKJV

I first met Bishop Julius Oyet in November 2005 and visited him in his nation of Uganda the following spring. Bishop Oyet believes that God is able to do exceedingly more than we can ask or think because of the power that works within us.

For 17 years, the LRA (Lord's Resistance Army) destroyed millions of innocent lives, wrecked the economy and left thousands of homesteads burned and destroyed through a man named Joseph Kony in Oyet's homeland of northern Uganda.

Just as God led Gideon to tear down demonic altars, God led Julius to do the same in his nation. First, Julius proclaimed in a public meeting, "You cannot fight spiritual strongholds with bullets!" Then a number of events transpired that led Julius to meet the president of his nation, which allowed him to share what he believed God was saying about the war.

On Saturday, March 1, 2003, Julius led an "Operation Gideon" team of 22 persons to the first of several sites to conduct onsite prayer vigils with pastors, an army battalion and intercessory prayer leaders. They tore down sacred altars they believed had spiritual powers for the rebel army.

As a result of these actions, a great turning point in the war took place with many rebel leaders surrendering and giving their lives to Jesus Christ. The impact of Julius's and his team's actions has resulted in the Lord giving great favour to the nation of Uganda.[49] Like Gideon, God is using this servant to turn the tide of evil in his nation.

Has God called you to tear down some sacred altars?

JESUS WEPT FOR THE CITY

As he approached Jerusalem and saw the city, he wept over it and said,
"If you, even you, had only known on this day what would bring you peace—
but now it is hidden from your eyes."

Luke 19:41-42

Jesus was making His triumphal entry into the city of Jerusalem when the Pharisees complained about the exuberance of His disciples, who were rightly celebrating a life that had blessed them and countless others: "When he came near the place where the road goes down the Mount of Olives, the whole crowd of disciples began joyfully to praise God in loud voices for all the miracles they had seen: 'Blessed is the king who comes in the name of the Lord!'" (Luke 19:37-38).

Jesus was saddened by the response of the Pharisees. He knew what His presence could do for the city. But He also knew that the Pharisees would not change. The city would reject His presence and crucify Him. His presence would bring peace to the city if they embraced who He was—the author of peace. Now, it would be hidden from their eyes because of unbelief.

Every city can be blessed by the presence of Jesus, but city leaders must invite the presence of Jesus into their city in order to experience His peace. Jesus' presence also has the potential to divide city leaders because of unbelief and political correctness.

Does your city need the presence of Jesus? Do you desire to see peace in your city? Begin to pray for city leaders to understand how the presence of Jesus can impact your city in dramatic and positive ways.

Pray for peace in Jerusalem and in your own city.

IS THERE HIERARCHY IN CALLING?

Now you are the body of Christ, and each one of you is a part of it.
1 CORINTHIANS 12:27

All legitimate work matters to God. God even describes Himself as a worker. Work is a gift from Him to meet the needs of people and of creation: "You made him ruler over the works of your hands; you put everything under his feet: all flocks and herds, and the beasts of the field, the birds of the air, and the fish of the sea, all that swim the paths of the seas" (Psalm 8:6-8).

Despite God's clear affirming word on work of all kinds, there is often an unspoken hierarchy that positions clergy (missionaries, evangelists, pastors and clergy) at the top, the "helping" professions (doctors, nurses, teachers, educators and social workers) in the middle, and "secular" workers (business executives, salespeople, factory laborers and farmers) at the bottom.

So what determines the spiritual value of a job? How does God assign significance? The hierarchy above assumes sacred and secular distinctions, and assigns priority to the sacred. But does God view vocations that way? No, He does not.

God creates people to carry out specific kinds of work in order to meet human needs. God uniquely designs each of us, fitting us for certain kinds of tasks. He distributes skills, abilities, interests and personalities among us so that we can carry out His work in the world. That work includes "spiritual" tasks but also extends to health, education, agriculture, business, law, communication, the arts, and so on.

Paul, for example, was a leader in the Early Church but a tentmaker by occupation along with his friends Aquila and Priscilla. Other church leaders practiced a wide variety of professions and trades. There's no indication that God looks at vocations in the form of a spiritual hierarchy.[50]

The next time you consider your vocation to be a second-class spiritual calling, consider what God says. Your work matters to God, and He values your work, no matter what it is, when you do it as unto Him.

"YOU'RE DIFFERENT"

But he said to me, "My grace is sufficient for you,
for my power is made perfect in weakness."
2 CORINTHIANS 12:9

Angie and I were in Switzerland visiting an acquaintance that I had met briefly almost 10 years earlier at a Christian conference on the island of Cyprus. We had stayed in contact over the years as he had become a big fan of *TGIF* and had the devotions translated into German.

I was sitting in the kitchen talking with my friend when I said, "You are different. There is a different spirit about you than when I met you 10 years ago on the island of Cyprus. I have to admit, I thought you were a bit aloof," I confessed to him.

"Hmm, you know, Os, I thought the same about you." We both chuckled at our observations.

There was a difference in both of us because something dramatic had happened in both of our lives. My friend was a very successful businessman in Switzerland and was running a family business when things went very wrong. He lost millions as a result. Although his fortune was not totally wiped out, it impacted him greatly. It brought a humility and newfound trust in God that had not been there before.

I had a similar story. I had gone through a seven year "pit experience" in which I had major losses in family, business and personal income. Now, we were both on the other sides of our "pits." We could recognize something in each other that had resulted from our experiences. There was a level of humility that was not there before.

I often tell others, "You can get humility voluntarily or involuntarily. It is much easier if you get it voluntarily."

"Humble yourselves before the Lord, and He will lift you up" (James 4:10).

GOD OWNS MY BUSINESS

So if you have not been trustworthy in handling worldly wealth,
who will trust you with true riches?

LUKE 16:11

Although he has been an innovator in the reclamation of silver in the photographic process, Stanley Tam of Lima, Ohio, is best known for his commitment to Jesus Christ. Tam, who has traveled throughout the country and world to testify about his Christian faith, is one who is willing to put his money where his mouth is. Although his business success could have made him a millionaire many times over, he and his wife, Juanita, draw only modest salaries from U.S. Plastics. All profits are channeled through the Stanita Foundation, where the funds are designated for a variety of Christian ministries, primarily overseas missions.

Tam's business calling began in the fall of 1954 when he was speaking at a revival meeting in Medellin, Colombia. At the meeting, God confronted Tam in a supernatural way. God let him know that He wanted Tam to turn the business over to Him completely and to become His employee. On January 15, 1955, Stanley Tam ceased being a stockholder in either of the companies he founded, States Smelting and Refining Corporation and United States Plastic Corporation.

Before Tam was ready to make this commitment, God had to deal with one specific area of his life. He states:

> I have always enjoyed making money, and God knew that. Had He left me undisturbed in this area, I could have become a proud, materialistic, self-centered spiritual misfit. In asking of me the submission of the greatest drive of my life, He removed a blighting influence and replaced it with an inner peace and satisfaction such as I could never have known otherwise. I don't think there is such a thing as a part-time Christian; we are all in full-time ministry. We each need to ask God to take our vocation and make it a ministry. And if we ask Him, He will do it.[51]

Does God own your business or your work life? If not, why not make that decision today, and let Him use your work life for His glory.

THE POWER OF INFLUENCE

Now I want you to know, brothers, that what has happened to me has really served to advance the gospel.

PHILIPPIANS 1:12

"Money talks." "He who has the gold rules." Both of these statements have truth in them.

When Jesus was crucified, there was a question about where He would be buried. Those who hurried Him to the cross designed for Him to be buried with the wicked, but God designed that He should be placed in a grave with the rich (see Isaiah 53:9). And so, Jesus was.

In order for Jesus to be buried with honor, a man of influence had to take the body of Jesus. This man was Joseph of Arimathea, a person of influence who owned a burial cave reserved for the rich. He had a personal relationship with Pontius Pilate, the Roman governor in Jerusalem.

Joseph of Arimathea was an honorable counselor, a person of character and distinction, and worked in an office of public trust. Some think he was a member of the state and that he was one of Pilate's privy council, but his post seems to have been in the religious establishment. He was a member of the great Sanhedrim of the Jews, one of the high priest's council.[52]

The Bible says that God desires His people to be the head, not the tail. If we are to influence the culture, there must be men and women of influence, like Joseph of Arimathea, whom God uses to impact the culture. If you are a successful person, consider the words of Paul: "what has happened to me has served to advance the gospel" (Philippians 1:2). Although Paul was referencing adversity in this statement, it can equally be said that each of us needs to ask if our prosperity has served to advance the gospel.

Are you using your influence to impact your workplace, city or nation for the sake of the gospel?

"GO TO CHRIST CHURCH"

The Lord told him, "Go to the house of Judas on Straight Street and
ask for a man from Tarsus named Saul, for he is praying."

ACTS 9:11

Angie and I stepped into the cab to take our first drive to downtown Jerusalem. It was an exciting time for us! Our cab driver's name was Moses. "When in doubt, just call out 'Moses!' and there is a good chance someone will answer," he said.

Moses offered to drive us throughout the city and surrounding area, and we agreed. Our cab driver began to talk openly with us when he discovered we were believers in Jesus. He was a born-again Jew. His father was a rabbi, and Moses had been disinherited from his family for his belief that Jesus is the Savior. Because of his faith, his marriage was in trouble and holding on only by a thread. His salvation had cost him deeply. He used to work on the family farm for his father-in-law but now drove a cab.

The Jewish-Palestinian conflict had cut tourism by 90 percent, so as a cab driver, Moses had plenty of time on his hands. He began to share his story with us:

> I'd been questioning my purpose in life. I began thinking there had to be more. My Jewish laws didn't satisfy something in me. I became very depressed. Then one day a remarkable thing happened. I was in my bedroom. Suddenly, I heard a voice in my room that said, "Go to Christ Church!" I thought I was imagining things. Then, I heard it a second time!
>
> I looked in the yellow pages and discovered that Christ Church was located downtown in the "Old City." The people there explained to me what happened. Jesus was calling me to know Him. I have known Him ever since. Now I have meaning and purpose. Things are still very difficult, but now I have a peace inside that I didn't have before.

Friend, Jesus is still reaching out to those who want to know Him. Do you have a faith that is willing to be rejected and ostracized by those close to you? Jesus said that we are to follow Him even at the expense of losing our father and mother, if need be.

TRUTH IN THE INWARD PARTS

Surely you desire truth in the inner parts;
you teach me wisdom in the inmost place.

PSALM 51:6

A popular story is told of how Sir Arthur Conan Doyle, the author of the Sherlock Holmes popular mystery series, once played a practical joke on 12 respected and well-known men. He sent out 12 telegrams with the same message on each: "Flee at once. All is discovered." Within 24 hours, all those to whom he had sent the telegram had left the country!

In 1923, the most powerful men of the day ruled the world of money. Charles Schwab was the president of the largest steel company in America. Samuel Insull was the president of the largest utility company. Howard Hopson was president of the largest gas company. Arthur Cutten was the great wheat speculator. Richard Whitney was president of the New York Stock Exchange. Albert Fall was Secretary of Interior in President Harding's cabinet. Jesse Livermore was the great "bear" on Wall Street. Ivan Krueger was head of the world's greatest monopoly. And Leon Fraser was president of the Bank of International Settlements.

These men were movers and shakers, the kind many people envy and wish to be like. Yet something went terribly wrong with these men's lives. Twenty-five years later, Charles Schwab had gone bankrupt. Samuel Insull had died in a foreign land, penniless and a fugitive from justice. Howard Hopson was insane. Arthur Cutten was insolvent and had died abroad. Richard Whitney had just been released from Sing-Sing prison. Albert Fall had just been pardoned from prison and had died penniless at home. And Jesse Livermore, Ivan Krueger and Leon Fraser had all committed suicide.[53]

Something went wrong during the process of these men's lives. It began in the inner man. Truth in the inner man is where integrity battles are won or lost. Pray that God allows you to live a life of integrity and honesty before Him.

PRAY FOR THOSE IN AUTHORITY

I urge, then, first of all, that requests, prayers, intercession and thanksgiving be made for everyone—for kings and all those in authority.

1 TIMOTHY 2:1

In 1 Timothy 2:1, Paul exhorts his young protégé to make prayer and intercession for those in authority the first work of the Church.

Whereas we once thought that those in politics, military, religion and economics controlled the earth, today we recognize the enormous influence wielded by those in the workplace. Our mindsets are changing: We now count those in the workplace, including business leaders, as authorities. They, too, are among those Paul exhorted Timothy to cover in prayer.

God is transferring His anointing to be placed upon all saints to get His job done. This requires the local church to focus on equipping men and women to live out their faith in the workplace. It is not surprising that the Lord would begin such a major shift in the modern-day Church. If we are going to see a major harvest in the last days, it will have to come through the largest segment of the Body of Christ—those who are Christ's representatives in government, business and education.

The book of Acts provides us with many examples. Lydia, a businesswoman, was God's instrument to introduce the gospel to Europe. The Ethiopian eunuch who was in charge of the treasury of Candace, Queen of the Ethiopians, introduced the gospel to Africa. Peter launched the gospel into the Gentile world through Cornelius, a Roman centurion. These workplace ministers reached Europe, Africa and much of the East for Christ. These examples indicate the importance of the workplace influence and why intercession is so important for leaders in places of authority.

Today, pray for those leaders in government, business and education.

OCTOBER 14

SERVING KINGS

Do you see a man skilled in his work?
He will serve before kings; he will not serve before obscure men.
PROVERBS 22:29

I was sitting in a room of 400 business people from 75 different nations to begin an international conference. After a time of worship, a man stood up and exhorted Christians in the United States to pray for their president. It was a difficult time in our nation, because President Bill Clinton was in the midst of a scandal.

The man who challenged us to pray was pastor Romain Zannou from the small African nation of Benin. Zannou had earned the right to exhort us. Many years ago, God had given him a burden to pray for his Marxist dictator president, Mathieu Kerekou. For 10 years he prayed for two hours a day for Kerekou's salvation and for God to give Kerekou wisdom to lead the nation. One day while he was praying, Zannou felt that the Lord had a message for the president. Within 24 hours, he was standing in a room with Kerekou to deliver the word of the Lord.

Although Kerekou and Zannou had agreed to meet regularly for a time of Bible study after their first free elections, the former president refused to meet with Zannou after only a few meetings. Almost every day after that, Zannou went to Kerekou's home, only to be told that Kerekou did not wish to see him. Each day he said, "I will wait," and stood outside the wall for hours, many times in the rain and heat, in hopes that Kerekou would let him in.

After a year and a half of these unsuccessful visits, the now-former president finally received him and greeted him with the words, "Pastor Zannou, you are a very persistent man." From there, they began an in-depth study of the Bible. Through this study of the Word of God, the former president received Christ.

Romain Zannou is one of many unknown leaders being used to impact nations through a workplace calling. These leaders are an unlikely group of people—pastors, flower shop owners, builders, industrialists and even a former golf pro and advertising executive (me).

Be skilled in what you do. You may be standing before a king in the future.

THE POWER OF GIVING

*Give, and it will be given to you. A good measure, pressed down,
shaken together and running over, will be poured into your lap.
For with the measure you use, it will be measured to you.*

LUKE 6:38

Oprah Winfrey is an African-American woman who overcame great obstacles in her life to become one of the most successful and wealthy TV personalities in America. Her daytime program is the most watched show on American television.

She is known for doing unusual acts of kindness for her 300-plus guests who attend each live television show. However, in the fall of 2006 she outdid herself. She decided to give $1,000 to every guest in the studio that day. But there was a catch: Instead of keeping the money, each recipient had to give the $1,000 away to someone they felt needed the money. They were given a video recorder to capture the results of their giving.

The creativity exercised by her guests was amazing. One teacher decided to give shoes to each of her students from low-income families. A shoe company heard what she was doing and decided to match her gift.

Another woman gave money to a needy family with several children whose father had a major illness. The newspaper ran the story and a flood of generosity began to come in from corporate sponsors and the local community. More than $200,000 was actually given to the family—and it all started with $1,000!

The stories were truly amazing. Each one was unique and creative. In each case, the giver testified to the tremendous blessing he or she received from this endeavor.

It does not matter whether or not you are a Christian—the principle of giving is a Kingdom principle that is an absolute law. What if every church gave their members $100 and told them to bless someone that day in the name of Jesus? Imagine the impact!

Today, ask God how you might give to someone else. You will be amazed at how the blessing will be poured back into your lap, running over.

WORK TO PLAY, WORK TO ACQUIRE

I have brought you glory on earth by completing the work you gave me to do.
JOHN 17:4

A popular TV commercial comes on the screen raising this question: *Why do you work long hours?* Meanwhile, the screen flashes beautiful pictures of a luxurious car. The message is clear: We work in order to acquire.

Another TV commercial comes on showing tantalizing aqua blue ocean waves and an attractive couple lounging on white sandy beaches. "Come to Jamaica," invites the soothing voiceover. The message here is that a vacation to Jamaica is the ultimate reward for your work.

People have many motivations to work. Some might say they are motivated simply to put food on the table, but George Barna, the American researcher on religious habits, found disturbing results from his study on the motivations of many Christians in American society:

> We are not a society that simply enjoys its time off. We are driven by our leisure appetites. It is increasingly common to hear of people turning down job offers because the hours or other responsibilities would interfere with their hobbies, fitness regimens and other free time activities. Even our spending habits show that playing has become a major priority. The average household spends more money on entertainment than it does on clothing, health care, furniture or gasoline.[54]

His study also found that many people define success in surprisingly non-Christian terms. He found that 66 percent of Americans define success in life as the acquisition of sufficient money, education, material possessions or career prestige, while only 7 percent related success to their faith condition and its influence on their life. "The Christian Church has stagnated, largely due to its comfort with routines and rituals that are neither challenging nor relevant for millions of people," said Barna.[55]

Have you ever asked yourself why you work? Jesus had a work to do that was given to Him by His heavenly Father. You too have a work that you are called to do. Ask God to give you a renewed sense of the work you are called to do today.

TRANSFORMING A WORKPLACE

Do not conform any longer to the pattern of this world,
but be transformed by the renewing of your mind.
ROMANS 12:2

A cab driver in the Philippines who was radically saved was taught that he now had the power of God in his life to transform his community. Because he had not had any prior religious training to the contrary, he took a literal approach to believing what the Bible says about prayer and miracles.

He decided that the best mission field for him was the local bar in his neighborhood, so he began to visit this bar to find someone he could minister to. He met the bartender and determined that he was a great prospect—he was a gay drug addict and a pimp to 65 prostitutes. The cab driver visited the bar regularly and got to know the bartender while drinking his "usual"—Coke.

Eventually, the power of God moved greatly in the bartender and he was delivered from his homosexual lifestyle. He began to change his life and shared Jesus with the prostitutes. All 65 of them became Christians, too, and they all began to meet in the bar for Bible study.

Soon, the owner of the bar began to notice the change in these people and he also was saved. The bar eventually became a church and the group started 10 cell-group churches in the neighborhood. Now *that* is a miraculous transformation!

No matter what situation we find ourselves in, we should always remain aware that God wants to intervene. He desires a moment-by-moment relationship with us, and He wants to demonstrate His loving power to others through us. We can approach God about any situation, for there is nothing that is too small or too great for Him.[56]

Ask God to be a transformer in your workplace and city.

PRAYER AT WORK

*Call to me and I will answer you and tell you great
and unsearchable things you do not know.*
JEREMIAH 33:3

Julian Watts and Warren Sinclair, who operate an international company called Markets Unlocked in Guildford, England, have learned how important intimacy and the presence of God are to fulfilling God's purposes for their business.

In 1999, Julian founded an Internet company that specialized in connecting businesses that wanted to buy and sell to each other. He set about building the new company, focusing on commercial fundamentals and occasionally praying for God's help to get the task done.

The business grew very quickly, riding on the crest of the Internet wave. But the dotcom crash that followed in the year 2000 was brutal, and the company was all but wiped out. The Christian directors started praying together—monthly at first, then, as things continued to worsen, weekly, and finally, as desperation set in, daily!

The directors' daily routines began to change. At first, Julian had his personal time with the Lord from 5:00 A.M. to 7:00 A.M. each day. Then, from 8:00 A.M. to 9:00 A.M., all the company directors would meet to worship and pray. From 9:00 A.M. to 2:00 P.M. every weekday, one director would worship and intercede for the company; and every Tuesday from 10:00 A.M. to 12:00 P.M., everyone in the company would meet, along with local pastors and intercessors, to worship and intercede.

By late 2001, the company had passed through the wilderness of the dotcom crash. In the process, all the commercial aspects of the company had been completely transformed—including its business strategy, organization structure, people, operational processes and location.

Today, the directors see that the Lord is increasingly establishing their company's corporate identity and defining characteristic as *corporate intimacy with Him*. Markets Unlocked is now expanding rapidly around the world, with customers in over 80 countries.

Is there an area in your workplace that could use prayer? Why not begin praying today for your company and see where God takes it.

SEEING BACKWARD

O LORD, when you favored me, you made my mountain stand firm;
but when you hid your face, I was dismayed.
PSALM 30:7

It is often difficult to recognize the hand of God when we are in the midst of adversity. During these times, we often feel that God has hidden His face from us. However, we must press into God with all we have when we face adverse situations. When the Lord takes us through deep valleys, He will bring us fruit that we cannot imagine.

God uses deep valleys in our lives to create a change in our nature, not just a change in our habits. The depth and width of our valley is often an indicator of the level of calling and influence we will have on others in the future. Our adversity is not just for us but also for others who will be in our future path of influence. This is not a very comforting sentiment when we are in the middle of the valley, but we need to know that suffering for the sake of others is a truth in the Kingdom.

It is often not until years later that we understand the timing and wisdom of God and why He intentionally led us through the dark valley. It is not until we are down the road, standing on a mountain and looking back through the valley, that we can appreciate the terrain that God has allowed us to scale.

From the mountaintop perspective, we can more clearly see the spiritual deposits He made in our life while we were in the valley. "He reveals the deep things of darkness and brings deep shadows into the light" (Job 12:22). When we begin to realize this, we can sit back and breathe a sigh of relief because we finally know that God was in control all along.

Do you ever find yourself in the valley? Now is the time to fully trust Him to guide you to higher ground.

JEHOVAH JIREH

But I think it is necessary to send back to you Epaphroditus, my brother, fellow worker and fellow soldier, who is also your messenger, whom you sent to take care of my needs.

PHILEMON 2:25-26

I got onto the bus with the other delegates attending a workplace conference in South Africa. It was a season in my life in which I had experienced many losses, both financially and relationally. God was stripping away the old wineskin and creating a new one in my life. One of the things He was teaching me was that He—not my skills, not my work—is my financial provider.

God provided me the means to attend the conference when, one day before the registration deadline, a man came to my office and told me that I was to go. He placed an envelope into my hand and said, "Here, God says I'm to give this to you." Inside I found 10 crisp $100 bills—$1,000!

Every believer needs to come to know Christ as his or her provider. In Hebrew, the phrase *Jehovah Jireh* means "God is my provider." This name for God was first used when the Lord called the Israelites from their place of slavery to walk through the desert. There was no way to earn a living in the desert, so God provided manna for them each day. Sometimes, He even brought forth water from rocks.

In the desert, the Israelites experienced a new way of gaining provision that was not rooted in sweat and toil. God demonstrated His faithfulness as *Jehovah Jireh* to His people.

Do you know God as your provider? Do you have a need? Place your need before the Lord today and ask Him to demonstrate His faithfulness as *Jehovah Jireh*.

COMING SIGNS OF PERSECUTION

*"Come," they say, "let us destroy them as a nation,
that the name of Israel be remembered no more."*
PSALM 83:4

God calls us to know the signs of the times. The final end-time conflict will arise when nations of the world come against Israel.

The Bible is clear that Jesus will return to the physical place of Jerusalem to collect His bride—represented as all those who believe and trust in Jesus, the Messiah. The book of Revelation offers a glimpse into what that event might look like: "Let us rejoice and be glad and give him glory! For the wedding of the Lamb has come, and his bride has made herself ready . . . I saw the Holy City, the new Jerusalem, coming down out of heaven from God, prepared as a bride beautifully dressed for her husband" (Revelation 19:7; 21:2).

In the meantime, Israel will always be a place of conflict in the world, because Satan knows that this is the place Jesus must come back to in order to collect His bride. Only when Jesus returns will Satan's influence on the earth end. Until then, Jerusalem will be in a tug of war among the nations.

There will grow an even greater intolerance in the world for anyone who has a belief system in absolutes. Christians will be viewed as rigid, inflexible and intolerant of other faiths. There will be a season of political moderate philosophy among many nations and individuals. This will open the door to the influence of the antichrist to come against any group—specifically Christians—that believe in absolutes.

A growing religious persecution will emerge against Jews and committed Christians. Christians will be called to stand with their brothers and sisters in Israel. When this happens, many Jews will believe in the Messiah.

There has been a season of peace for followers of Christ in the Western, European and Asian world. But a season of persecution is to come. "However, if you suffer as a Christian, do not be ashamed, but praise God that you bear that name" (1 Peter 4:16). Pray that you will be faithful.

REFLECTING THE LIGHT

John was a lamp that burned and gave light,
and you chose for a time to enjoy his light.
JOHN 5:35

The moon is lovely on a clear night only because it reflects the light of the sun. It has no light of its own. Without the sun shining onto its surface, you and I would never see the moon. It would simply be a dark object in the sky.

Like the moon, a diamond is designed to reflect light to reveal its true value. The cut of a diamond determines its brilliance. There is no single measurement of a diamond that defines its cut, but rather a collection of measurements and observations that determine the relationship between a diamond's light performance, dimensions and finish.

Jesus came to bring the light of His love and grace to each of us. However, we are born into a world dulled by the sin created by Adam and Eve: "For all have sinned and fall short of the glory of God" (Romans 3:23). In contrast, those who allow Jesus' life to live in them will live in the light amidst darkness. When you invite Jesus Christ to live in your heart, it is as though a light is shining upon your life in order to reflect the glory of God's Son through you.

Jesus calls you to be a vessel to reflect the brilliant light of His love to others. The workplace is a great place to reflect His glory. How are your reflective qualities? Ask Him to make your life a continual reflection of His light to others.

WE ALL NEED OUR "PURAHS"

*If you are afraid to attack, go down to the camp with your servant
Purah and listen to what they are saying. Afterward, you will
be encouraged to attack the camp.*

JUDGES 7:10-11

The Israelites did evil in the eyes of the Lord, and as a consequence, He gave them into the hands of the Midianites for seven years. Because the power of Midian was so oppressive, the Israelites prepared shelters for themselves in mountain clefts, caves and strongholds. God heard their prayers and decided to deliver them from their oppression through an unknown farmer named Gideon.

God came to Gideon through an angel and addressed him as "mighty warrior," which was quite a stretch of characterization from Gideon's perspective. Gideon was very insecure about his assignment from God to be a warrior, especially after God reduced his troop size from 22,000 to 300. But the Lord was using this event to ensure that Gideon knew where his victory came from.

Even after an angel spoke to Gideon, he was not convinced about the battle, so God did two more things to help ease Gideon's anxiety. He told him to go into the camp during the night to eavesdrop on the Midianite soldiers. He promised Gideon that what he would hear there would encourage him. God also sent a trusted friend and soldier named Purah with Gideon in order to ease his nerves.

God knew that Purah (probably one of the 10 who had helped Gideon to break down the altar of Baal) was the person Gideon could confide in. The Lord used Purah to be a witness of what Gideon heard from the Midianites and then to provide the faith to enter the battle. With Purah's help, Gideon went on and won the battle.

We all need Purahs in our lives. We need people who are willing to take risks and who can be used by God to bring our faith up to a level of greatness.

Has God called you to a daunting assignment? Perhaps He has also placed a Purah in your life to encourage you.

THE COMING WEALTH TRANSFER

But the wealth of the sinner is stored up for the righteous.
PROVERBS 13:22, *NKJV*

In the last days there will be a transfer of wealth into the hands of the righteous for the purpose of funding a great harvest of souls and for believers to have greater influence on society in the name of Christ. This will happen in at least four ways.

(1) *Supernatural transfer.* Like the Israelites leaving Egypt, Christians and non-profit organizations will receive major gifts from individuals or foundations to carry out their Christian mission. In 2004, the Salvation Army received one of the largest gifts for Christian ministry: $1.5 billion from Joan Kroc, the now-deceased wife of the founder of McDonalds.

(2) *Power to make wealth.* God is going to inspire believers throughout the world with clever inventions that will generate wealth. This phenomenon has already begun: "But remember the LORD your God, for it is he who gives you the ability to produce wealth, and so confirms his covenant, which he swore to your forefathers, as it is today" (Deuteronomy 8:18).

(3) *Social entrepreneurship.* Just as Joseph was entrusted with the resources of Egypt to solve a societal problem, God is going to transfer money to believers who are solving societal problems. God will fund private enterprises because the government alone is not able to solve society's many crises.

(4) *Wealthy individual "conversions."* Finally, many wealthy non-believers will become Christians in these last days and will begin to use their wealth for Kingdom purposes.

The transfer of wealth is designed to accelerate God's activity on the earth, not to make believers wealthy. Pray that God uses your work to accelerate His kingdom on Earth. And pray that God raises up good stewards of the wealth He will pour out.

REGAINING THE ART OF COMMUNITY

But if we walk in the light, as he is in the light, we have fellowship with one another, and the blood of Jesus, his Son, purifies us from all sin.

1 JOHN 1:7

I have a friend who spent three months living in Israel with Jewish believers. During one of his conversations there, a Jewish man noticed how often my friend came to visit him only to discuss a project. One day, he turned to my friend during dinner and admonished him, "You Western Christians! You always seem to need a program or an event to get together. Why can't you fellowship with one another just because you love each other?"

My friend was convicted by his Jewish friend's assessment. They began to talk about how Jesus modeled love for the disciples and how He simply hung out with them because of their mutual love. "A new command I give you: Love one another. As I have loved you, so you must love one another. By this all men will know that you are my disciples, if you love one another" (John 13:34-35).

Love for one another is one of the greatest signs of faith in Christ. However, the pace of life often contributes to our tendency to live for the next event instead of a relationship rooted in the love of Christ.

Jesus often spent unhurried times of fellowship with the disciples. They shared countless meals together. It is often during such times that we get to know others at a deeper level.

How many relationships do you have in your life that would allow you to fellowship simply because you cared for someone?

THE TIPPING POINT

It was he who gave some to be apostles, some to be prophets,
some to be evangelists, and some to be pastors and teachers.
EPHESIANS 4:11

Malcolm Gladwell authored a secular marketing book entitled *The Tipping Point*. A tipping point is the moment when an idea, product or movement is accepted by the masses. Gladwell says that the tipping point is "the best way to understand the emergence of fashion trends, the ebb and flow of crime waves, or, for that matter, the transformation of unknown books into bestsellers."[57]

Gladwell also says that ideas, products, messages and behaviors spread just like viruses do, but he has discovered that there are usually three types of people involved in the marketing process of a tipping point. He calls these people connectors, mavens and salesmen.

Connectors are people with a special gift for bringing the world together. They know people who have an ability to make an impact. Mavens are people who accumulate knowledge about a particular area. They are information brokers who like to get information and share it with others to help solve problems. Salesmen have an ability to persuade us when we are unconvinced. They are critical to the tipping point because they spur word-of-mouth epidemics.

These three characters correlate to three biblical personalities as well: the apostle (connector), often defined as "one who is sent"; the prophet (maven), defined as "one who proclaims truth"; and the evangelist (salesman), "one who wins the lost"—all described in Ephesians 4:11.

John Wesley used a structure similar to the maven-connector-salesmen framework when he founded Methodism in the 1780s. He was a connector (apostle) who stayed in a city after he preached to form small groups from the most enthusiastic of the followers. He used connectors (apostles) and salesmen (evangelists) to get people to his meetings. The community that resulted contributed to his success in starting the Methodist movement.

Mavens, connectors and salesmen make an idea contagious by working together to spread the message. Consider bringing these three types of people together to see real success on your next project.

HIS VISION, HIS WAY, IN HIS TIMING

*Then God said, "Take your son, your only son, Isaac, whom you love,
and go to the region of Moriah. Sacrifice him there as a burnt offering
on one of the mountains I will tell you about."*

GENESIS 22:2

Have you ever wanted something so badly that you would do almost anything to get it? Have you ever gotten so close to fulfilling a dream only to have it disappear right before your eyes? Such was the case for Abraham.

God promised Abraham that he would be the father of many nations. He promised Abraham that even though his wife was barren, he would have a son with her. However, Abraham panicked when Sarah aged beyond childbearing years, so he tried to help God by fathering Ishmael through Sarah's servant. Eventually, despite Abraham's disobedience, Sarah bore Isaac, the promised son.

Later, God gave Abraham another chance to obey Him. He told Abraham to sacrifice his son, Isaac, on an altar to demonstrate his obedience to God. Truly, this was one of the hardest instructions given to one of God's people in all of Scripture. It compares only to the heavenly Father sacrificing His own Son. Abraham obeyed, but just as he was about to sacrifice Isaac, God intervened and allowed a lamb to take Isaac's place as a prophetic sign of what was to take place in the future on the cross.

God often births a vision in our lives only to allow it to die before the purest version of the vision is manifested. Oswald Chambers observed, "God's method always seems to be vision first, and then reality, but in between the vision and the reality there is often a deep valley of humiliation. How often has a faithful soul been plunged into a like darkness when after the vision comes the test. When God gives a vision and darkness follows, waiting on God will bring you into accordance with the vision He has given if you await His timing. Otherwise, you try to do away with the supernatural in God's undertakings. Never try to help God fulfill His word."[58]

When God's vision is finally birthed, nothing will stop it. Our job is to allow God to birth *His vision* through us *His way* and in *His timing*.

WORKPLACE MINISTER

And whatever you do, whether in word or deed, do it all in the name of the
Lord Jesus, giving thanks to God the Father through him.

COLOSSIANS 3:17

More than 70 percent of our time is spent in the workplace, yet our training and teaching in local churches focuses on areas where we spend much less time. The workplace is the greatest mission field of our day and represents the greatest opportunity for societal transformation, yet we do not train workplace believers how to effectively integrate their faith life into their work life. The wall between Sunday and Monday still exists, and most workplace believers do not understand that all of life is spiritual, not just church life on Sunday.

Our studies show that an alarming 90 percent of Christians do not feel that they've been adequately trained to apply biblical faith in their work life. But God is removing the wall of separation by speaking to pastors and workplace believers all over the world.

A pastor recently shared how his church ordains their workplace believers for their calling to the workplace. Another pastor described his church's commitment to integrating training for workplace believers on the theology of work. Another told how they began a workplace ministry within their church for their workplace believers, and even integrated Sunday School programs specifically geared to help workplace believers understand their calling in the workplace.

We are entering a new era in the Church in which workplace believers will be seen as a remnant of the Body of Christ that needs to be mobilized and trained for the work of the ministry in the workplace. We are reversing the 80/20 rule in the 9 to 5 window from 20 percent of people doing workplace ministry to 80 percent.

Are you one of the men or women God is raising up for this task? Pray that God will help local church leaders understand and affirm this calling, and pray that they will respond by training their people for ministry in the workplace.

RETIREMENT OR A NEW ASSIGNMENT?

For a man may do his work with wisdom, knowledge and skill.
ECCLESIASTES 2:21

One man famous for his work in politics didn't begin his most well known job until he was 69 years old. He had already had a successful Hollywood movie career, but he decided in his late 60s to try his hand at politics. Eventually, this man became known as one of the United States' greatest statesmen. He had a faith that was genuine but not intruding or very public. He always treated people, even his detractors, with grace. He was known for his extraordinary love for his wife.

His name was Ronald Reagan, and I'll say it again: He did not begin his greatest work until he was 69 years old! By this season of life, most are thinking of retirement in Florida. Ronald Reagan, however, decided to run for president of the United States, and successfully served two terms as our fortieth president.

Reagan's faith led him to see the Soviet Union as an "evil empire," and he is remembered as the president who brought down Communism. Reagan's Christian faith also gave him the quiet confidence and self-certainty that made him a great leader and earned him the title "the great communicator."

Author Paul Kenger notes, "Where did he get his spiritual values? There were a number of influences. First and foremost was his mother, Nelle Reagan. I'm confident that had Nelle Reagan died in the winter of 1918-19—a near-victim of the devastating influenza epidemic that killed millions of healthy, middle-aged mothers around the world—Ronald Reagan very likely would not have become President. It was Nelle who insisted her boy go to church—a request he happily obliged—and it was in church that Reagan picked up not only those core beliefs and values, but also the intangibles so vital to his success: his confidence, his eternal optimism (which he called a 'God-given optimism'), and even his ability to speak. Indeed, history has also overlooked the fact that the Great Communicator found his first audiences in a church. He learned to speak in a church."[59]

Consider this: Your greatest work may yet be ahead of you. Don't let age keep you from being used by God.

WORSHIP AND WORK

One man considers one day more sacred than another;
another man considers every day alike.
ROMANS 14:5

Avodah, a Hebrew noun used in the Bible, is derived from the Hebrew verb *La'avod* that has two distinct yet intertwined meanings: worship and work. The dual meaning offers powerful wisdom for how we are to view our work lives.

Work, if done with integrity and unto God, is a form of worship in the biblical Hebrew context. The concept of segmenting our work from our faith life has never existed in the Bible. Instead, the Bible says that it is in the realm of the sacred to bring God into our everyday life. The Hebrews did not set aside a day of worship, such as Saturday or Sunday, but everyday was a place and time of worship.

The idea of separating our faith life from our work life is a Western idea. In Middle Eastern and Asian cultures, faith is never separate from work. When people come to faith in Christ from this area of the world, they have an easier time assimilating their faith into their work, because they have always understood the sacred and secular to be integrated.

God calls us too, to do our work as an act of worship to Him. Our work is not to be a place of sweat and toil but an expression of our love, faith and adoration of Jesus Christ.

Today, before you work, ask God to help you see your work in a new way—as worship to Him.

RELATING TO THOSE DIFFERENT FROM US

*The Samaritan woman said to him, "You are a Jew and I am a
Samaritan woman. How can you ask me for a drink?"*
JOHN 4:9

Do you find it difficult to relate to others who are different than you? Do you shy away from interacting with those who may have a different belief?

Jesus interacted with those in His culture who thought differently than He did. When Jesus met the Samaritan woman at the well it was much like an interaction that might happen today between a Christian and a Muslim, or a Jew and a Palestinian.

In order to influence our culture, it is vital that we engage with those unlike us. We often assume that others who come from different cultures do not want to engage with us. This is a deception from Satan. Many who grow up in other faiths do so as a cultural tradition, not because they have strongly held beliefs. For instance, many Muslims do not personally read the Koran; they simply believe what they are taught based on tradition. Every person is looking for a genuine relationship with God.

Jesus operated based on that assumption. Notice how Jesus engaged with the Samaritan woman: "Everyone who drinks this water will be thirsty again, but whoever drinks the water I give him will never thirst. The woman said to him, 'Sir, give me this water so that I won't get thirsty and have to keep coming here to draw water.' He told her, 'Go, call your husband and come back.' 'I have no husband,' she replied. Jesus said to her, 'You are right when you say you have no husband. The fact is, you have had five husbands, and the man you now have is not your husband. What you have just said is quite true.' 'Sir,' the woman said, 'I can see that you are a prophet'" (John 4:13-19).

Once Jesus established a rapport with the woman, He began to engage with her. He spoke supernaturally into her life, which broke through the religious spirit and prevented a theological debate. This led to faith in Christ and even the city being impacted.

Why not seek out a relationship with someone different from yourself? You'll be surprised at how God might use you.

THE QUEEN OF HEAVEN

The children gather wood, the fathers light the fire, and the women knead the dough and make cakes of bread for the Queen of Heaven.
JEREMIAH 7:18

If you want to change the spiritual climate of your city, you must address the principalities that rule that city. Such was the case for the apostle Paul when he went to the city of Ephesus, a center for magic and the occult. There was a territorial principality named Diana of the Ephesians that was worshiped by the people of Ephesus. The people gave money to this false god, and because of this, Diana strongly influenced the economy.

Her temple in Ephesus was listed as one of the Seven Wonders of the Ancient World—the most outstanding and opulent example of architecture in the whole city. Her followers called her "magnificent," "great goddess," "savior" and "Queen of Heaven."

Paul preached in Asia for two years and had great success in confronting this territorial principality. He began to neutralize the Queen of Heaven's power so much through the gospel that the common people began to notice. They stopped worshiping and sacrificing to her, and the silversmiths who manufactured her idols were going out of business.

Many who were converted burned all of the idols and magic books. Paul records, "When they calculated the value of the scrolls, the total came to fifty thousand drachmas. In this way the word of the Lord spread widely and grew in power" (Acts 19:20). Based on the U.S. economy today, the pile of magic paraphernalia that was burned would have been worth four million dollars![60]

In order for you to impact your city, you must identify and break down the ruling principalities that may be hindering the gospel there. Common principalities in the Western world include the religious spirit, the spirit of mammon, pride, and freemasonry, to name a few.

Ask God for wisdom and discernment as you prepare to deal with your local and regional principalities.

GOD IS NOT ABOUT *YOUR* SUCCESS

I tell you the truth, unless a kernel of wheat falls to the ground and dies,
it remains only a single seed. But if it dies, it produces many seeds.
The man who loves his life will lose it, while the man who hates his life
in this world will keep it for eternal life.

JOHN 12:24-25

God is all about your death so that *His* success can be realized through you!
This is why the Church is having such little impact—there are too many
believers who have not yet died to their old natures so that Christ can live
fully through them. When believers come to the end of themselves, they
lose their lives to Him, live through the power of the Holy Spirit and begin
to see the reality of a living gospel that impacts lives, workplaces, cities and
nations.

"Much of modern Christian enterprise is 'Ishmael.' Born not of God,
but of an inordinate desire to do God's will in our own way—the one thing
our Lord never did," wrote Oswald Chambers. The psalmist describes what
it means to live in our own strength:

Unless the LORD builds the house, its builders labor in vain. Unless
the LORD watches over the city, the watchmen stand guard in vain.
In vain you rise early and stay up late, toiling for food to eat—for he
grants sleep to those he loves (Psalm 127:1-2).

How can we die so that Christ can be our all and all? It usually takes a
crisis of significant proportions for most people to relinquish the control of
their lives. We must come to the end of ourselves and our striving to control
the events in our lives; we must finally come to the place where we can say,
"Lord, I surrender. Please take full control of my life."

Have you come to this place with God in your life? Let go and let God
make you a success His way.

"I CAN'T BELIEVE YOU THINK THAT!"

Who is wise and understanding among you? Let him show it by his good life, by deeds done in the humility that comes from wisdom.
JAMES 3:13

"I can't believe you think I said that," I complained to my wife. "I was simply trying to explain that I don't have the same feelings about that issue as you do." Her response left little empathy for my position because of the tone in which I responded to her. We resigned ourselves to agree to disagree.

We all see things through our own set of glasses. Men view things differently than women. Bosses see things differently than employees. One ethic group will see a situation totally differently than another. Our life experiences, our past treatment of circumstances and our personalities all contribute to how we view situations in daily life.

Perception is often each person's reality, whether that reality is true or not. Your perception of a situation is going to dictate your response more than the actual reality of the circumstances.

Whenever conflict arises from viewing things differently, there is really only one way to resolve the difference: If the other person is offended, offer a few words—"I'm sorry. Will you forgive me?"

Humbling ourselves is the only way to resolve the relational breach. This does not mean that you must agree with the other person's position; it simply means you acknowledge their right to their position and apologize for the manner in which you responded to their statements. This will usually allow most conflicts to avoid a breach in the relationship.

Is there someone you need to seek forgiveness from for taking an adversarial position?

TRANSFORMING YOUR WORKPLACE

This, then, is how you should pray: "Our Father in heaven, hallowed be your name, your kingdom come, your will be done on earth as it is in heaven."
MATTHEW 6:9-10

What would your workplace look like if this prayer were answered today where you work?

"Transformation" is a powerful word. Just hearing it, one almost automatically thinks of radical conversions and incredible change. But is it possible to transform your workplace into something Christlike? Jesus thinks so.

In *Anointed for Business,* Ed Silvoso tells the story of a Filipino businessman who owned a hotel chain. God saved this man and began an amazing transformation in his life and in his large-scale hotel.

The man owned a 1,600-room hotel that covered three buildings. Because of its rates and location, the hotel had become a haven for prostitution. There were over 2,000 employees, and the primary clientele was more than 3,000 prostitutes.

One of Silvoso's associates shared with the owner a formula for winning the lost. The businessman hired 40 pastors and told them to follow these instructions: (1) Speak peace to the wolves; bless those who curse you. (2) Eat and drink with the sinners; become their friends. (3) Pray for them and their needs.

The pastors were not to share the gospel until they'd met these three requirements for *two years.* What an investment! Ultimately, it paid off. The pastors followed these three rules and saw every single one of the 2,000 employees become saved. The hotel was upgraded to an executive level, raising the rates and forcing the prostitutes out because they could no longer afford it. The owner even added a prayer chapel with 24/7 prayer available to anyone by dialing "7" on the telephone. Two years later, 10,000 guests had received the Lord on the property.[61]

That's transformation! And that's the kind of transformation we can see in our workplaces. We just have to find the vision and the willingness to ask God, "Lord, what wilt Thou have me do?"

MARTHA'S BAD RAP

As the body without the spirit is dead, so faith without deeds is dead.
JAMES 2:26

Mary and Martha were entertaining Jesus in their home when Martha complained to Jesus about Mary sitting at His feet rather than assisting her with the needs of the meal. Many a preacher has condemned Martha for her focus on *doing* rather than sitting at the feet of Jesus as Mary did. However, let me ask you an important question: Who would you rather hire—Mary or Martha?

I can tell you, I would rather hire Martha in my business. There are times in the Body of Christ when we come and worship and then go away, failing to activate our faith lives in practical expression. The truth is, we need to model both Mary and Martha in our Christian lives.

There are times when we are called to sit at the feet of Jesus and worship Him. But we must always have an outlet for expressing the love of God through practical deeds. This is our point of contact to reach the world with the gospel.

My friends Dennis and Megan Doyle are committed believers who own one of the largest commercial real estate companies in Minnesota. After noticing that many corporations had overstocks and overruns of merchandise and food that could be used to help the poor, they began to collaborate with corporations to get the excess goods for distribution through various ministries across the world. The ministry, called Hope for the City, became very successful and has given more than $300 million in the past three years.

Like the Hope for the City ministry, we all need to model devotion and deeds—both aspects of the lives of Mary and Martha. And we all need a point of expression for our faith that the world can see. What type of expression might the Lord call you to have?

DO YOU NEED A BREAKTHROUGH?

*While I was still in prayer, Gabriel, the man I had seen in the earlier vision, came
to me in swift flight about the time of the evening sacrifice. He instructed me and
said to me, "Daniel, I have now come to give you insight and understanding."*

DANIEL 9:21-22

There are times in our lives when we need a breakthrough from God. Maybe
you need a new job or a breakthrough in your finances, direction on a big
business deal, or maybe physical healing from an illness. Sometimes we
need to hear from God directly.

Daniel sought God to understand why the nation had been in captivity
for 70 years. He began to fast and pray. At the end of this time, an angel of
the Lord appeared to him. It is clear that the angel came to Daniel because
of his fasting and prayer, and because he was seeking God for answers.

The prophet Jeremiah says, "You will seek me and find me when you seek
me with all your heart" (Jeremiah 29:13). The problem with most of us is that
we are unwilling to seek God for the answers—we are too lazy to spend time
in prayer and fasting, focusing intentionally on God.

Bill Bright, the founder of Campus Crusade for Christ, said:

I believe the power of fasting as it relates to prayer is the spiritual
atomic bomb that our Lord has given us to destroy the strongholds
of evil and usher in a great revival and spiritual harvest around the
world. The longer I fasted, the more I sensed the presence of the
Lord. The Holy Spirit refreshed my soul and spirit, and I experienced the joy of the Lord as seldom before. Biblical truths leaped at
me from the pages of God's Word. My faith soared as I humbled
myself and cried out to God and rejoiced in His presence.[62]

Do you need a breakthrough? Consider committing to a time of fasting
and prayer.

SIMPLY OBEY

But Naaman went away angry and said, "I thought that he would surely come out to me and stand and call on the name of the LORD his God, wave his hand over the spot and cure me of my leprosy."

2 KINGS 5:11

Naaman was an army general who needed healing from leprosy. A young servant girl suggested that the prophet Elisha could heal him. He followed her advice, and Elisha sent a message to him to do the following: "Go, wash yourself seven times in the Jordan, and your flesh will be restored and you will be cleansed" (2 Kings 5:10).

Like many of us, Naaman expected God to perform his miracle through Elisha in a dramatic and "religious" way. The instructions that came instead must have seemed ridiculous to him. Sometimes we fail to recognize that God can work through a simple act of obedience that may seem unrelated to our problem.

God told Joshua to walk around Jericho seven times to win the battle. Jesus put mud on a man's eyes to heal his blindness. Peter was told to catch a fish to find the money to pay his taxes.

Sometimes in order to receive a breakthrough from God, we need to change our diet or go see a doctor to see a change in our health. Sometimes we need to change the way we are doing our work to get a breakthrough in our careers.

Samuel the prophet told King Saul that obedience is better than sacrifice. He was right. Learning to listen to the Lord and following His instructions are the keys to success in life with God. Sometimes God chooses the dramatic, and sometimes He chooses the ordinary. In either case, both are miracles because God is the God over all creation.

Ask Him what steps you are to take for your breakthrough.

"I'M NOT READY!"

But he said to me, "My grace is sufficient for you, for my power is made perfect in weakness."
2 CORINTHIANS 12:9

If there is one thing that is consistent throughout Scripture, it is this: God calls people when they are not ready. God will never call you into service when you think you are prepared. This is intentional on God's part.

When God calls you, you may have a response similar to Saul when he was called to be the first king of Israel. Or maybe you will react like Gideon when he was called to take down the idols in his nation, or like Moses when he was called to deliver his people from Egypt.

Saul answered, "But am I not a Benjamite, from the smallest tribe of Israel, and is not my clan the least of all the clans of the tribe of Benjamin? Why do you say such a thing to me?" (1 Samuel 9:21).

"But Lord," Gideon asked, "how can I save Israel? My clan is the weakest in Manasseh, and I am the least in my family" (Judges 6:15).

But Moses said to God, "Who am I, that I should go to Pharaoh and bring the Israelites out of Egypt?" (Exodus 3:11).

When God calls, you will probably be in the most *unlikely* circumstances to receive that call. You will be in the midst of a crisis, you will lack resources and you will not have the skills you think you need. This is the way of God.

God works this way because He wants you to know that your call is based on His ability, not yours. When you think it is based on you, you possess a false humility, which is unbelief and disobedience on your part.

Has God called you to something you have failed to do because you felt you were not ready? Repent before the Lord, and let God accomplish great things through you today.

PLAYING TO ONE CONDUCTOR

*The eye cannot say to the hand, "I don't need you!" And the head
cannot say to the feet, "I don't need you!" On the contrary,
those parts of the body that seem to be weaker are indispensable, and the
parts that we think are less honorable we treat with special honor.*

1 CORINTHIANS 12:21-23

I watched as the conductor looked over to the violin section, then the percussion, then toward a seemingly insignificant lady standing way back in the corner waiting to play her one or two notes on a chime-looking instrument. *Who would even notice if she didn't play her instrument?* I wondered to myself. *The conductor would*, said the still voice in my spirit.

An orchestra is a great picture of the way the Body of Christ should operate. It is made up of different people with different gifts, all being led by the one Great Conductor, telling us when to use our gift in the right time.

I am sure the lady in the back of the room who only plays a few notes must think she doesn't measure up to the great violinist who sits right up close to the conductor. But imagine if you slowly removed each member of the orchestra one at a time. At first you may not notice any difference without a trained ear, but as you remove more and more members, you begin to miss the powerful and melodic sound of many instruments playing together.

Imagine if these instruments tried to go out and play songs all by themselves. Imagine if the tuba tried to play a solo. Or if the oboe did the same. You get the idea.

Each member in the Body of Christ matters. Every job matters to God and contributes to our great Conductor's grand plan to fulfill His purposes on the earth. Your contribution matters to God, and He has no hierarchy of importance.

Play your instrument to the glory of God in unison with the other instruments God has raised up for His purposes.

PICKING FRUIT

So I gave you a land on which you did not toil and cities you did not build; and you live in them and eat from vineyards and olive groves that you did not plant.

Joshua 24:13

I live on a golf course. Golf has been a part of my life since I was 11 years old. I went to college on a golf scholarship and later turned professional for three years. During the course of my life, golf has taught me many life lessons.

I often walk at sundown for exercise and use this time to pray. It is a quiet and beautiful time of day for walking. When I walk, I usually find one or two golf balls along the way. But one time was different.

On this particular walk, I began to find golf balls everywhere I looked. First I collected 5, then 8, then 10—and finally my pockets were stuffed with 13 golf balls! I noticed how strange it was to find so many balls on one walk, so I prayed, "Lord, what are You saying through this?" The answer came quickly: "I have called you to walk a specific path. I will bring the fruit to you. All you will have to do is pick it up and stay on My path for you. That is what it means to abide in Me."

The people of Israel conquered the Promised Land as a result of obedience, not sweat, toil or natural talent. In our work-life call, God desires to give us fruit from our calling when we fulfill the unique purpose for which God made us.

When something unusual happens in our daily life experience, it is a time to tune in to our spiritual antennae. God is often at work. We need to abide completely in His presence and purpose for our life so that we can pick the fruit He desires to bring into our path. Remember, His nature is to do exceedingly beyond what we can think or imagine.

THE FALLACY OF FULL-TIME CHRISTIAN WORK

And whatever you do, whether in word or deed, do it all in the name of the Lord Jesus, giving thanks to God the Father through him.

COLOSSIANS 3:17

Jonathon was a 25-year-old pastor's son who worked in his local Christian bookstore. He had started seminary but was unable to finish because of a lack of finances. He was okay with working in the bookstore but felt that it was a second-best type job. In fact, sometimes he felt that he had missed his calling.

Then one day a young woman wandered into the store. She was not a believer, and she was distressed. Her husband had just left her, and she did not know where to turn. She was walking through the mall when she noticed the store and decided to walk in, not knowing why.

"Hello, may I help you?" said Jonathon.

"Well . . . I don't know. I saw your sign and just came in." Right then, she began to cry. She told Jonathon about her plight, not knowing why she would do such a thing with a perfect stranger. Jonathon listened and began to talk with her. Before the conversation was over, Jonathon had prayed with the woman and led her to faith in Christ.

That night Jonathon pondered what had happened that day. He realized that he had personally led a woman into eternity by being available in his workplace. He felt a new sense of purpose behind what he thought was simply a job to put food on the table until he could get to his *real* ministry. He confessed his wrong view of his work to the Lord and realized for the first time that working at a bookstore was ministry, too.

We have incorrectly elevated the role of the vocational Christian worker as holier and more committed than the person who serves in other arenas. Yet the call to any workplace is as important as any other calling. God needs His people in every sphere of life. Otherwise, many would never come to know Him.

Wherever you are called, serve the Lord in that place. Let Him demonstrate His power through your life so that others might experience Him through you today.

GRACE ABOUNDS

And God is able to make all grace abound to you, so that in all things at all times, having all that you need, you will abound in every good work.

2 CORINTHIANS 9:8

God always knows what we need before we even ask. I recall a few years ago when God allowed my business to dry up—it happened in order to lead me to an entirely new calling. At the time, this was a scary proposition because I had many outstanding obligations to banks and others, and I had to have a significant cash flow to make these payments.

I thought I was at the end of my rope when a consulting contract with a client was ending and I saw no prospects for replacing it. But days before the contract expired, I received a call from a new ministry that was consistent with the calling I sensed God was leading me to. They asked me to consult with them for the next year, and I took their offer. At the end of that year, I learned that God had spoken to the ministry's founder, telling him to pay my entire salary out of his own pocket in order to meet the needs I had at that time. This was no insignificant amount, either.

At the conclusion of my contract with them, I was wondering where my income was going to come from for the next year. The day before I was informed that their commitment would decrease by 50 percent, I received a call from the administrator of our foundation. They informed me that a supporter had given $20,000 to our ministry. God encouraged me through this gift to know that He was my provider.

God equips us to fulfill the mission He has for us. Whenever there is a lack of resources, God is either teaching us to trust Him in greater ways or He is using the experience to direct our path to new sources of income. Trust the Lord to bring you what you need in the timing that He determines.

THE VALUE OF AGE AND WISDOM

But Rehoboam rejected the advice the elders gave him and consulted the young men who had grown up with him and were serving him.

2 CHRONICLES 10:8

Age and wisdom don't always go hand in hand—but most of the time, they do.

King Solomon became heavy-handed in his employment practices by placing an overbearing burden on the workers, which caused a problem with the northern tribes, equivalent to the threat of a labor strike in modern times. Jeroboam, Solomon's son, was like the head of the labor union and had to flee to Egypt from his father's anger. After Solomon's death, another of his sons, Rehoboam, became king, and Jeroboam appealed to his brother on behalf of the working people.

To make a decision, Rehoboam asked for advice from the older men who had been a part of Solomon's reign and then asked for advice from his younger contemporaries. The elders advised Rehoboam that if he lightened the load his father had put on the people, they would be loyal workers throughout his reign. The younger advisors, on the other hand, told Rehoboam to tighten the reigns even more than his father.

Rehoboam took the younger advisors' advice, and as a result, the northern tribes rebelled, and the kingdom of Israel was permanently divided.

Today there still exists a tendency to discount input from older people. However, God has placed wisdom in older people from which the young can learn a great deal. Do not despise input from those who may be considerably older than you. God has placed a level of wisdom in them that can help you to avoid major mistakes.

BEING LED INTO THE DESERT

Then Jesus was led by the Spirit into the desert to be tempted by the devil.
MATTHEW 4:1

After Jesus had been baptized by John the Baptist, the Holy Spirit led Him into the desert to be tempted by the devil. Jesus came to Earth as a human, with the same limitations as you and I. In the desert Jesus was tempted as a man, not as God. But Satan tempted Jesus because he wanted Jesus to come out of His human condition and to exercise His identity as God. It was Jesus' first real test under human limitations.

Some people think that God would never lead His people into the desert to be tested—but if Jesus is our example, this is obviously not true (see Matthew 4:1). Some would say that temptation is the devil's doing. The fact is, God actually uses Satan and desert experiences to test His servants, in order to develop obedience in their lives.

God led the people of Israel into the desert to learn something about themselves. They learned about their level of obedience when life became difficult: "Remember how the LORD your God led you all the way in the desert these forty years, to humble you and to test you in order to know what was in your heart, whether or not you would keep his commands" (Deuteronomy 8:2).

When God led Jesus into the desert, Jesus had to tap into the power of the Holy Spirit, just like we must, in order to have victory over temptation. Jesus was not allowed to be God in the desert, because God was testing His obedience. For the rest of Jesus' life, the miracles He performed were the result of seeing what the Father was doing and obeying His commands. Jesus told us that we would do even greater works than He did because we have the same access to the Father as He did.

When God leads you into the desert, He is allowing you to learn something about yourself. We all need to learn how we will respond to temptations in our lives. As we press into God during these times, the roots of our faith are forced deeper and deeper into the soil of His grace.

Do not fear being led into the desert. This too is the way of God.

MARKETPLACE FORGIVENESS

See to it that no one misses the grace of God and that no bitter root
grows up to cause trouble and defile many.
HEBREWS 12:15

Bill once had a business partner who took advantage of their relationship and embezzled money from their firm. This man was caught, but Bill decided to drop the charges if his friend agreed to repay the money he had stolen. The forgiveness Bill extended in this situation allowed both men to regain freedom in spite of the wrong that Bill's friend had committed.

In business and in life, we are given plenty of opportunities to grow bitter from relationships that bring hurt and pain. The writer of the Hebrews passage above admonishes us not to miss the grace of God so that we don't take up bitterness as a response to life's pain. He cautions us against this because he knows that a bitter root grows and grows until it eventually begins to poison others. If bitterness is allowed to take root, we become imprisoned to it. God's grace will no longer have as great an effect in our lives. We become ineffective, insensitive and spiritually dead when we harbor bitterness. We can even become physically ill from it. God does not live in bitterness—He lives in grace and has provided grace for every person to walk in.

One day, I was challenged to deal with an individual who had hurt me terribly. I was faced with a decision: Would I choose bitterness or would I choose grace? Oh, how my natural tendency wanted to choose bitterness! But God provided the courage to choose grace. With that grace came freedom—a freedom to love and even accept the person who was the source of my pain.

This is the real place where Christ's power is revealed. We cannot live without His supernatural grace. Are you in need of grace today? It is there for the receiving. It will take courage to accept it and to walk in it, but it will be your step to freedom.

PREPARATION IN ARABIA

*Nor did I go up to Jerusalem to see those who were apostles before I was,
but I went immediately into Arabia and later returned to Damascus.*
GALATIANS 1:17

The apostle Paul clearly understood the call that Jesus placed on his life at his conversion. He did not have to consult other men to verify his calling. But before he was released to begin his own mission, Paul went to Arabia for three years. Why did Paul have to go to Arabia for three years before he met with any of Christ's other apostles?

The Scripture does not tell us plainly why Paul spent three years in Arabia. No doubt, Paul had plenty of time there to consider what had taken place in his life. His journey to Arabia gave him three years' time to develop an intimate knowledge and relationship with his newfound Savior.

So often when God places a call on one of His children, the ability to answer the call requires a separation between the old life and the new life. We are called away from the old in order to prepare our heart for what is to come.

This can be a painful and difficult separation. Joseph was separated from his family. Jacob was sent to live with his uncle Laban. Moses was sent to the desert. Perhaps God has placed you in your own desert period. Perhaps you cannot make sense of the situation in which you find yourself. If you, like Paul, will get intimate with God during this time, He will reveal the purposes He has for you. The key is pressing into Him. Seek Him with a whole heart, and He will be found.

God may have a special calling and message that He is building in your life right now. Trust in His love for you, that He will fully complete the work He has started in you.

"I NEEDED POWER"

If you then, though you are evil, know how to give good gifts to your children, how much more will your Father in heaven give the Holy Spirit to those who ask him!
LUKE 11:13

It is good for us to know about the struggles that others have in their faith journeys. Here is Oswald Chambers's story of how he struggled to understand the role of the Holy Spirit in his life:

I was in Dunoon College as a tutor in philosophy when Dr. F. B. Meyer came and spoke about the Holy Spirit. I determined to have all that was going, and went to my room and asked God simply and definitely for the baptism of the Holy Spirit, whatever that meant . . .

At a little meeting held during a mission in Dunoon, a well-known lady led our meeting and set us to prayer, and then sang "Touch Me Again, Lord."

I rose to my feet in an effort to receive that prayer then sat down. The lady worker, who knew me well, said: "That is very good of our brother, he has spoken like that as an example to the rest of you." Up I got again and said: "I got up for no one else's sake, I got up for my own sake; either Christianity is a downright fraud, or I have not got hold of the right end of the stick." And then there I claimed the gift of the Holy Spirit in dogged commitment to Luke 11:13.

I had no vision of heaven or angels, I had nothing. Then like a flash something happened inside of me, and I saw that I had been wanting power in my own hand, so to speak, that I might say—"Look what I have by putting my all on the altar." . . . Love is the beginning, love is the middle and love is the end. After He comes in, all you see is "Jesus Only, Jesus Ever."[63]

The Holy Spirit has the power to change us. Even though the moment we experience the Holy Spirit might not be all we had envisioned it to be, He does begin a work in our lives the moment we invite Him in.

COME OUT OF THE STRONGHOLD

Do not stay in the stronghold. Go into the land of Judah.
1 SAMUEL 22:5

David and his fighting men were hiding in the cave of Adullam and many of Israel's down-and-out had joined them to flee from Saul. David was content to stay in the stronghold of safety, but one day God's prophet came to David and told him that he must leave the stronghold and go into the land of Judah, which means "praise."

When life beats down on us and we want to hide in a cave, God often places people in our lives who prod us into moving in the right direction. He does not want us to remain in the place of discouragement. He wants us to move into the land of praise.

I recall a difficult time in my own life. It seemed to drag on and on with no change until I wanted to retreat into a cave and forget pressing on. It was a great time of discouragement. But then, a godly man came to me and said, "You must keep moving! There are too many who are depending on you in the Kingdom."

I didn't totally understand what he meant at the time. Now, however, I know that he was telling me that God prepares each of us to be the vessel He wants to use in the life of another person, but we will never be that vessel if we give up and hide in our cave of discouragement. Not only must we keep moving, but also we must move into a new realm. Our attitude must move from discouragement to praise:

He has sent me to bind up the brokenhearted, to proclaim freedom for the captives and release from darkness for the prisoners . . . to comfort all who mourn . . . a garment of praise instead of a spirit of despair. They will be called oaks of righteousness, a planting of the LORD for the display of his splendor (Isaiah 61:1-3).

It is only when we move past discouragement and into praise that we begin to live above our problems. Make a decision today to go into the land of Judah.

MADE FOR HEIGHTS

*The Sovereign LORD is my strength; he makes my feet like the feet
of a deer, he enables me to go on the heights.*

HABAKKUK 3:19

The book of Habakkuk encourages us to question what God is doing in our lives. When we are thrown into suffering for a period of time, or when our enemies are prospering while we are just barely getting by, we might wonder about the fairness of God and life. Habakkuk affirms that God is God and that we are made to scale the mountains of adversity. We just need to be still and know that He is at work, because He is Who He says He is, and He keeps all of His promises.

God equips His people to scale the heights in the midst of great challenges. He enables us to go to the higher places with Him, where we are set apart from the world. Sometimes the way we have to go to get there is through suffering and sorrow, but if we rest in Him and trust Him, we come out where He wants us.

Jesus sent the Holy Spirit to the disciples (and to us today), in order for them to scale the mountain of adversity with a new form of power that they had not yet experienced:

> But you will receive power when the Holy Spirit comes on you; and
> you will be my witnesses in Jerusalem, and in all Judea and Samaria,
> and to the ends of the earth (Acts 1:8).

If you find yourself doubting God and His plan for your life, know that this is a normal aspect of your journey in faith. Remember, God has made available His Holy Spirit in order for you to accomplish the tasks that lie ahead.

Ask the Holy Spirit to enable you to achieve the heights for which He has created you.

TWO PILLARS

He erected the pillars in the front of the temple, one to the south and one to the north. The one to the south he named Jakin and the one to the north Boaz.

In 2003, I took my first trip to Israel. I visited the Wailing Wall, the only portion left of the original Temple built by David's son, Solomon. I took an underground tour of the Temple, which allowed me to see the incredibly huge, square boulders that were used to lay the actual foundation.

On top of these enormous stones, pillars were erected to provide the height and strength needed to connect the roof to the lower foundation. What's remarkable is the name of the two pillars that stood at the front of the Temple: Jachin, which means "he establishes," and Boaz, which means "in him is strength." Jachin was a priest, while Boaz was a businessman—also known as a "king" in the Scriptures. He was also Ruth's kinsman-redeemer, whose lineage can be traced to Christ (see Matthew 1:5). Worshipers at the Temple had to pass through these soaring columns to enter.

Seeing these two pillars, I was struck that today God is using the same combination of priestly leadership (the Jachin pillar) and market leadership (the Boaz pillar) to bring His presence into a place that was formerly forbidden territory: the workplace.

It is only when this partnership cooperates in unity, mutual respect and affirmation that we will see God's power released. Together, like the pillars of Jerusalem's Temple, we can support the presence of God and bring it into all spheres of society to transform workplaces, cities and nations.

CHECK YOUR ARMOR

That is why the Israelites cannot stand against their enemies.

JOSHUA 7:12

Battle commanders want to know where their forces' defenses are weakest. CEOs want to know where their companys' profit margin is at risk. In the same way, Christians should want to know where we are spiritually vulnerable.

This is the message God told Joshua when he attempted to go against a small army at Ai, which was the Israelites' second battle in the Promised Land. From Joshua's vantage point, everything seemed to be going just as it should for the Israelites. So when his army was soundly defeated, Joshua cried out to God, "Ah, Sovereign LORD, why did You ever bring this people across the Jordan to deliver us into the hands of the Amorites to destroy us?" (Joshua 7:7).

The people were defeated because one person had violated the covenant with God. The army was told not to take any possessions from the first battle, but one person failed to be obedient and everyone suffered.

Sin makes our armor vulnerable to attack from Satan, who then gains permission from God to attack us in the area where we have failed to uphold righteousness. If we break down in moral purity, Satan comes in and establishes a stronghold. If we give place to bitterness and unwillingness to forgive, we break fellowship with God and others. If we become money-focused, we fall into greed and deception. Sin is a vicious cycle that leaves us weak and vulnerable to ever more sin.

Examine your armor today. Make sure you are not susceptible to attack. Begin from a solid spiritual foundation and your chances of success will be great.

DISCERNING ROAD BLOCKS

You need to persevere so that when you have done the will of God,
you will receive what he has promised.
HEBREWS 10:36

How do you know when the obstacles in your path have been placed by God to protect you, or by Satan to hinder God's purposes in your affairs?

I was once in California, traveling four hours to a speaking engagement, when terrible fires broke out and many of the highways were shut down. As a result, I had to detour to a small town and was questioning whether I should turn around and go back home or continue on to my meeting. I stopped at a convenience store to pray and consider, and a woman pumping gas next to me said that the interstate was closed and if I was going north I would never get there—and even if I *did* get there, I'd have difficulty getting back.

Suddenly, fear struck me with the prospects of being stranded in a strange place. I quietly prayed, asking the Lord whether this was a warning for me to turn back or Satan's hindrance. I went into the convenience store to inquire about a map. While I was standing there a man walked up to me and said, "Where are you trying to go?" I told him my dilemma and he explained that the interstate was open just north of where we were. In fact, he had to go to the exact spot I was headed and would be glad to guide me there.

This man took me through all sorts of side roads in very unfamiliar areas. I would never have reached my destination by myself, nor would I have made the attempt.

When we came to the interstate ramp just above where the fires were, he waved as he sent me on my way. I had no more trouble. I arrived at the luncheon on time and ministered to the businessmen.

I often look at that situation and wonder if God sent His angel to lead me where I was to go. Immediately after I had prayed at that convenience store, the man approached me and gave me the answer.

Do you have a situation in which you're having trouble discerning whether God is protecting you or Satan is hindering you? Ask God to show you His way.

RECOGNIZING THE SOURCE OF SUCCESS

Now then, tell my servant David, "This is what the LORD Almighty says:
I took you from the pasture and from following the flock
to be ruler over my people Israel."

2 SAMUEL 7:8

When David neared the end of his life, God used the prophet Nathan to remind David of the journey he had made from his humble beginnings. God reminded David that *He* had taken David from pasturing sheep in the fields to pastoring a nation. God also reminded David that *He* had cut off all of David's enemies for David's sake and for the sake of his nation.

Have you ever felt tempted to look at your accomplishments with pride, as if you were the reason for your success? Have you ever thought that your prosperity was due to your ingenuity? Or has your material success been a testimony to others that God is the ruler of all aspects of your life, even the material side?

The greatest temptation some of us will ever face is the pride of ownership. If we think our success is a result of our own efforts, we affront God and open the door to pride. "A man's pride brings him low, but a man of lowly spirit gains honor" (Proverbs 29:23).

Success can be a greater test than adversity. "Not every man can carry a full cup. Sudden elevation frequently leads to pride and a fall. The most exacting test of all to survive is prosperity," said Oswald Chambers. Success can be a breeding ground for complacency with God and pride of ownership.

Do you have a proper understanding of who you are? Do you understand that it is God who has given you the ability to work and to achieve? He is the source of all good things. Ask God today if your life models this belief.

COMPLETE THE WORK

*Tell Archippus: "See to it that you complete the work
you have received in the Lord."*
Colossians 4:17

Have you ever driven by a construction project that had been abandoned when it was only half-finished? These sites are lasting testimonies of a vision, an investment, and an event that killed the project.

Why do projects fail to be completed? There may be a number of reasons. There could have been a failure to raise adequate funds. There could have been a fall-out among management. The project could have been simply ill conceived.

Good planning is a key to estimating what it takes to complete a project. We must conceive of a project and then clearly write out the vision with detailed specifications that identify what will be needed to complete it.

Entrepreneurs have a tendency to conceive a project without estimating the financial and manpower requirements necessary for completion. Many a project has died because of this trait among entrepreneurs.

Great entrepreneurs, on the other hand, understand their need to have detail-oriented people around them. These are wise entrepreneurs who have learned to complement their weaknesses with those who can help them achieve their vision.

Do you have a vision for a work that God has called you to do? Identify what will be needed to achieve success and get started (but don't forget to complete the vision).

"FOR ONLY $19.95"

His divine power has given us everything we need for life and godliness through our knowledge of him who called us by his own glory and goodness.

2 PETER 1:3

During my career in advertising I worked with many well-known companies such as American Express and Steinway Pianos. I also created direct-response TV commercials for different kinds of products.

A direct response TV commercial is a television commercial that offers a product or service via a free call. While working on these ads, I learned that the "magic" price point for a product is $19.95. Anything over this amount significantly reduces viewer response.

Another key to direct response commercial success is that the product has to demonstrate an ability to solve a viewer's felt need. Household items that solve common problems or improve the viewer's ability to perform a task are the most successful.

Advertising is usually designed to appeal to people's wants versus their needs. What we perceive as a need is often simply a want. Peter tells us that the gospel provides us a way to distinguish between wants and needs. According to Peter, the gospel provides every believer with divine power to receive what he or she *needs* for life and godliness. In order to access this power, believers must develop a knowledge of Christ.

The Bible says, "the truth will set you free" (John 8:32). When we know about the gifts Christ has provided for us, we are able to access those gifts to meet a need or solve a problem. However, if we do not study the Scriptures daily, we will never know what is available to us and will not be able to use God's gifts to meet our daily needs.

Make a commitment to study God's Word daily, and spend time reflecting on His work in your life. Then you will discover that "the truth shall make you free."

GOING BEYOND YOUR PARADIGM

*So Saul went to Naioth at Ramah. But the Spirit of God came even upon him,
and he walked along prophesying until he came to Naioth. He stripped off his
robes and also prophesied in Samuel's presence. He lay that way all that day
and night. This is why people say, "Is Saul also among the prophets?"*

1 SAMUEL 19:23-24

Saul had just been anointed to be the first king of Israel. He was being
launched into a whole new calling. Because of this new calling, he started to
hang out with the spiritual leaders of the nation—and to prophesy.

When the new king began to speak words of prophecy, the prophets
wondered if he, too, was a prophet. The fact was that Saul was *not* a prophet—
God was simply doing a new thing through Saul, activating something in
him that had previously been dormant.

When God calls you into a new endeavor, you may find that God
anoints what you considered your weakest traits. God turns shepherds like
Moses into leaders of nations. He turns farmers like Gideon into reformers.
He turns impetuous and unstable personalities like Peter into leaders that
can transform a culture and lead a movement.

Whenever God does a new thing in a life, people notice the change.
Quiet people become bold. Poor speakers become great communicators.
Those who were never leaders before become leaders. This is the way of
God: When God looks at an individual, He looks at his or her future, not
his or her past. He is always looking at the person He has created you to
become, not the person you are now.

How do you think God views your life? What is the destiny you believe
He has chosen you to fulfill?

UNWHOLESOME TALK

Do not let any unwholesome talk come out of your mouths,
but only what is helpful for building others up according to
their needs, that it may benefit those who listen.

EPHESIANS 4:29

The way you interact with fellow employees at work can often determine whether you will be the leaven for Christ in your workplace or be viewed as one of the multitudes.

Two defining situations in the workplace involve joke-telling and derogatory discussions about employees and bosses. If we laugh at off-color jokes, we communicate to the person telling the joke that it is okay to do so. If we fail to laugh, however, we discourage this behavior.

When someone is about to tell a joke in your presence, stop that person and ask, "Is this a clean joke? If not, I don't want to hear it." This defines future situations with that person, and word will spread to others in the office because of your response.

The other defining workplace situation involves how you talk about management in front of other employees. In a workplace it can easily become an "us vs. them" culture. When this happens, you violate Paul's command to honor those who employ you. He says, "Teach slaves to be subject to their masters in everything, to try to please them, not to talk back to them, and not to steal from them, but to show that they can be fully trusted, so that in every way they will make the teaching about God our Savior attractive" (Titus 2:9-10).

Remember, you are always a witness at work, whether you use words or not. As the psalmist wrote, "LORD, who may dwell in your sanctuary? Who may live on your holy hill? He whose walk is blameless and who does what is righteous, who speaks the truth from his heart and has no slander on his tongue, who does his neighbor no wrong and casts no slur on his fellow-man" (Psalm 15:1-3).

THE POWER OF SERVING OTHERS

Each one should use whatever gift he has received to serve others,
faithfully administering God's grace in its various forms.
1 PETER 4:10

There is a Kingdom principle that few people really understand: When you focus on serving others, God often meets your own need.

The law of sowing and reaping comes into play in these two Kingdom principles: "Sow for yourselves righteousness, reap the fruit of unfailing love" (Hosea 10:12) and "Remember this: Whoever sows sparingly will also reap sparingly, and whoever sows generously will also reap generously. Each man should give what he has decided in his heart to give, not reluctantly or under compulsion, for God loves a cheerful giver. And God is able to make all grace abound to you, so that in all things at all times, having all that you need, you will abound in every good work" (2 Corinthians 9:6-8).

When God calls me to serve another person with my time and resources, I notice that God measures unrelated resources back to me. Sometimes it comes through an unexpected donation to our ministry or a speaking engagement or a new opportunity. It is uncanny how I am consistently blessed when I serve others.

Serving is a great way to steer clear of viewing people or organizations as competition, because through serving we place others above ourselves. Besides, the Bible says that God has already assigned our portion. We cannot manipulate outcomes anyway:

> LORD, you have assigned me my portion and my cup; you have made my lot secure. The boundary lines have fallen for me in pleasant places; surely I have a delightful inheritance (Psalm 16:5-6).

We don't serve others to gain on our own behalf. However, when we do serve others, there is a Kingdom principle that works on our behalf as fruit of our service. Is there someone you need to serve today?

BUILDING A MIGHTY TEAM

These are the names of David's mighty men.
2 SAMUEL 23:8

David and Jesus each built teams that were made up of the unlikeliest people. David's small army of men became known as "David's mighty men" because of their extraordinary exploits. However, they were the rejects of society. Jesus' team was made up of common men who would never have been chosen by other rabbis, yet they were chosen by the superstar of up-and-coming teachers: Jesus.

We can learn three key things from David in particular about building a mighty team. First, David's men came to him as a result of battle. They fought together and learned firsthand about one another's capabilities. They had covered one another's backs on several occasions, and they trusted each other.

Second, David modeled servant-leadership with his men. When three of his mighty men risked their lives to obtain drinking water for him during a battle, David refused to drink it, choosing instead to pour it out onto the ground. This no doubt made a big impression on his men and only drew greater devotion to him because of his own sacrifice.

Finally, David and his men experienced God-sized victories when they were the underdogs. They defeated bigger armies and more resourceful enemies than themselves, and because of their underdog status, they saw God's hand in their victories.

Keep these things in mind as you build your own team. Learn to trust those on your team, and take a lesson from David's management style by modeling his servant-leadership.

A PROPHET WITHOUT HONOR

"Where did this man get these things?" they asked. "What's this wisdom that has been given him, that he even does miracles! Isn't this the carpenter? Isn't this Mary's son and the brother of James, Joseph, Judas and Simon? Aren't his sisters here with us?" And they took offense at him. Jesus said to them, "Only in his hometown, among his relatives and in his own house is a prophet without honor."

MARK 6:3-4

In the eyes of His family and community, Jesus was more qualified to be a carpenter than the Son of God. It was too difficult to change their old perceptions about someone they knew so well. It is the same for your family members.

Have you ever noticed how difficult it can be to spiritually impact your immediate circle of friends and family? Jesus warned us of this phenomenon. We often relate to family and friends differently than with acquaintances, because we share a history with them that no one else has. "After all—you're just my sister or brother, with whom I fought, played and lived everyday life," we might say. The sad result of this mindset is that we often do not experience the same fruit of ministry in our family's lives that we do outside this circle.

Ultimately, it is God who determines the fruit of our lives. Do not allow spiritual pride to prevent you from freely giving to your family and friends when they do not accept you in the way you think they should.

Many did not receive Jesus. Therefore, many will not receive you. Nevertheless, allow God to touch the few in your circle that He chooses to touch through you.

ADORNED BY THE DOCTRINE OF GOD

Exhort bondservants to be obedient to their own masters, to be well pleasing in all things, not answering back, not pilfering, but showing all good fidelity, that they may adorn the doctrine of God our Savior in all things.

TITUS 2:9-10, *NKJV*

The island of Crete was known for its corruption and many false gods. It was also the center of the jewelry trade. In the above passage, Paul challenges Titus and the Cretan church to *adorn their lives* with the doctrine of God, rather than the jewelry that was so much a part of their culture.

Whenever you are challenged by an environment that is corrupt and ungodly, you have an opportunity to let your light shine before those in that culture. The greater the corruption, the greater your light can shine. It is not a time to flee; it is a time to shine brighter. Paul addressed five unique things believers could do:

1. *Be obedient to their masters*—submit to their authority structures.
2. *Be well pleasing in all things*—do their work with excellence.
3. *Not answer back*—handle conflict with wisdom and courtesy.
4. *Not pilfer*—model integrity.
5. *Show all good fidelity*—demonstrate loyalty and dependability.

Do you find your environment difficult to work in? The answer is to live to glorify the Lord in the midst of your culture. An industry survey revealed the average person will come in contact with 300 people over the course of a year through their work. What better opportunity to let your life be adorned by the doctrine of God? St. Francis of Assisi agreed—he encouraged believers in his day to "preach the gospel always."

INSECURE LEADERSHIP

When Herod realized that he had been outwitted by the Magi, he was furious, and he gave orders to kill all the boys in Bethlehem and its vicinity who were two years old and under, in accordance with the time he had learned from the Magi.

MATTHEW 2:16

Any leader who is not secure in God will be insecure in their leadership actions. King Herod was such a leader. He feared the loss of power and had to control every aspect of the people he was ruling. When Herod heard about Jesus' coming birth, his insecurity spun out of control and led to decisions that threatened and ended many lives in Jerusalem and Bethlehem.

Herod had deep-seated control issues, rooted in the fear of losing power, money and prestige.

When a leader has control issues rooted in fear, he or she tends to argue with, manipulate and confront his or her subordinates. However, a leader who has yielded his or her life and work to God can relinquish outcomes to the Lord and let God change things that may go astray. A secure leader realizes that God is the source of his or her power and leadership, and that leader does not need to fear others who may demonstrate leadership qualities. Instead, Christ-following leaders are able to affirm others for the sake of the organization as a whole.

Pray that God makes you a leader who is secure in your God-given position.

AVOID THE ESCAPE MENTALITY

Praise be to the LORD my Rock,
who trains my hands for war,
my fingers for battle.
PSALM 144:1

One of the best-selling American fiction series of all time focuses on the end times, called *Left Behind*. It deals with the rapture of Christians from the earth before the final end-times crisis takes place and the anti-Christ rules.

If we are not careful, we will fall into the mindset that says that we're simply buying time until Jesus calls us home. No matter what the end-times Scriptures teach, it is clear that believers should model a behavior that is more like a soldier desiring to take land than a person awaiting an airlift.

Today in the Church of Jesus Christ, we often have a cruise-ship mentality instead of a battleship mentality. Our army is often ill equipped to take the land that God has provided through His Son. This is why believers in the workplace must see their work and calling as an assignment from God. They are to demonstrate His power in all of society in order to restore His rule upon the earth. That is the key reason Jesus died on the cross—to restore that which was lost (see Luke 19:10).

Are you engaged in the battle?

THE MARKETPLACE PSALM

LORD, who may dwell in your sanctuary?
Who may live on your holy hill?

PSALM 15:1

In February 2001, *Sales and Marketing* magazine did a survey and found that among those surveyed 58 percent cheat on expense reports, 50 percent work a second job on company time, 36 percent rush closed deals through accounting before they were really closed, 22 percent list a "strip bar" as a restaurant on an expense report, and 19 percent give a kickback to a customer.

If Psalm 15 were the core value of every business plan and purpose statement and if it were reviewed with every employee before hiring, the workplace would be a very different place:

> He whose walk is blameless and who does what is righteous, who speaks the truth from his heart and has no slander on his tongue, who does his neighbor no wrong and casts no slur on his fellow-man, who despises a vile man but honors those who fear the LORD, who keeps his oath even when it hurts, who lends his money without usury and does not accept a bribe against the innocent. He who does these things will never be shaken (Psalm 15:2-5).

Are you blameless in your approach to your work life? Are you truthful in all your dealings? Do you treat customers, vendors and fellow employees as your neighbor? Do you say what you do truthfully and do what you say? Do you follow through even if the outcome may not be positive? Will you lend money without usury to a friend and refuse a bribe? If you can say yes to these questions, then you are a Psalm 15 man or woman, and you can dwell on God's holy hill.

Friend, pray that God makes this psalm a part of your life. Ask God to show you how to live this chapter in all you do. Amen.

LEARN FROM GOD'S CREATION

For since the creation of the world God's invisible qualities—his eternal power and divine nature—have been clearly seen, being understood from what has been made, so that men are without excuse.

ROMANS 1:20

Have you ever heard someone say, "I don't see any evidence of God. How can a person believe in someone they can't see or prove even exists?"

The Bible tells us that God is revealed in His creation every day. Look at the human body and consider how thousands of body parts automatically work together. Someone created it to work this well. If it were a manufactured product, it would be in the repair shop all the time because of all the moving parts required to make it work.

The twelfth-century Scottish Christian mystic Richard of St. Victor said, "The whole of this sensible world is like a book written by the finger of God." Think about how the seas know their boundaries. Ponder the beauty of the mountains and the balance of rain and oxygen that stabilizes the ecosystem. Consider God's signature, the rainbow. Look at nature and wonder at the creative design of the hundreds of thousands of species of animals like the tiger, the elephant, the great whales and the millions of species of birds, just to name a few.

Consider the planet we live on. As author Mike Taylor notes:

The Earth is a rough sphere about eight thousand miles in diameter, which means that it's about four thousand miles straight down to the center. We're accustomed to thinking of it as a ball of rock, but that's not so: the great majority of the Earth is liquid—molten rock called magma swirling, incredible slowly, beneath our feet. The solid part of the earth that we live on, and in whose hollows the sea sits, is called the crust, and on average it's only a few miles thick—maybe ten miles. That's like a layer a third of a millimeter thick coating a football. We live on that incredibly fragile, thin layer of plates floating on the subterranean sea of magma.[64]

Yes, God has revealed Himself in His creation.

LABOR ALONE WILL NOT SATISFY

All the labor of man is for his mouth, and yet the soul is not satisfied.
ECCLESIASTES 6:7, *NKJV*

How would you feel about yourself if your job were revoked tomorrow? Let's imagine that your income wouldn't change, just what you do everyday.

One of the schemes that Satan uses in the life of Christian workers is to get them to base their value solely on the type of work they do and how well they do it. We call this performance-based acceptance. It says, "As long as I have a good job and as long as I do it well, I have self-esteem."

This is a slippery slope, and Satan can use these thoughts to keep our focus on *our* performance rather than on Christ. In reality, we are not meant to find our value in what we do. Instead, our value is based solely on who we are in Christ.

The apostle Paul wrestled with this after he came to faith in Christ. He had grown to the top of his field as a Jewish leader, and it was probably difficult for him to surrender his stature to identity in Christ:

> If anyone else thinks he has reasons to put confidence in the flesh, I have more: circumcised on the eighth day, of the people of Israel, of the tribe of Benjamin, a Hebrew of Hebrews; in regard to the law, a Pharisee; as for zeal, persecuting the church; as for legalistic righteous-ness, faultless. But whatever was to my profit I now consider loss for the sake of Christ. What is more, I consider everything a loss compared to the surpassing greatness of knowing Christ Jesus my Lord, for whose sake I have lost all things. I consider them rubbish, that I may gain Christ and be found in him, not having a righteousness of my own that comes from the law, but that which is through faith in Christ—the righteousness that comes from God and is by faith (Philippians 3:4-9).

You'll never really know the degree that your self-esteem is rooted in your work until your work is removed from the picture. Why not evaluate where you are in this area of your life? Affirm with God your desire to be known by your identity in Christ, not what you do to earn a living.

PERSEVERANCE FOR SUCCESS

And we rejoice in the hope of the glory of God. Not only so, but we also rejoice in our sufferings, because we know that suffering produces perseverance; perseverance, character; and character, hope.

ROMANS 5:2-4

Perseverance is the key to every great accomplishment—nothing of lasting value has ever been achieved without it. Industrialist Henry Ford is one of the great success stories of American history, but he failed in business five times before he succeeded. A Ford Motor Company employee once asked his boss the secret of success, and Henry Ford replied, "When you start a thing, don't quit until you finish it."

The path ahead of you is strewn with obstacles. People will oppose you. There will be financial setbacks, time pressures, illnesses and misfortunes. Some of the biggest obstacles will be inside of you: self-doubt, insecurity, procrastination and worry. Despite all these factors, you must give yourself permission to succeed.

When we persevere through adversity, we win the approval of our Lord Jesus Christ, who told the suffering church at Ephesus, "You have persevered and have endured hardships for my name, and have not grown weary" (Revelation 2:3).

Perseverance is a refusal to quit. It's falling down 100 times and getting back up 101 times. We need to remember that perseverance is not a matter of forcing doors to open; it's standing in front of the doors as long as it takes before God chooses to open them.

Life is a marathon, not a sprint. The race doesn't go to the swiftest, but to those who don't give up. We need endurance in order to deal with the stress of adversity. We must maintain a balanced diet, exercise regularly and get plenty of rest. People give up or give out when they feel depleted—when they physically, emotionally and spiritually run out of gas.

When going through adversity, watch out for pessimists, blamers and toxic personalities. Beware of people who try to talk you out of your dreams and goals. Spend time with optimists and encouragers. Seek out people of faith. Persevere to the end.

USING JERRY SPRINGER TO PREACH CHRIST

On hearing this, Jesus said, "It is not the healthy who need a doctor, but the sick.
But go and learn what this means: 'I desire mercy, not sacrifice.'
For I have not come to call the righteous, but sinners."
MATTHEW 9:12-13

Linda Rios Brook is a businesswoman who desires to impact the culture with the good news of Jesus Christ. Linda lives on the front lines of the fast-paced world of business. A former president and general manager of a network television affiliate in Minneapolis, Linda resigned her position after making comments about her faith in her local newspaper, which subsequently resulted in a company policy that precluded officers and managers from publicly identifying with a specific faith.

After her resignation, Linda was approached by a Christian foundation with the opportunity to purchase a television station in her local market. The idea of managing a religious television station did not appeal to her in the least because she knew that such a format would not sustain a for-profit business model. But she took the offer anyway.

After losing hundreds of thousands of dollars every month in attempting to attract a Christian audience, she realized that the station could not survive without a more mainstream programming lineup. An opportunity arose to get the Rush Limbaugh program from a competitor, but only if she also took *The Jerry Springer Show*. Linda struggled, knowing that the religious community would criticize the decision to take on both shows. Then the Lord gave her an idea.

She decided to place a rolling statement across the bottom of the page that said, "Need a friend? Call 555-5555." She decided to use *The Jerry Spring Show* as bait for ministering to those who might be watching the program, who, she concluded, represented a ripe field for the gospel. Her insight proved true. The phones began to ring off the hook and many people came to Christ as a result.

Sometimes we need to get out of our religious boxes to see how we can impact the culture using even the most negative societal influences to do it.

TRUSTING IN CHARIOTS

Woe to those who go down to Egypt for help, who rely on horses, who trust in the multitude of their chariots and in the great strength of their horsemen, but do not look to the Holy One of Israel, or seek help from the LORD.

ISAIAH 31:1

It is human nature to want to use every means available to succeed. However, a conflict arises when we place our trust in ourselves instead of in God. The idea of maintaining a proper balance between trust and obedience to God, versus dependence upon our natural skill and resources, has created problems since the time of Genesis. We are prone to build strong defenses through our natural gifts to avoid failure and to gain success. However, we often do this at the expense of the supernatural in our lives.

When it comes to receiving from God, it is important that we don't make the same mistake Moses made when God told him to speak to the rock in order to receive water for the people. Instead of doing what God commanded, Moses struck the rock and thus failed to enter the Promised Land. The people of Israel often fell back to trusting in their own abilities, and God had to send a reproof (in this case Moses' disobedience) into their lives.

How do we avoid the trap and maintain a proper balance between the natural and the spiritual? The rule of thumb is to submit every activity to God and to use your skill as God directs you. Be sensitive to God's leading in all your activities. Avoid trying to build resources for the sake of insulating yourself against calamity that is rooted in fear.

Finally, follow Solomon's advice: "Trust in the LORD with all your heart and lean not on your own understanding; in all your ways acknowledge him, and he will make your paths straight" (Proverbs 3:5-6).

ANEMIC FAITH

For we also have had the gospel preached to us, just as they did; but the message they heard was of no value to them, because those who heard did not combine it with faith.

HEBREWS 4:2-3

I run into anemic Christians everyday. They have a form of religion but fail to mix their belief with faith and obedience. The apostle Paul described these Christians when he said that these people have a form of godliness but deny its power (see 2 Timothy 3:5).

What are the telltale signs of anemic faith? When you no longer pray about decisions, you have anemic faith. When you fail to speak to others about their relationship with God, you have anemic faith. When you're unwilling to spend time with God everyday, your faith has become anemic. Christian anemia is when you no longer have a living faith.

God spoke to John the apostle through a vision and told him about some anemic Christians who were part of the church in Laodicea:

To the angel of the church in Laodicea write: These are the words of the Amen, the faithful and true witness, the ruler of God's creation. I know your deeds, that you are neither cold nor hot. I wish you were either one or the other! So, because you are lukewarm—neither hot nor cold—I am about to spit you out of my mouth. You say, "I am rich; I have acquired wealth and do not need a thing." But you do not realize that you are wretched, pitiful, poor, blind and naked. I counsel you to buy from me gold refined in the fire, so you can become rich; and white clothes to wear, so you can cover your shameful nakedness; and salve to put on your eyes, so you can see (Revelation 3:14-18).

We are all susceptible to growing cold and anemic in our faith. Today, ask God to revive your heart and to restore the fire of your faith so that you will experience a vibrant and active faith that impacts the kingdom of darkness.

WHEN HOPE IS DEFERRED

So Satan went out from the presence of the Lᴏʀᴅ and afflicted Job with painful sores from the soles of his feet to the top of his head. Then Job took a piece of broken pottery and scraped himself with it as he sat among the ashes. His wife said to him, "Are you still holding on to your integrity? Curse God and die!"

Jᴏʙ 2:7-9

I walked into the room and Angie burst out crying. "I'm so discouraged! I don't know what else to do. Will I ever get better?" After three years of fighting a medical condition and six months of treatment, the doctor had just told her that no progress had been made. Instead, alternative treatment was needed that might have more severe side effects.

Great men of God with healing ministries had prayed for her. Thousands of others had prayed for Angie through our ministry. A string of doctors had failed to yield any positive results.

When hope is deferred, the psalmist says, the heart becomes sick. During these seasons, we can only do one thing: We must hang onto whatever faith we have to get through each day and entrust our lives to Him.

> Though the fig tree does not bud and there are no grapes on the vines, though the olive crop fails and the fields produce no food, though there are no sheep in the pen and no cattle in the stalls, yet I will rejoice in the Lᴏʀᴅ, I will be joyful in God my Savior (Habakkuk 3:17-18).

When faith doesn't see results, it challenges what we believe. We must pray as Job prayed: "Teach me what I cannot see" (Job 34:32).

Later that day, Angie talked to a friend who had overcome the same medical problem. He told her, "Angie, God is going to reveal things to you through this season of adversity that you would never receive had you not gone through this. This is part of your calling even though Satan is the instrument. God is always bigger than Satan's afflictions."

Our greatest tests are when we cannot perceive positive results coming from our faith and obedience. In such cases we must die to our expectations and entrust them to our Lord.

GREAT IS YOUR FAITHFULNESS

Pour out your heart like water in the presence of the Lord.
LAMENTATIONS 2:19

Recently Angie and I were playing Bible Challenge, a Bible trivia game, with some friends. We got the question "Who is the author of Lamentations?" Angie shouted out "Jeremiah!" I thought the author was someone else, but she spoke with such conviction, I went with her answer. It turned out she was right.

Angie laughed and said, "You know you're bad off when you're looking for comfort in the book of Lamentations!" Angie had been walking through three years of medical challenges and felt like she was still no closer to resolution than when she started her journey. At times she was discouraged to the point of despair and felt totally abandoned by a God she knows loves her. And yet in the midst of all of it she found comfort in Jeremiah's words in Lamentations 3:2-24:

> He has driven me away and made me walk in darkness rather than light; indeed, he has turned his hand against me again and again, all day long. He has made my skin and my flesh grow old . . . Even when I call out or cry for help, he shuts out my prayer . . . I have been deprived of peace; I have forgotten what prosperity is. So I say, "My splendor is gone and all that I had hoped from the LORD." I remember my affliction and my wandering . . . I well remember them, and my soul is downcast within me. Yet this I call to mind and therefore I have hope. Because of the LORD's great love we are not consumed, for his compassions *never* fail. They are new every morning; *great is your faithfulness*. I say to myself, "The LORD is my portion; therefore I will wait for him" (emphasis added).

If you are at the point of despair, do what Jeremiah did and pour out your heart to God. Then call to your mind the fact that God's faithfulness is *great*. He has not abandoned you—He loves you. Don't allow Satan to deceive you into thinking anything else. God will be faithful in your life.

SPIRITUAL HARASSMENT

Your enemy the devil prowls around like a roaring lion looking for someone to devour.
1 PETER 5:8

I was 20 years old when I approached the first tee in the sectional qualifying round of the Professional Golfers Association's U.S. Open, one of the most prestigious golf tournaments in the world. I was a college golfer and was teeing it up with the world's best golfers to win one of only a handful of spots available to get into the tournament.

I had just teed up my ball when something unusual happened: As I looked down at my ball, I noticed someone standing no more than two feet from where I was about to tee off. I thought to myself with great irritation, *Who in the world is standing this close to me?* I looked up and saw that it was Sam Snead, still one of golf's greatest players. This man was known for intimidating tactics. But this was beyond belief! Here he was trying to intimidate a young college player. I ignored his presence and hit the ball straight down the fairway.

In the spiritual realm, we deal with spiritual harassment from Satan and his legions. The Bible says that "our struggle is not against flesh and blood, but against the rulers, against the authorities, against the powers of this dark world and against the spiritual forces of evil in the heavenly realms" (Ephesians 6:12). It is important to recognize when we are coming against these forces. We often trivialize the reality of the spirit realm of evil, but Satan really does attempt to distract us from our calling and destiny in life.

To combat spiritual harassment, Paul tells us that we must set our minds to deal with the spiritual realm of evil when it impacts our lives. He writes, "Therefore put on the full armor of God, so that when the day of evil comes, you may be able to stand your ground, and after you have done everything, to stand" (Ephesians 6:13).

The next time you feel that obstacles have been placed in your life that are designed to distract you from your God-ordained mission, remember Paul's words and stand firm in Christ.

FORGIVING THOSE WHO JUDGE YOU

*After Job had prayed for his friends, the LORD made him prosperous
again and gave him twice as much as he had before.*

JOB 42:10

Have you ever been wrongly judged? Have people ever assumed that there was sin in your life because of the troubles you may have experienced? Or perhaps others have wrongly judged your motives. What if the people judging you were your closest friends?

All of this is exactly what happened to Job. His friends did not understand how a godly person could ever go through his degree of adversity unless God was judging him for his sin.

Sadly, nothing has really changed after thousands of years. I recall going through my own seven year "Job" experience. Friends in the marketplace could not understand why I would experience the calamity that I underwent unless I had made poor choices. Those in the church often wrongly equated my trouble with sin. Sometimes troubles are a result of sin, but often trouble is simply a consequence of a call on our life that we have ignored.

The root cure in the face of troubles is forgiveness—especially when our adversity is brought on by the judgment of others. Joseph was required to forgive his brothers. Jesus was required to forgive Judas and the disciples for betrayal. You and I are required to forgive those who wrongfully judge us. Forgiveness is often the most important step in gaining restoration in our own lives. The Scripture above reveals that it was not until Job prayed for his friends who had judged him that he was restored in the things he had lost.

Is there someone in your life you need to forgive? It may be the missing piece of your puzzle for restoration.

GETTING A HAIRCUT

There I will give her back her vineyards, and will make the
Valley of Achor a door of hope.

HOSEA 2:15

I walked into the local hair salon for only the second time and sat down to get a haircut. "Hello, Donna, how are you?" I said pleasantly. All of a sudden she looked sad-eyed at me and began to cry uncontrollably with her head on my shoulder. "Donna, what's wrong!?"

Donna began to tell me how her marriage was in a crisis and how her husband was abusing her. She told tale after tale of his years of drug use as the other customers quietly sat in their chairs. When Donna began to settle down, we talked more and eventually we prayed together right there in the hair salon.

I gave Donna a few books to read and invited her to our house for a prayer gathering we were having. I knew that it would be months before Donna could do anything but vent about her husband and the pain she was experiencing. Our home fellowship group prayed for Donna that night. Every two weeks thereafter, I got the latest on her situation.

Donna had been a church-going person up to this point but understood little about walking with God. Gradually, though, Donna gained strength. Ultimately, her husband divorced her and she became free of the abusive relationship.

In this process, God came to Donna through different people. First, He sent a man (me) to sit in her salon chair who could share the love of God. Then God sent ladies who invited her to a Bible study that began to build a spiritual foundation in Donna. Soon after joining the study, she made a recommitment to her life and became baptized.

Donna is the first to admit that it took the Valley of Achor (trouble) to bring her to the end of herself where finally she chose to seek God with her whole heart. Today Donna is a different person. She has broken free of her co-dependent, abusive relationship and has entered a new, love relationship with her Savior. Now Donna is a servant of Jesus masquerading as a hair stylist.

BEING AN OVERCOMER

How long, O LORD? Will you forget me forever? How long will you hide your face from me? How long must I wrestle with my thoughts and every day have sorrow in my heart? How long will my enemy triumph over me?

PSALM 13:1-2

Have you ever heard someone jokingly say, "It's not easy being me"? Well, it wasn't easy being King David.

His was a life of extreme highs and extreme lows. He was a shepherd, a political leader, a builder, a prophet, a businessman, a warrior, a lover, a giver and a worshiper. In each of these roles, he achieved things for God, but he also failed God on many occasions.

When David wrote his psalms, he was honest about what he was feeling. When he feared his enemies, he expressed it. When he could not understand why God was silent, he expressed it, as in the psalm above. When he was excited, he danced almost naked and unabashedly before the Lord (see 2 Samuel 6:14).

Though David had a passionate personality characterized by mood swings, he never stayed in the place of despair. He often ended his psalms like this: "But I trust in your unfailing love; my heart rejoices in your salvation. I will sing to the LORD, for he has been good to me" (Psalm 13:5-6). David chose to focus on what God had done for him, not on what He had *not* done.

If you are waiting for a breakthrough with God, be honest with Him about your hopes and dreams. Affirm your faith and trust in Him to accomplish His purposes through your life. Be an overcomer.

BEING THE REAL THING

For the devious are an abomination to the LORD;
But He is intimate with the upright.

PROVERBS 3:32, *NASB*

Years ago, Coca-Cola had an advertising slogan that said, "It's the real thing." The world is desperately looking for the real thing. We live in a day when technology can make us believe that something that isn't actually is. Animation in movies today, for instance, is so advanced that it makes us see and believe extraordinary things. It is the ultimate deception.

There was one thing that angered Jesus more than anything else. It was hypocrisy—when religious people did things that were inconsistent with what they taught. Hypocrisy is a form of deception designed to make you believe something that isn't real. Hypocrisy angered Jesus, because it is impossible to violate God's ways through deceit and hypocrisy and expect to have an intimate relationship with Him.

In Matthew 15:7-9, Jesus said to the Pharisees, "You hypocrites! Isaiah was right when he prophesied about you: 'These people honor me with their lips, but their hearts are far from me. They worship me in vain; their teachings are but rules taught by men.'" He later said, "Woe to you, teachers of the law and Pharisees, you hypocrites! You clean the outside of the cup and dish, but inside they are full of greed and self-indulgence. Blind Pharisee! First clean the inside of the cup and dish, and then the outside also will be clean" (Matthew 23:25-26).

Believers in the workplace have an opportunity to demonstrate "the real thing" to the world. The apostle Peter prayed that our faith "may be proved genuine and may result in praise, glory and honor when Jesus Christ is revealed" (1 Peter 1:7).

Ask God to make you a follower of Jesus who is genuine in all you say and do. As you do so, you will discover that your intimacy with the Lord will grow, and others will see you and your faith as the real thing.

CONSIDERING YOUR INVESTMENTS

Each of you should look not only to your own interests,
but also to the interests of others.

PHILIPPIANS 2:4

It's rewarding to get a good return on an investment. In business we invest money, time and people into promoting a product or service in hopes of a return on those investments. We make financial investments, for example, in hopes that we can gain a monetary return.

The apostle Paul understood another kind of investment: investing in the spiritual lives of people. Paul particularly invested his life in a man named Epaphras. When writing to the Colossians, Paul makes reference to his influence on Epaphras. He says, "You learned it from Epaphras, our dear fellow servant, who is a faithful minister of Christ on our behalf, and who also told us of your love in the Spirit" (Colossians 1:7-8). Paul knew that it can be rewarding to invest in other people's lives.

One day Angie and I received this note from a friend in whom we had made an investment: "The two of you have had a tremendous influence on my life. For that, I will be forever grateful and love you as well." Sometimes we don't realize the difference we can make in another life. Investing in people through love can easily become a natural way of operating. We may not even think we are doing anything unusual. Then one day, we receive a note like the one my wife and I received, and our lives are changed forever.

Are you investing in lives that are in your sphere of influence through your workplace call? The returns on these investments are considerable.

ZIG WHEN OTHERS ZAG

Therefore the Pharisees also asked him how he had received his sight.
"He put mud on my eyes," the man replied, "and I washed, and now I see."
JOHN 9:15

Before I owned my own advertising company, I worked for another agency. The owner was a man who was very creative and who taught me that if you want to be remembered and want to stand out among the crowd, you must "zig" when others "zag." This was another way of saying, "Do something very different so that your work will stand out in the crowded marketplace."

When I owned my own firm, we created several award-winning ad campaigns. One ad we created for a new brand of plush carpet won international marketing awards. It featured a white Persian cat. You could only see the head of the cat, as if the plush carpet were so thick that he'd sunk right in. People wrote us and thought we had killed a cat to make our point. (We hadn't—it was all trick photography.) Our awards are still on the wall in my office.

Likewise, Jesus did things that caused people to talk. One miracle that caused a buzz was when He healed a blind man. Instead of saying a religious prayer, Jesus reached down, grabbed some mud and put it on the man's eyes. When the mud was washed off, he could see.

When the Pharisees asked *how* he was healed, the man told them exactly what had happened. The Pharisees must have been totally confused! Jesus did this to confront the religious spirit among the Pharisees and to keep things focused on the source of the miracle, not the way it was done.

Be aware when God does things outside of your paradigm of experience. Don't jump to conclusions about the ways of God just because they don't fit your paradigm. Jesus rarely does things the same way twice. He likes to work through many means in order to keep us trusting in His power, not His ways.

HIS PRESENCE

And you will again see the distinction between the righteous and the wicked,
between those who serve God and those who do not.

MALACHI 3:18

"Good morning," I said to the woman behind the counter as she asked if she could take my order. "You're a Christian, aren't you? I can see Him in you!" I proclaimed.

"Yes, I am," she replied with a beaming smile. I could literally see the presence of God in her countenance in the way she related to me and others.

When Moses led the people out of Egypt, he had several crisis moments. His greatest crisis was when he came back from the mountain and discovered that the people had made an idol—a golden calf. It was after this that he came to a profound conclusion. He said to God, "If your Presence does not go with us, do not send us up from here . . . What else will distinguish me and your people from all the other people on the face of the earth?" (Exodus 33:15-16). Moses realized that he had to have the presence of God with him to lead such a people.

The difference between a Christian in the workplace and a non-believer should be that the Christian brings the presence of God with her to work. However, this is not always the case. A Christian can shut out the presence of God by her behavior.

Like the Israelites who experienced great miracles in their lives but began to worship idols, we can move away from God. Sin separates us from God. We move away from His presence when we live sinful lives.

The prophet Malachi said that a day is coming when we will be able to recognize a clear difference between the righteous and the unrighteous. Would your coworkers be able to recognize a difference in you from others? Ask God to fill you with His overflowing presence in all you do today.

GOD GIVES US A DESIRE FOR OUR WORK

You shall call, and I will answer You; You shall desire the work of Your hands.
JOB 14:15, *NKJV*

Did you know that God has already pre-wired you for the work He created you to do? The psalmist says, "All the days ordained for me were written in your book before one of them came to be" (Psalm 139:16). We all have things inside of us that excite us when we think about them. God is the source of these passions. However, our career path may require many stepping stones before we reach the work for which we were ultimately created.

When it was time to design the Ark of the Covenant to contain the sacred Ten Commandments, God prepared a man to perform the important work:

> Then the LORD said to Moses, "See, I have chosen Bezalel son of Uri, the son of Hur, of the tribe of Judah, and I have filled him with the Spirit of God, with skill, ability and knowledge in all kinds of crafts—to make artistic designs for work in gold, silver and bronze, to cut and set stones, to work in wood, and to engage in all kinds of craftsmanship" (Exodus 31:1-5).

We do not know much about Bezalel, but you can be sure he had many jobs leading up to this most important assignment. He was also the first man mentioned in all of Scripture to be "filled with the spirit of God."

When your work is empowered by the Spirit of God, you will be hand-picked for some of the most important assignments. The Lord says that the skilled worker will even serve before kings (see Proverbs 22:9). God will see to it that your skills will be used for His ultimate purposes. This is the call of God for each of us—to be fulfilled in our work and to use our work to fulfill His purposes on the earth.

He seals the hand of *every* man, that *all* men may know His work.

CONFRONTING LEADERS

Moses' father-in-law replied, "What you are doing is not good.
You and these people who come to you will only wear yourselves out.
The work is too heavy for you; you cannot handle it alone."

EXODUS 18:17-18

There comes a time when every great leader may need to be confronted about a blind spot in his or her leadership style. When Moses' father-in law, Jethro, came to visit him in the desert, he watched his son-in-law in action and noticed a major flaw in his management style. Moses was spending his time from morning until night judging disputes among the people. Jethro could see that this was going to burn Moses out if it continued:

> The work is too heavy for you; you cannot handle it alone. Listen now to me and I will give you some advice, and may God be with you. You must be the people's representative before God and bring their disputes to him. Teach them the decrees and laws, and show them the way to live and the duties they are to perform. But select capable men from all the people—men who fear God, trustworthy men who hate dishonest gain—and appoint them as officials over thousands, hundreds, fifties and tens. Have them serve as judges for the people at all times, but have them bring every difficult case to you; the simple cases they can decide themselves. That will make your load lighter, because they will share it with you. If you do this and God so commands, you will be able to stand the strain, and all these people will go home satisfied (Exodus 18:18-23).

This was wisdom from a wise sage. And because the advice came from someone older and someone Moses respected, he heeded the advice. Even now, when a leader needs to be confronted, the correction must come from someone whom the leader respects and from whom the leader is willing to receive instruction. Correction must also be done in a spirit that is designed to help the leader to improve rather than a spirit intending to shame the leader for poor performance.

WORK REWARDS

For He repays man according to his work, and makes
man to find a reward according to his way.
JOB 34:11, *NKJV*

There is a belief held by many in the Body of Christ that says, "If I'm not doing something that has an inherent spiritual value, then it has no value at all." This sacred/secular dichotomy impacts believers every day as they go into their secular workplace. They believe that their secular work is simply a means of supporting the real ministry carried out by local churches, ministers, missionaries and vocational ministries.

However, this has no biblical basis. Some of the most important leaders in the Early Church had secular jobs. And they did not see them as jobs only to support other ministry. They considered their own jobs ministry.

Consider Dorcus (also known as Tabitha), a clothing manufacturer who was "abounding with deeds of kindness and charity which she continually did" (Acts 9:36, *NASB*). When Dorcus died, it was immediately brought to the attention of Peter, who tells us that she was very important to the Early Church leaders: "Peter went with them, and when he arrived he was taken upstairs to the room. All the widows stood around him, crying and showing him the robes and other clothing that Dorcus had made while she was still with them" (Acts 9:39).

Dorcus was known equally for her business as well as her ministry among the people. However, she was also known for being raised from the dead: "Peter sent them all out of the room; then he got down on his knees and prayed. Turning toward the dead woman, he said, 'Tabitha, get up.' She opened her eyes, and seeing Peter she sat up. He took her by the hand and helped her to her feet" (Acts 9:40-41).

What type of ministry in the workplace do you suppose Dorcus had after this event? Dorcus is a great reminder for every worker in the secular marketplace that "He repays man according to his work, and makes man to find a reward according to his way" (Job 34:11, *NKJV*).

"MAY IT BE"

"I am the Lord's servant," Mary answered.
"May it be to me as you have said." Then the angel left her.

LUKE 1:38

Have you ever had a boss come to you and give you an assignment that had rules you had never heard of? Not only were the rules different, but he also asked you to agree to them without knowing the outcome or impact it would have on your life. That must have been the way Mary, the mother of Jesus, felt.

Mary was handpicked to give birth to the Christ-child. Can you imagine? In order to do so, she would have to be pregnant while yet unmarried, something totally taboo in her culture. In fact, women were stoned to death if they were found to be fornicators. When Mary heard the assignment and responded by saying, "May it be," this tells us what a courageous woman of faith she must have been.

She did not understand the implications of what she was about to do, but she placed her total trust in God and knew that if He had chosen her for such an assignment, she could trust the outcome to Him. She would even have to trust the explanation to Joseph, who was not going to understand. In fact, when Joseph discovered that Mary was pregnant, he immediately considered divorce proceedings.

Because of Joseph's immediate response, God sent an angel to explain the situation through a dream. I am sure the time between Mary telling him about her pregnancy and Joseph's clarifying dream must have been difficult for both of them.

Mary did not know that God was going to solve the problem. This is another example of her faith and courage. I would imagine most women might have responded to the angel like this, "I won't do it unless you tell my husband!"

Do you have an assignment from God that seems impossible on the front end? Is God calling you to trust Him for the outcome? Take a lesson from Mary and release the outcome to God.

RECOGNIZING THE SIGNS OF THE TIMES

Magi from the east came to Jerusalem and asked, "Where is the one who has been born king of the Jews? We saw his star in the east and have come to worship him."
MATTHEW 2:1-2

God is looking for leaders who recognize the signs of their times. Such was the case of the three wise men who were so in tune with their times that they were able to pinpoint when the long-awaited Messiah was born. They recognized that God had come in their midst.

These three men may have been philosophers, priests or astronomers, and they probably lived in Persia or Arabia. They were marketplace ministers of the Eastern nations devoted to astronomy, religion and medicine. The magi were held in high esteem by the Persian court, were admitted in the king's presence as counselors, and followed the camps in war to give advice. They came from the professional ranks in society and were authorities in their fields of expertise.

The wise men were likely aware of the prophecy of Balaam, which said that a "star" would come out of Jacob (see Numbers 24:17). When the prophecy was fulfilled at Jesus' birth, they came and gave three distinct gifts: gold, frankincense and myrrh. Each of these gifts had prophetic significance.

Frankincense was a white resin or gum obtained from a tree by making incisions in the bark to cause the gum to flow out. It was highly fragrant when burned and was often used in worship as a pleasant offering to God. Myrrh (a name that indicates bitterness) was obtained from a tree in the same manner as frankincense. It was used chiefly in embalming the dead to preserve bodies from putrefaction.

Like the men of Issachar who "understood the times and knew what Israel should do" (1 Chronicles 12:32), the three wise men were aware of God's activities in their times.

Are you recognizing God's activity in your times?

LIKE A SHEPHERD

*He tends his flock like a shepherd: He gathers the lambs in his arms
and carries them close to his heart.*

ISAIAH 40:11

Sometimes Christ is modeled in the most unusual ways. Gerry, our neighbor, is a shepherd to the neighborhood dogs. Once Buddy, the roving black lab of the neighborhood, discovered that Gerry was a wellspring of treats, he began to bring other dogs on his visits to Gerry's house. They made themselves welcome in his front foyer.

One of them was an older cocker spaniel named Joe Cocker. Unlike Buddy, Joe didn't leave after 30 minutes—he stayed for two days! Gerry finally called the number listed on his dog tag and found out that Joe's owner lived up the road. Gerry walked him home, but Joe stopped as soon as he reached the hill because he was too weak to climb it. So Gerry picked him up and carried him home. It was not a short walk, and Joe was not a small dog.

Day after day this routine continued, and I was amazed at how much Gerry grew to love that dog. He let Joe stay at his house for days at a time. Joe was content to just hang out with Gerry and loved to sleep on top of the dirty laundry.

Then one day Gerry got a call from Joe's owner, who let him know that Joe had died. When Angie called Gerry to see how he was, he choked back the tears as he talked about the old spaniel.

Jesus is often referred to as the Good Shepherd in the Scriptures, and His followers are referred to as sheep that He carries close to His heart. There are times in our lives when Jesus knows that we cannot make it up our own hill in life. It may be because we are facing financial ruin, debilitating health or insurmountable grief. No matter what the reason, we can trust that Jesus is there to carry us.

Allow Him to pick you up so that you can find rest in His arms and comfort in hearing His heartbeat as He carries you close to His heart.

THE WAY OF THE CROSS

Come down from the cross and save yourself!
MARK 15:30

God calls each of us daily to the cross so that we may die to the worldliness of our flesh. Daily we are also invited by the enemy of our souls to love ourselves and come away from the cross.

In the words of Francois de Fénelon, who was considered on of the most godly men of the 1600s, "When God starts to deal with the old nature He heads straight for the center of all that you hold most dear. Allow Him to bring you to the cross in the very center of who you are. Don't grumble and become agitated when the process starts: Silence and peace will help you much more than being upset. To bear the cross simply, without letting your self-love add all sorts of dilemmas to it, will make your life easier. When you accept the cross simply allow it to do the work God intended, you will be happy because you will see what good fruit is produced in you."[65]

The apostle Paul sums up the way of the cross this way:

> For, as I have often told you before and now say again even with tears, many live as enemies of the cross of Christ. Their destiny is destruction, their god is their stomach, and their glory is in their shame. Their mind is on earthly things. But our citizenship is in heaven. And we eagerly await a Savior from there, the Lord Jesus Christ, who, by the power that enables him to bring everything under his control, will transform our lowly bodies so that they will be like his glorious body (Philippians 3:18-21).

What are the signs that you have come off the cross? When you are overly concerned with appearance, you have come off the cross. When the words of others cause you to react and defend, you have come off the cross. When you strive to have your world in perfect order, you have come off the cross. When you complain about circumstances, you have come off the cross.

The way of the cross means letting go and letting God have His way in every matter, every relationship and every outcome. Let the cross have its way in you.

THE GOD OF TIME

For there is a proper time and procedure for every matter,
though a man's misery weighs heavily upon him.
ECCLESIASTES 8:6

How we use our time is a good indicator of the God we choose to serve. There is a god whose name is "the urgent" that can rule our lives if we are not diligent. The wrong use of time can lead to misery. The right use of time can result in fulfillment.

Francois de Fénelon, a seventeenth-century Christian leader, once wrote, "Take time to turn to God. Do not pray only when you have set aside time to do. The busier you are, the more you must practice turning to God. If you wait until the time is convenient, there is little doubt that you will end up spending little time with God. Try to come before God both in the morning and the evening. Pray during and between all your other jobs as much as you can. You cannot retire too much from the mindless chatter of the world. Learn to steal this time in little snatches, and you will find these moments the most precious part of your day."[66]

The amount of time we spend with any person or any activity is a good indicator of the value we place on that person or activity. The way we use our time is the physical evidence of what is at the center of our lives.

We generally *make* time for what we want to do. Neglecting time with God is not due to a lack of available time but to a lack of will to set priorities for the time we have. Time can be the evidence that convicts our soul that our devotion has waned.

What does the evidence of time tell you about yourself? Today, give God the time needed to develop a relationship that is meaningful for both of you.

LOVING YOUR ENEMY

*You have heard that it was said, "Love your neighbor and hate your enemy." But I
tell you: Love your enemies and pray for those who persecute you, that you may be
sons of your Father in heaven. He causes his sun to rise on the evil and the good, and
sends rain on the righteous and the unrighteous.*

MATTHEW 5:43-44

If you are a leader, you will have conflict sooner or later. How you manage conflict will determine how good of a leader you will be. Dr. Martin Luther King,
Jr., father of the United States' civil rights movement, modeled conflict management in the following way:

> On Christmas Day, 1957, Dr. Martin Luther King, Jr. delivered a ser-
> mon at the Dexter Avenue Baptist Church in Montgomery, Alabama.
> It was based on this passage [Matthew 5:43-44] and the sermon title
> was "Loving Your Enemy." Through the course of his sermon, Dr. King
> suggested three ways by which we can do just that.
>
> First, we must develop and maintain the capacity to forgive. Such for-
> giveness doesn't mean that we ignore the wrong committed against us.
> Rather it means that we will no longer allow the wrong to be a barrier to
> the relationship. Forgiveness, according to King, "is a catalyst creating the
> atmosphere necessary for a fresh start and a new beginning."
>
> Second, we must recognize that the wrong we've suffered doesn't
> entirely represent the other person's identity. We need to acknowledge
> that our opponent, like each one of us, possesses both bad and good
> qualities. We must choose to find the good and focus on it.
>
> Third, we must not seek to defeat or humiliate our opponent, but to
> win his or her friendship and understanding. Such an attitude flows not
> from ourselves, but from God as his unconditional love works through us.
>
> As followers of Christ who seek to lead as He led, we must remem-
> ber that the more freely we forgive, the more clearly we reveal the nature
> of our Heavenly Father.[67]

Today, be proactive about forgiving those who have been the source of pain
in your life.

AVOIDING CONFLICT

Then Joab went to Geshur and brought Absalom back to Jerusalem.
But the king said, "He must go to his own house; he must not see my face."
So Absalom went to his own house and did not see the face of the king.

2 SAMUEL 14:23-24

Many people hate conflict to the extent that they will never confront a wrong. Taking this path, though, will only lead to later hardship. Such was the case for Absalom and his father, King David.

Amnon, also a son of David, raped his sister Tamar. When this happened, David was furious but did not punish Amnon for his actions. Absalom, on the other hand, saw this as a terrible injustice for his sister and plotted to kill Amnon at the right time. He patiently waited for two years before he set up a situation to have him killed.

After Amnon's death, David was heartbroken and held Absalom responsible. At the same time, David desired to have a relationship with Absalom, but because he failed to address the situation with Amnon when it happened, it led to more serious consequences in the family. Absalom was banished for three years because of David's anger toward him, and his banishment allowed seeds of resentment to grow in his heart. Absalom then conspired to overthrow David's kingdom.

David and Absalom's example shows us that it is imperative to confront problems when they arise no matter how uncomfortable it might be. We are called to speak the truth in love (see Ephesians 4:15-16). Failure to confront in love allows the enemy to sow greater seeds of conflict.

Is there someone in your life that you need to confront in love? Make plans now to get with this person and work through the issues that divide you.

THE FINAL BATTLE

*I saw heaven standing open and there before me was a white horse, whose rider
is called Faithful and True. With justice he judges and makes war.*

REVELATION 19:11

I used to love old western movies growing up. Often the main characters
would get into trouble, and just in the nick of time the cavalry would show
up, blowing their trumpets to announce that they had come to save those in
trouble.

Throughout our lives, a battle is waged between Satan and God's kingdom. But there is a final battle coming that will see Jesus and His army defeat
the enemies of His kingdom. It will be the great climax to thousands of years
of warfare, and it will put those western movies to shame:

> He is dressed in a robe dipped in blood, and his name is the Word
> of God. The armies of heaven were following him, riding on white
> horses and dressed in fine linen, white and clean. Out of his mouth
> comes a sharp sword with which to strike down the nations. "He
> will rule them with an iron scepter." He treads the winepress of the
> fury of the wrath of God Almighty. On his robe and on his thigh he
> has this name written: KING OF KINGS AND LORD OF LORDS
> (Revelation 19:13-16).

We are all moving toward a day in which we will be judged (see Revelation
20:12-13). Ultimately, we will all reign with Christ in a new heaven and earth
(see Revelation 21). How you live your life now will determine your role in the
new heaven and earth.

Your life on Earth is a mere blink on the scale of time. Whatever hardships
you've faced on Earth will pale in comparison to the glory that is to be
revealed when the marriage of the Bride of Christ takes place on that final day.

Be faithful. Stand firm. And see the glory of the Lord. Amen.

ENDNOTES

1. Marketplace Leaders provides a process to help every believer discover his or her unique purpose. Visit our website at marketplaceleaders.org and click on "Discover My Purpose."
2. Os Guinness, *The Call* (Nashville, TN: Word Books, 1998), pp. 4, 48.
3. Henry Blackaby and Claude King, *Experiencing God* (Nashville, TN: Lifeway Press), pp. 33-34.
4. F. B. Meyer, *The Life of Joseph* (Lynnwood, WA: Emerald Books, 1995), p. 45.
5. Adapted from John Woodridge, ed., *More Than Conquerors* (Chicago, IL: Moody Press, 1992), p. 311.
6. Adapted from study notes from the *Word in Life Study Bible,* copyright 1993, 1996, by Thomas Nelson, Inc. All rights reserved. Used by permission.
7. Adapted from "Work-World Stories Describe the Kingdom," *Word in Life Study Bible.* http://www.ivmdl.org/wil.cfm?study=43 (accessed January 2007).
8. Bill Johnson, *When Heaven Invades Earth* (Shippensburg, PA: Destiny Image, 2003), p. 29.
9. Adapted from a presentation by Ken Blanchard at the 2004 His Presence in the Workplace Conference held in San Antonio, Texas.
10. James Rutz, *Mega Shift* (Colorado Springs, CO: Empowerment Press, 2005), pp. 4-5.
11. Watchman Nee, *The Latent Power of the Soul* (Newspeak, NY: Christian Fellowship Publishers, 1972), p. 85.
12. Oswald Chambers, *Not Knowing Where* (Grand Rapids, MI: Discovery House Publishers, 1989), p. 143.
13. James Rutz, *Mega Shift* (Colorado Springs, CO: Empowerment Press, 2006), pp. 6-7.
14. *The Leadership Bible* (Grand Rapids, MI: Zondervan Publishing House, 1998), p. 1378.
15. Elmer Towns, *Understanding the Deeper Life* (Old Tappan, NJ: Revell, 1988), pp. 214-215.
16. C. Peter Wagner, ed., *Freedom from the Religious Spirit* (Ventura, CA: Regal Books, 2005).
17. Os Hillman, *Upside of Adversity* (Ventura, CA: Regal Books, 2006), p. 59.
18. Tom Watson, "My Shot: Tom Watson," interview by Guy Yocom, *Golf Digest,* July 2004. http://www.golfdigest.com/majors/britishopen/index.ssf?/majors/britishopen/gd200407my shot.html (accessed May 2006).
19. "A Business Strategy Portal for One and All," *Franteractive—A Web 3.0 Strategy Portal.* http://www.franteractive.net/coke.html (accessed February 2007).
20. "Born Again Christians," *The Barna Group.* http://72.14.253.104/search?q=cache:kCdTGu9cIxQJ :www.barna.org/FlexPage.aspx%3FPage%3DTopic%26TopicID%3D8+35-40%25+of+U.S.+popu lation+is+born+again&hl=en&ct=clnk&cd=1&gl=us&client=firefox-a (accessed February 2007).
21. Elaine L. Chao, "Remarks Prepared for Delivery by U.S. Secretary of Labor Elaine L. Chao, Capitol Connection Forum Louisville, Kentucky," U.S. Department of Labor, August 12, 2005. http://www.dol.gov/_sec/media/speeches/20050812_CCF.htm (accessed April 2007).
22. Frederick Nohl, *Luther* (St. Louis, MO: Concordia Publishing House, 1962), p. 26.
23. Ed Silvoso, *Anointed for Business* (Ventura, CA: Regal Books, 2002), p. 123.
24. Henry T. Blackaby, *Experiencing God* (Nashville, TN: Broadman and Holman Publishers, 1998), p. 132.
25. Kenneth Lay, quoted in Michael Novak, *Business as Mission* (New York: The Free Press, 1996), p. 22.
26. Pat Williams and Jay Strack, *The Three Success Secrets of Shamgar* (Deerfield Beach, FL: Health Communications, Inc., 2004), p. 103.
27. Adapted from Richard Ehrlich, *Mothers: 100 Mothers of the Famous and the Infamous* (New York: Paddington Press, 1976).
28. Rick Heerela, personal story shared with the author.
29. Bob Rotella, *Golf Is Not a Game of Perfect* (New York: Simon and Schuster, 1995), p. 117.
30. Anglican Church Assembly, "Towards the Conversion of England," London, 1945.
31. "Pulling Out of the Nosedive," Christian Research English Church Census 2005, September 18, 2006. http://www.christian-research.org.uk/intro.htm (accessed April 2007).
32. Michael Hout and Andrew M. Greeley, "The Center Doesn't Hold: Church Attendance in the United States, 1940-1984," *American Sociological Review*, vol. 52, no. 3 (June 1987), pp. 325-345.

33. "Unchurched Population Nears 100 Million in the U.S.," *The Barna Update,* March 19, 2007. http://www.barna.org/FlexPage.aspx?Page=BarnaUpdateNarrow&BarnaUpdateID=267 (accessed April 2007).

34. Mark Markiewicz, summary notes from a presentation delivered at a YWAM conference, 2004.

35. John Woodbridge, *More Than Conquerors* (Chicago, IL: Moody Press, 1992), p. 312.

36. Mother Teresa, "Whatever You Did Unto One of the Least, You Did Unto Me," address at the U.S. National Prayer Breakfast, February 3, 1994. http://www.ewtn.com/New_library/breakfast.htm (accessed March 2007).

37. Elmer Towns, *Understanding the Deeper Life* (Grand Rapids, MI: Zondervan Publishing House, 1984), pp. 224-225.

38. Brother Lawrence, *Practicing the Presence of God* (Pittsburg, PA: Whittaker House, 1982).

39. Billy Graham, *Answers to Life's Problems* (Nashville, TN: Word Publishing, 1988), pp. 251-252.

40. Allan Luks, "Helper's High: Volunteering Makes People Feel Good, Physically and Emotionally," *Psychology Today*, October 1988. http://www.findarticles.com/p/articles/mi_m1175/is_n10_v22/ai_6652854 (accessed March 2007).

41. Adapted from Peter Drucker, *The Effective Executive* (New York: Harper Collins Publishers, 1994) and *The Leadership Bible* (Grand Rapids, MI: Zondervan Publishing House, 1998), p. 653 study notes.

42. "Prayer of an Unknown Soldier," quoted in Austin Pryor, "Trusting God to Answer Our Prayers," *Crosswalk.com*. http://www.crosswalk.com/family/finances/1386973.html (accessed March 2007).

43. Os Guinness, *The Call* (Nashville, TN: Word Books, 1998), p. 101.

44. Princeton Religion Research Center, study published in the *Wall Street Journal,* December 1983.

45. Daniel Workman, "Starbucks Global Sales: American Coffee Around the World," *Suite 101: Enter Curious.* http://internationaltrade.suite101.com/article.cfm/starbucks_global_sales (accessed March 2007).

46. "ETV Remembers September 11th with the Documentary *For the Love of Their Brother,*" *ETV,* August 17, 2005. http://www.myetv.org/about_etv/pressroom/highlights/2005/sep/BROTHER.cfm (accessed March 2007).

47. John Woodbridge, *More Than Conquerors: Portraits of Believers from All Walks of Life* (Chicago, IL: Moody Press, 1992), p. 337.

48. Oswald Chambers, *My Utmost for His Highest* (Grand Rapids, MI: Discovery House Publishers, 1992), entry for January 19.

49. If you would like to learn more about Julius's impact in Uganda, his story is documented in a video entitled *An Unconventional War* (Lynnwood, WA: TransformNations Media, 2006).

50. Adapted from study notes from the *Word in Life Study Bible* (Nashville, TN: Thomas Nelson, Inc., 1996).

51. Stanley Tam, quoted in Robert J. Tamasy, ed., *The Complete Christian Businessman* (Brentwood, TN: Wolgemuth & Hyatt Publishers, Inc., 1991), n.p.

52. Matthew Henry, *Commentary on the Whole Bible: New Modern Edition* (Peabody, MA: Hendrickson Publishers, Inc, 1991).

53. Paul J. Meyer, *My Work Is My Ministry* (Waco, TX: Paul J. Meyer Resources, 2004), p. 18.

54. George Barna, *Boiling Point* (Ventura, CA: Regal Books, 2001), p. 223.

55. Ibid.

56. Os Hillman, *The 9 to 5 Window* (Ventura, CA: Regal Books, 2005), p. 143.

57. Malcolm Gladwell, *The Tipping Point* (New York, Little Brown and Company, 2000).

58. Oswald Chambers, *Not Knowing Where* (Grand Rapids, MI: Discovery House, 1989).

59. Paul Kengor, "The Intellectual Origins of Ronald Reagan's Faith," The Heritage Foundation, Lecture #832, April 30, 2004. http://www.heritage.org/Research/PoliticalPhilosophy/hl832.cfm (accessed March 2007).

60. C. Peter Wagner, *Confronting the Queen of Heaven* (Colorado Springs, CO: Wagner Books, 2001), pp. 14-17.
61. Ed Silvoso, *Anointed for Business* (Ventura, CA: Regal Books, 2006).
62. Bill Bright, "7 Basic Steps to Successful Fasting & Prayer," Campus Crusade for Christ. http://www.billbright.com/7steps/ (accessed March 2007).
63. V. Raymond Edman, *They Found the Secret* (Grand Rapids, MI: Zondervan Publishing House, 1984), pp. 33-34
64. Mike Taylor, "What God Is Like, part 6: Omnipotent, Omniscient, Omnipresent," February 21, 2003. http://www.miketaylor.org.uk/xian/omni.html (accessed March 2007).
65. Francois de Fénelon, *100 Days in the Secret Place* (Shippensburg, PA: Destiny Image Publishers, 2001), p. 24.
66. Ibid., p. 117.
67. Dr. Sid Buzzell, Dr. Kenneth Boa and Bill Perkins, eds., *The Leadership Bible* (Grand Rapids, MI: Zondervan Publishers, 1998), p. 1119.

Additional Resources
by Os Hillman

FREE Email Devotional

Start your day by reading an email that encourages you to experience the Lord's presence at work. *TGIF Today God Is First* is a free daily email subscription which has a scripture verse and brief devotional applied to a workplace situation. Subscribe by going to: *www.marketplaceleaders.org*

Marketplace Mentor

Twice a month, receive more in-depth Biblical teaching on various topics related to your workplace calling, marketplace tips, proven business principles, and free and discounted resources via this email e-Zine. *When you subscribe you'll receive five free ebooks by Os Hillman.*

TGIF Today God Is First

365 Meditations on the Principles of Christ in the Workplace.

The daily email devotional in book form! *Today God Is First* provides daily meditations that will help you focus your priority on knowing Jesus more intimately every day.
Hardback, 400 pp.

TGIF Paperback

180 devotionals presented by topics that range from God's will for your life to adversity. The smaller size and weight allows you to carry it with you wherever you go.
Paperback, 286 pp.

TGIF Small Group Bible Study

The popular *TGIF Today God Is First* book is now a 12-week, small group Bible study that is ideal for workplace groups. This study includes discussion questions; a workplace application with added scriptures that will allow the leader to extend or reduce the study time. Booklet, 48 pp.

Faith & Work: Do They Mix?

When you have an intimate relationship with Jesus, you will understand that your faith and work are not separate in God's eyes. This book will help you understand why your work IS your ministry.
Paperback, 128 pp.

Some products are not available in stores
See one of our websites to order:
www.marketplaceleaders.org or
www.faithandworkresources.com